# Managing Einsteins

## Leading High-Tech Workers in the Digital Age

# Managing Einsteins

## Leading High-Tech Workers in the Digital Age

**DR. JOHN M. IVANCEVICH**
Cullen Research
Professor of Management
The University of Houston

**DR. THOMAS N. DUENING**
Adjunct Professor of
Entrepreneurship
The University of Houston

**McGraw-Hill**
New York   Chicago   San Francisco   Lisbon   London
Madrid   Mexico City   Milan   New Delhi   San Juan
Seoul   Singapore   Sydney   Toronto

**Library of Congress Cataloging-in-Publication Data**
Ivancevich, John M.
  Managing Einsteins : leading high-tech workers in the digital age / by John M.
  Ivancevich and Thomas N. Duening.
      p. cm.
  Includes index.
  ISBN 0-07-137500-7
  1. Knowledge management.   I. Duening, Thomas N. II. Title.

  HD30.2 .I93 2001
  658.3—dc21                                            2001045234

1 2 3 4 5 6 7 8 9 0   DOC/DOC   0 9 8 7 6 5 4 3 2 1

ISBN 0-07-137500-7

*Printed and bound by R.R. Donnelley & Sons.*

McGraw-Hill books are available at special quantity discounts to use as premi-
ums and sales promotions, or for use in corporate training programs. For more
information, please write to the Director of Special Sales, Professional Publishing,
McGraw-Hill, Two Penn Plaza, New York, NY 10121-2298. Or contact your local bookstore.

This book is printed on recycled, acid-free paper containing a minimum of 50%
recycled, de-inked fiber.

# Contents

# Preface

The economy and the world of work are changing. For managers these changes are exciting, challenging, stressful, and occasionally so sudden that catching up to them is almost impossible. One of the obvious changes is the race to attract, hire, motivate, and retain talented workers who can keep the technology working on time without causing delays, breakdowns, and crashes. This book is about these geniuses who can make computers hum and who can, through a form of mystical magic, help the not-so-gifted, less technologically savvy, use the technology in a somewhat proficient way. We call these supersmart wizards and technology lifelines *Einsteins*. Yes, Einsteins named in honor of history's most famous genius, Albert Einstein.

Some refer to Albert Einstein as the greatest scientific genius of the twentieth century. He is recognized throughout the world as being super intelligent, revolutionary, and an outspoken critic of command and control governments, military regimes, and bureaucracies. The Einsteins of today, like their namesake, are also super intelligent, possess revolutionary ideas, and dislike authority or power exerted over them by bureaucratic, only by-the-rules non-Einstein managers and organizational rules, policies, and rituals.

The need for Einsteins to lead the way in understanding and applying technology is reshaping industries, economies, and educational systems. The digital revolution has accelerated the speed with which information is processed, disseminated, and used. The ability to shape, direct, and redirect information rests with Einsteins. Although the book is about these Einsteins, it is written for individuals who have a responsibility to *manage*, *lead*, and *facilitate* the super intelligent, talented individuals and teams to accomplish organizational missions, goals, and programs.

Busy managers who have built careers around working in stable environments with relatively predictable worker behavior patterns are now being asked to manage, lead, and facilitate the needed and talented Einsteins. In most cases the majority of Einstein managers are from a different background, experience, intelligence level, and place in time than the Einsteins. The old command and control management-directed orders and approach just will not be effective with Einsteins.

This book will offer firsthand views, research findings, suggestions, and advice to help Einstein managers grasp and take control of the challenges they are facing or will eventually have to address. Reading this book will not turn managers into Einsteins. This is not possible. What it will do is provide guidelines that will prove beneficial in winning the battle to find, hire, motivate, retain, lead, and support Einsteins. If managers use one suggestion offered in this book to help them make better use of their Einsteins, we will consider this a worthwhile endeavor. If these same managers refer to the book a number of times in the future, we will consider the book a diamond. The test of this book's value will be what managers do with what is presented to generate greater levels of satisfaction, productivity, and innovation among the Einsteins in their workplace. Managing Einsteins effectively can create a respect, appreciation, and image that managers can be geniuses themselves in fitting this important pool of talent, skill, and creativity into the organization.

# Acknowledgments

The Einsteins we have observed, worked with, and talked to provided examples, ideas, and critiques for the book. They served as up close Einsteins who offer fascinating insight into what makes members of these diverse Einstein tribes' unique individuals tick. We came to realize that Einsteins come in many different packages that run against the grain of mythology. The pocket protectors, "geeky glasses," and benign facial expressions just do not fit the twenty-first century Einsteins

Special thanks to Peggy Adams, who helped provide the word processing, smoothing over, graphical nuances, and patience with change after change after change that authors must have. She stuck with us through encryption of bizarre notes, scribbles, and drawings. Ginger Roberts also endured our outlines, changes, requests, and deadlines. We acknowledge their support and help and thank them for always doing so with a pleasant demeanor.

In addition, we want to thank Kevin Spears of Speartoons, Inc., who provided the excellent cartoon panels that appropriately fit the content. Kevin (www.kevinspear.com) used drafts of the book and created some enjoyable and funny cartoons.

# Introduction

# Einsteins in the Workplace

## Preview Einstein Story

### Einsteins Are in Demand

This book is about Einsteins, that special group of intelligent, curious, often introverted, technologically literate and proficient geniuses who keep everything operating. They are the must-have engineers, software developers, systems analysts, technical support experts, and wizards who keep the computers functioning, connected, and humming like birds every day. Even with a changing labor market, these geniuses are still in short supply. Not only are recruiters seeking Einsteins in traditional ways, they now have a number of techniques for finding Einsteins using the Internet. Some of these techniques are:

**Flipping:** By flipping a site, recruiters find résumés or conference rosters with links to a particular company. These listings also often yield biographies, e-mail addresses, and other juicy details about potential job candidates.

**X-Raying:** Using this technique, recruiters can identify key employees by traveling to those places on a company's website that aren't directly accessible via links on the main public home page.

**Peeling:** Embedded inside many Web addresses are what may be links to staff directories or content lists. Many Web addresses are filled with clues for recruiting searches.

**Anchor Search:** Many internal corporate Web pages include some telltale words as part of the address, such as "view résumés." As such, using the command "anchor" and those words can uncover a stash of employee information.

"Raiding Talent Via the Web," *Wall Street Journal*, October 3, 2000, B1

Some leading thinkers have declared that the Internet and its related technologies have ushered in a "new economy," one that is dominated by "intellectual capital." Steadily driving the modern economy is a continuous introduction of cool technotoys, gotta-haves, and wow software products. Work settings around the world are being turned upside down by computers and the people who fix, prime, and apply the hardware, connectivity, and software.

---

### Einstein Wisdom

The world is competing for knowledge workers wherever they are, and everybody needs more. Our collective knowledge is changing much faster today than it was when we designed our business practices and developed our employment relationships. And we still need what we always needed: Employees who know how to do what needs to be done now in order to keep the business competitive. In the important sense, a knowledge worker is anybody who must use their head on the job.

Rick Dove, Senior Fellow, Paradigm Shift International

---

Despite the severe downturn in the stock market during the first year of the new millennium, it is difficult to dispute that information and knowledge have become and will remain exceedingly important factors of production in the modern economy. Where once land, labor, and capital were the predominate factors, knowledge and information now lead the way.

There's a funny thing about information and knowledge, however: they require people to be useful. You can't eat information, or build a skyscraper with bricks made of knowledge. These ethereal and intangible assets require humans—we call them Einsteins—to give them life. If knowledge and information have become the predominate factors of production in the modern economy, then the Einsteins who give life to them must also predominate. In fact, many scholars have identified and written at great length about this new class of worker. In *The Work of Nations*, Robert Reich spoke of the "symbolic analysts." These are the educated men and women whose workday finds them bestride computers—working primarily with words and other symbols. Peter Drucker has for decades presaged the rise of the "knowledge worker." To Drucker, knowledge workers are those persons who adds more value to the firm by application of their intellect rather than their physical strength. Tom Stewart of *Fortune* magazine wrote a book on *Intellectual Capital*. In fact, some theorists have gone so far as to attempt to develop a calculation to identify the intellectual assets that reside within a firm. *Tobin's Q* is the measure of a firm's market cap less the value of its physical assets. The remainder is intellectual capital.

## Einsteins Everywhere

Probably no one would deny that the modern economy has become increasingly dependent upon smart people to keep it moving. Departing from the more dramatic terms such as *symbolic analyst*, we identify and profile intellectually gifted people who make the economy function as *Einsteins*. We use this term because the class of employee we describe in this book has many characteristics of Albert Einstein. Perhaps the greatest physicist that ever lived, Albert Einstein is notable for his insatiable curiosity, disdain for social niceties, piercing wit, incredible focus on the problem at hand, and high degree of personal modesty. These characteristics, and others, are found in the Einsteins that populate the modern workplace. Einsteins can be found in the information technology (IT) department—they keep your network running. Einsteins can be found in the engineering department— they keep systems running. Einsteins can be found in the accounting department—they keep the cash flowing.

What is an Einstein? In our usage an Einstein is the new breed of worker, possessing deep technical knowledge, driven by an unyielding curiosity, unfettered by traditional norms, and characterized by an unending appetite for novelty and new technologies. The Einsteins on any staff are the ones who ask questions about why things are being done the way they are. They're the ones who are quick to adopt new technologies and apply them to work processes. They're the ones who flout authority, but who perform their work at a high level.

Einsteins are a unique breed of well-educated employees working alone or working in teams, solving problems, who combine their passion for learning and technology with a desire to participate in exciting ventures. Einsteins are characterized by divided loyalties. They are loyal first and foremost to their craft—the specific technical area in which they have studied, learned from others, and to which they have dedicated their lives. They are loyal secondly to their various Einstein tribes (e.g., programmers, systems analysts, database administrators, engineers). As you will learn throughout this book, Einsteins are tribal in nature. They may seem asocial to non-Einsteins, but they form strong bonds with those who share a reverence for their craft and who are working on the same projects. Third, Einsteins are loyal to the organization, but it's not their primary loyalty. Einstein managers must recognize their Einsteins' deep commitment to their craft and their desire to hone and perfect their skills. Organizations that purposefully or inadvertently block Einsteins from this will lose them. Einsteins who are blocked will either physically depart or psychologically depart these settings in which they are stymied or smothered from growing.

Successfully managing Einsteins requires an understanding of their diversity, divided loyalty, and intellectual capabilities and talents. It may be alarming to Einstein managers to realize that some of their most well paid and valuable employees are loyal first to their craft. However, accepting this truth about Einsteins is a necessary first step in being able to retain them for years of commitment, service, and value added to the organization. Like it or not, Einsteins are among the most mobile category of workers that has ever existed. They possess technical knowledge that can be transferred across organizations, across industries, and across oceans. Further, they are in high demand and short supply. You can bet that every one of the top Einsteins on your staff has been contacted by a recruiter, or headhunter, at least a few times in the past year.

The picture we have painted here at the outset is a bit frightening. We've done so deliberately in order to alert you about the talent wars for Einsteins. We've told you how important Einsteins are to your organization. You probably already knew this fact of life in the digital age. Einsteins are like electric power—you usually don't realize how vital they are until they're gone. You don't want to wait until Einsteins depart or psychologically disengage to realize how important they are to the organization and the accomplishment of its goals. So we've taken the preemptive step of reminding you about the supply and demand realities in the Einstein labor market.

## Managing Einsteins

What Einstein managers may not have been as aware of is the divided loyalties of Einsteins and their high level of mobility. Managers like to think that their Einsteins would have the same loyalty and commitment to the organization that they have. They don't, and they won't. There are things Einstein managers can do, however, to better the odds of finding the best Einsteins and keeping them—that's what this book is all about. The effective managers of Einsteins are proactive, action-oriented optimists who must learn how to become managers, leaders, and facilitators. This all-around person is referred to later in the book as an ideal manager, leader, and facilitator (MLF). Becoming an ideal MLF is difficult, challenging, and requires learning, practice, and patience. Some of what must be learned is common sense, some is research-driven, some is copied from others who are successful, and some will require taking risks and experimenting. Einstein managers who become MLFs have had successes and failures along the way.

Effectively managing Einsteins requires that you understand their background, intellectual capabilities, needs, wants, and divided loyalties. Einstein managers need to learn what and how Einsteins think, communicate, work, aggregate, and relax. They also must understand and respond to the desire of Einsteins to develop within their craft. Becoming an effective Einstein manager requires building a work environment that allows Einsteins to grow, thrive, and fulfill their needs and wants. Determining these needs and wants will require contact with, listening to, and working with Einsteins.

---

## Influence Tip

### The New Psychological Mandate

Power in the information age is defined by having the autonomy to work on what you want when you think it's best to do so. Knowledge workers' disdain for traditional rules of management forces traditional business executives to contend with a new "psychological mandate." Instead of allocating and controlling material goods and resources, managers must now satisfy knowledge workers' psychological needs. For a business to survive in the information age, executives must find ways to gratify the ambitions of workers who prefer the exhilaration of an ever-challenging web of knowledge, not merely material gain and status.

Steven Berglas, "To Keep Your Workers, Set Them Free," *Business 2.0*, December 12, 2000

---

Effectively managing Einsteins requires retention programs that are developed to match interests and tap into their high level of self-motivation. It requires developing, implementing, and monitoring reward and recognition programs that balance Einsteins' desire for creature comforts with their insistence that they be rewarded according to their individual contributions, teamwork, and value added to the organization. It requires that managers communicate openly, honestly, and ethically about the operating status of the company, and lead with a light touch that is considered fair.

Recruiting, hiring, retaining, rewarding, and developing Einsteins is one of the most vital links in a firm's value chain. Identifying, recruiting, hiring, and retaining smart, energetic, innovative Einsteins is essential in the new economy. There is no substitute for human intellect in the modern economy, and no replacement for the creative spark that only the human mind has flickering within. No amount of investment in information technology—hardware or software—can obviate the need for making a major investment in Einsteins. This investment involves applying astute managerial, leadership, and facilitative techniques in the right way and at the right time.

---

### Black Hole

*Traditional Perks Don't Work*

Knowledge workers—Einsteins—have created new challenges for the modern manager. Traditional career paths are unlikely to motivate them. Managers who attempt to motivate Einsteins with promises of job titles and perks will be disappointed. Instead of these traditional trappings of employment, Einsteins want to be involved in interesting, challenging, and life-changing projects. They view themselves primarily as practitioners of a "craft." Like any individual whose life revolves around their craft, their primary interest is becoming a "master." Anything that thwarts that quest or hinders personal skill development will be resisted. Einsteins are, above all, craftsmen, and the most effective "perks" managers can offer them will center on skill building and opportunities to exercise their skills.

---

## Plan for This Book

This book will take you through the entire process of identifying, recruiting, retaining, rewarding, and developing Einsteins. Along the way, you'll be exposed to many management and leadership ideas, theories, and approaches that have stood the test of time, been modified to fit Einsteins, or have been totally overhauled to work effectively with Einsteins individually and as members of teams and projects. The inclusion of old, modified, and new theories is necessary to serve as a reminder of their basic assumptions, and as an indicator that there are certain "laws of effective management" that are more than passing fads.

Four elements will be embedded in each chapter: Preview Einstein Story, Einstein Wisdom, Influence Tip, and Black Hole.

The *Preview Einstein Story* is a concise presentation of an example, situation, event, or illustration of a topic or area that will be covered in the chapter. It is "real," lively, and provides a chapter start that sets the tone for what will follow.

*Einstein Wisdom* is a witty comment, phrase, idea, or statement that originated from Einstein or from someone else, that has a bite, is common-sensical, or is provocative. These short items will provoke you to stop and reflect.

The *Influence Tip* is a positive "how to" perform guideline, suggestion, or recommendation. It is logical, practical, has been applied, and offers promise to Einstein managers.

The *Black Hole* describes things that should be avoided in working with and managing Einsteins. The Black Hole is the opposite of "how to do" or practice management. It should be avoided if at all possible.

You will also find a list of resources and reference information in the back of this book. This information has been organized into segments that will help you understand the nature of Einsteins, the wide range of career options available to them, and other resources dedicated to their effective management.

"I JUST FINISHED READING THAT BOOK. I DIDN'T THINK IT WAS THOROUGH ENOUGH."

Finally, we have also developed a banquet of new concepts and management techniques that you can apply immediately in your current situation. Some of these will fit and work perfectly, some won't. You can be the judge and jury. We are cautious in specifying where a specific technique may or may not apply. We cannot anticipate every situation or your unique circumstance. You'll find this book most useful if you are willing to apply some of its ideas in your workplace, fully aware that there is no standard recipe that will ensure success. Monitor the effects of your managerial initiatives and adjust them as conditions and Einsteins warrant. Remember, taking risks, experimenting, and practicing is going to be required. Einstein managers can't make a difference by simply knowing what should be done. They must implement knowledge about managing Einsteins and then monitor the impact of what is implemented.

In the following chapters the text follows a fairly straight path from identifying, through recruiting, hiring, rewarding, and developing Einsteins. Along the way you'll also find a large number of examples, anecdotes, and other useful pieces of information. These are intended to highlight the real-life applications that face Einstein managers. Although we have attempted to use a light and entertaining tone throughout, there should be no mistake about the seriousness of this topic. We repeat what we have already stated and what you probably already know: There is nothing more important to an organization's success than identifying, recruiting, hiring, retaining, rewarding, and developing Einsteins.

Einsteins, properly organized, motivated, rewarded, and developed can make mountains out of molehills, lemonade out of lemons. You will not need to worry about shifting economic winds or fickle investor sentiments if you have strong teams of Einsteins. Einsteins adapt. Let the world change. Let the market shift. A team of committed and loyal Einsteins will help pull you through.

Use this book, don't just read it. Each chapter contains guidelines, suggestions, and proven principles. We hope that you find it pleasant and even enjoyable to read. Our greater hope is that you find it *useful*. We have sifted through thousands of articles, spoken to hundreds of people, and have personally worked with Einsteins to develop the guidelines, ideas, and concepts in this book. Every new concept or insight that we discuss has been tested in conversations, validated by case studies, applied in work environments, and tested in different settings. The application theme of the book is purposefully prepared for the use of managers in whatever situation or circumstance they face.

# Managing Einsteins

## Leading High-Tech Workers in the Digital Age

# Realities of the Twenty-First Century

"MY DAD THOUGHT I WAS WASTING MY TIME PLAYING ALL THOSE VIDEO GAMES. NOW HE BRAGS ABOUT HOW THIS BUSINESS COULDN'T SURVIVE WITHOUT MY PROGRAMMING!"

# CHAPTER 1

# Profiling Einsteins

## Preview Einstein Story

### Tips on Managing Einsteins or "Geeks"

An article in *Fast Company*, titled "How To Manage Geeks," discusses the story of Eric Schmidt, CEO of Novell, Inc. He is a proud, card-carrying "geek" himself. (In this book we generally refrain from the use of the word "geeks" except to trace it historically and instead call these individuals "Einsteins.")

The *Fast Company* article explains Schmidt's approach to managing and getting the best out of his Einsteins. Schmidt contends that innovation drives business and you need to have your own teams of Einsteins. He proposes that a negative stereotyping of Einsteins has occurred. They are considered antisocial, but within their groups they are very social. It is also claimed that arrogance is a trait of Einsteins. Yes, they have egos, but they should be viewed as free agents with specialized talents similar to a pro basketball player.

Einsteins want to make a difference by solving challenging problems. They want credit for their successes, and this doesn't mean promoting them to become managers. Schmidt contends that most Einsteins would turn out to be terrible managers. But they need recognition more than money. He recommends the use of a dual career ladder. For example, at Novell he added the new title of "Distinguished Engineer" to provide another track for Einsteins.

Schmidt also offers advice that clearly indicates that managers can tell Einsteins what to do but should refrain from telling them how to do it. He also warns that the best evaluators of Einstein performance are other Einsteins. Having non-Einsteins in managerial positions conduct performance appraisals involving technical attributes is a mistake.

*Continued*

Schmidt is also an advocate of small, lean teams of Einsteins. Too many of them working together results in chaos, debates, and lower performance. The smaller the Einstein team, the faster the team members work. By creating a smaller team, the manager actually makes the schedule shorter.

These tips, suggestions, and insights about Einsteins are offered by a person who fits the profile that will be developed in this chapter. Eric Schmidt is a person who believes in the witty Silicon Valley phrase, "The geeks shall inherit the earth."

Source: Russ Mitchell, "How to Manage Geeks," *Fast Company*, June 1999, 174–176

There is a parlor game a lot of physics students' play: Who was the greater genius, Galileo, Kepler, Maxwell, or Bohr? Most claim that it was Maxwell, but it's a lot closer than you can imagine, according to the game participants. Maybe the physics students playing the game forgot about two intellectual superstars. There are two figures in history that are off the charts in terms of intelligence: Isaac Newton and Albert Einstein. It is a photo finish.

Newton's claim is apparent. He created modern physics. His system described the behavior of what is called the cosmos. His theories were mathematical, made specific predictions, and led to many experiments in the real world.

Einstein was also special in terms of intelligence and contributions. He was born on March 14, 1879, in Ulm, Germany. Since his mother loved music, Albert started playing the violin when he was six years old. From an early age he had a natural mechanical ingenuity. He wasn't a boy genius in mathematics and was referred to by his teachers as a dreamer. He was curious, but was a dreamer who preferred music over anything else.

Let's not gloss over Einstein's love and passion for music. He claimed in expressing his view of music and physics research that "both are forms of the same source and complement each other." Whenever he came to the end of the road in problem solving, Einstein took refuge in playing music. Playing music seemed to calm Einstein.

Two significant events put Einstein on the road to becoming a physicist. When he was about five, while sick at home from school, his father gave him a compass to pass the time. The compass needle's movement intrigued him. He was curious about what made the needle move.

The second notable occurrence came when his Uncle Jakob presented Einstein with a book on Greek mathematics. Einstein read about the Pythagorean theorem: in a right triangle, the sum of the squares of the perpendicular sides equals the square of the hypotenuse. He was impressed by the simplicity of the theorem. For three straight weeks he worked on proving the theorem to himself. He came up with a unique proof.

Einstein's early childhood experiences were filled with curiosity, violin playing, and mathematics. He taught himself how to play music he preferred. At the same time, he taught himself geometry. Galileo and Einstein both apparently had a deep passion for geometry at the same age.

Einstein's intelligence, curiosity, ability to handle multiple tasks, and a thirst for experimenting and trying new things establishes the theme for this book. Despite the awesome potential of the human brain, most of us non-Einsteins are hard pressed to multiply two-digit figures without using a calculator. Only the Einsteins, Galileos, da Vincis—a small segment of humanity—seem to use their intellectual brainpower efficiently. So superior are the intellectual powers of Einsteins that we are awestruck. However, non-Einsteins need to fight through being awed, and they have to in many situations manage and lead these intellectually gifted people.

---

### Einstein Wisdom

- It's not that I'm so smart; it's just that I stay with problems longer.

- As far as I'm concerned, I prefer silent vice to ostentation's virtue.

- The important thing is not to stop questioning. Curiosity has its own reason for existing.

---

## The Elusive Genius

Are geniuses like Einstein so different from the rest of us? Yes, they probably are different in many respects, including their early childhood experiences. Seldom do bona fide Einstein-type geniuses distinguish themselves in childhood. For example, the renowned mathematician Henri Poincaré did so poorly on the Binet IQ test that he was classified as an "imbecile." Thomas Edison, whose record 1,093 patents outshadowed every inventor in history, was slow in school.

Albert Einstein was considered slow, partly due to his dyslexia. He was a below average speaker and reader as a child. His Greek teacher told Einstein, "You will never amount to anything." Einstein was expelled from high school and flunked his college entrance exam.

When Einstein reached his twenty-sixth year the unexpected occurred. He published his Special Theory of Relativity, which contained the famous formula, $E = MC^2$. Sixteen years later he won a Nobel Prize and was on his way to international recognition. Even today, over forty-five years after his death, Einstein's piercing eyes, bushy mustache, wrinkled clothes, and shock of hair remain the image of genius. His name is a synonym for superior intelligence and is used to describe the modern-day knowledge worker for which this book is written.

## Current-Day Einsteins

The term "Einstein" has elegance, a link to a central historical figure, and connotes super intelligence to everyone. An array of terms to describe mysterious, intelligent, and curious people includes geeks, nerds, knowledge workers, techies, computerists, technolibertarians, cyberfreaks, and propeller heads. Of these terms, geeks and nerds are the most cited and the most referenced. The individual with the pocket protector, rumpled and stained shirt and pants, Coke-bottle-thick glasses, and socks that don't match provides a somewhat inaccurate image of the Einsteins of the new economy. Certainly, some of today's Einsteins fit the stereotype, but the majority do not provide these "geek"-type visual signals today. What non-Einstein managers definitely know is that the Einsteins of the world are vital to the functioning of technology, systems, and information within organizations. They are an essential part of the employee group that must be recruited, retained, motivated, and even occasionally disciplined and terminated.

The current-day Einsteins come in more than thirty-one flavors. They are young and old, male and female, short and tall, thin and overweight, conservative, liberal, and libertarian, and are born in and outside of the United States. Some are Caucasian, while others are Asian, Hispanic, and African. There are religious Einsteins and atheist Einsteins. There is no "one package" or set of characteristics or profiles that fits each and every one of the millions of Einsteins working in organizations. Some Einsteins dress in black or grunge, sport tattoos, and have nose rings. Others are dressed in buttoned-down shirts and suits with each and every hair in perfect, blown-dry, and proper-gelled place.

## Jargon-Filled World

Besides a super intelligence, which is quite common among Einsteins, there is also a whole new language that has been created. To ease communication between the elite Einsteins and to separate themselves from the non-Einsteins, they talk in slang, codes, and unique tongues which will be further discussed in Chapter 5. If you are managing Einsteins, you probably have tried to decrypt the Einstein languages. Unfortunately, there are languages that are associated with the jobs, work roles, projects, locations, and settings in which the Einstein is employed.

How about taking a brief test to determine if you are up-to-date on some of the jargon used by Einsteins. It is common knowledge that trying to fake or pretend to be an Einstein is going to be quickly uncovered by how you talk and your vocabulary. An important rule for non-Einsteins is to refrain from faking or trying to impress Einsteins. You will be considered a fake, a fool, a phony, and many other things. You will lose credibility among Einsteins, which could be impossible to recoup.

---

### Einstein Slang/Jargon Test

1. What does BDU mean?

2. What is a "nine to five" code?

3. Describe a SLIRK.

4. What is the lasagna syndrome?

5. What is a "code 18"?

---

How long did it take you to answer these questions? Did you answer any of these within a minute or so? Are your answers correct? How many did you get right?

## Einstein Slang/Jargon Answers

1. What BDU means is "brain dead user," or a person who didn't follow any documentation and is calling for technical support help.

2. A "nine to five" code is plain, vanilla software that just barely gets the job done; written during normal, "ho-hum" working hours—"nine to five."

3. A SLIRK is a smart little rich kid with great potential technical promise using the family money to play. SLIRKs know they are smart and are rich and wear these characteristics with pride.

4. A lasagna syndrome is software with too many dialog boxes overlapping each other.

5. A "code 18" is an error made by a user sitting 18 inches from the computer screen.

See www.sabram.com/site/tophtml for these answers and other Einstein jargon

If you scored a perfect 5 you probably are conversant and very knowledgeable in Einstein-type speaking. Anything below three correct answers indicates you are in the majority in society and are not a part of the Einstein tribe. Most managers would be hard pressed to get four or five correct. Why? Because most managers are not Einsteins and do not speak the language. Since the language is different, managers need to listen, observe, and not try to appear to be an Einstein.

## Einstein Work in Organizations

The concept of what is called a *knowledge economy* is too abstract for most people. Knowledge work is what Einsteins typically do. The worker in the U.S. Steel plant in Chicago, Pittsburgh, or Gary, Indiana, in the 1960s worked with his back, muscles, and physical strength. In the knowledge-oriented company, department, or project team the work is performed with information, data, concepts, and usually computers. The backbreaking steel mill jobs and work have largely disappeared, having been replaced by more automated, smaller, and leaner steel plants. The mill sweatshop is unknown by the current generation and is simply a part of labor history and folklore.

Today, more and more people spend their workday surrounded by computers, fax machines, personal digital assistants (PDAs), project teams, and analytical problem solving discussions. The physical strength jobs that represented over 80 percent of the U.S. workforce as the twentieth century began now represent, at best, only about 20 percent or less of the 125 million jobs.

Robert Reich, the former Secretary of Labor, in his book *The Work of Nations*, described three major job categories: routine production (factory labor, such as the steel mill jobs, back-office, clerical), professionals (lawyers, consultants, teachers and professors, and executives), and in-person services. The largest and growing groups include professionals and in-service workers who rely on knowledge and information. Included in these two categories are the Einsteins. It is estimated that "knowledge-dominated" companies such as Microsoft, Nortel, Cisco Systems, and Sun Microsystems account for about 30 percent of the total U.S. employment, or about 40 million workers.

Certainly, Einsteins exist in other countries throughout the world. Conservatively, if Einsteins make up about 3 to 4 percent of the U.S. work population, approximately the same proportion exists in the rest of the world. However, most countries do not have the same type of economic infrastructure and knowledge-dominated industry base as the United States. The world population of 6 billion has within it at least 200 million actual and potential Einsteins. Even if only 20 percent of the potential Einsteins are now working in organizations, it would mean about 40 million super-intelligent individuals are engaged in intellectually rich work and projects around the globe.

Dissecting the 40 million workers into Einstein and non-Einstein qualified segments is difficult to impossible. An educated guess as to the Einstein segment in the United States is about 4 to 5 million employees who are super-intelligent and fit the descriptions attached to geeks, nerds, and technolibertarians.

## The New Management Manifesto

The rise of the stature, presence, and need for Einsteins alters dramatically the agenda, processes, and concepts of managing and leading others in work settings. Managers are custodians who protect and care for the goals, mission, and assets of an organization. In the old economy the back, hands, and the specialized nature of work were geared to accomplish efficient, quantifiable results. The use of the "widget" (an imaginary end product) was the centerpiece of evaluating performance results. How many generators were produced in an eight-hour workday? How many files were completed today? In essence, how many widgets per worker, per day, were produced and at what cost—this was how work was measured, evaluated, and changed when necessary. Managers wanted firsthand answers to the "how many and at what cost" questions and looked over the workers' shoulders to make sure that goals were met.

Managers' work was described as planning, organizing, controlling, and directing the work, processes, and workers. Management by the "widget" numbers was what was expected from managerial practitioners. Frederick W. Taylor, a brilliant industrial engineer who is called the "father of scientific management," influenced this old economy (1890–1980s) era of management. Taylorism emphasized a carrot and stick approach to making sure that goals were met without cost boundaries. Henry Ford's assembly line is a 1920s example of applying Taylor's guidelines. At Ford the only intellectual power used was that of managers. The fount of knowledge rested with the managerial class.

Einstein work is totally different. It is based on knowledge, problem solving, analysis, the use of computers, and the actual results achieved. It is also fast-paced, unpredictable, continuous, and may occur on a 24/7 schedule. Most Einsteins are "smarter than their bosses," so old widget-counting management no longer is a feasible method of orchestrating positive results.

Telling, demanding, or haranguing Einsteins is not going to work. The new covenant between leaders who also are managers (protectors of the firm's assets) and Einsteins includes concern for values, empowerment, teamwork, respect, and personal growth and development. A more humane concern for the well-being of Einsteins and non-Einsteins is what leaders today have to perfect and refine. In a world in which Einsteins work, it is important for leaders to understand creativity, innovation, relationships, and consideration. In Taylor's world these human tasks were not important elements of management.

---

### Influence Tip

Leadership is a set of qualities that causes people (Einsteins) to follow. This simple view means that leadership requires two parties, a leader and a follower. A leader has the ability to inspire people to go beyond what they think they are capable of doing. Leaders inspire by:

- Building trust
- Displaying respect
- Acting consistently
- Motivating followers by words and deeds

"I DO MY BEST CREATIVE WORK WHEN I STAND LIKE THIS FOR THREE HOURS."

The job titles popular in the Taylor-dominated era of scientific management included mechanic, lathe operator, body shop specialist, mill foreman, lab supervisor, hod carrier, iron worker, blast furnace helper, and grain elevator loader. These specialist-type jobs were narrowly defined. That is, the tasks that a lathe operator performed were specific, could be learned with practice, and were expected to be performed the same each day.

A few of the popular titles (changing constantly) of Einstein work include programmer, designer, programmer analyst, software engineer, applications engineer, hardware engineer, network engineer, project manager, tech support, IT director, and systems integrator.

Einstein-type work involves creativity, problem solving, a wide and broad range of tasks, and uncertainty. It involves helping people who use computers (mostly non-Einsteins) solve their problems and guiding them away from computer mayhem (e.g., bugs, crashes, hacking, bombs, freezes).

In 1980 it was not fashionable to be talking about Einsteins in organizations and suggesting that these super-intelligent people must be managed and led. Until the late 1980s most organizations played by the rules of top-down management. Today, however, with the advent of rapid technology changes, diversity among employees, globalization, and intense competition, Einsteins are revered because they are needed. If a firm wants to compete, survive, and grow, it must have Einsteins who are managed effectively and led elegantly and with finesse. These are the obvious facts and the reality of twenty-first century organizations. If proper management and leading is going to occur, a sound understanding of what distinguishes Einsteins from non-Einsteins is required. The starting point of this understanding is knowing something about intelligence.

## Intelligence

Standardized intelligence testing is still alive and prospering in developed countries. Americans have grown so accustomed to taking tests to prove themselves competent that most people don't bother to question the tests' accuracy, legitimacy, or value. The American intelligence testing system has encouraged a so-called meritocracy.

There appear to be distinct differences in the critical thinking, problem solving, analytical, and mathematical competencies of Einsteins and non-Einsteins. However, there is no perfect intelligence test available that can pick out exactly who is an Einstein and who is not. Intelligent people come in many varieties. What managers observe is that Einstein intelligence typically comes in the form of analytical and critical thinking competencies.

Charles Spearman, a father of intelligence testing, wrote that "an accurate measurement of everyone's intelligence would seem to herald the feasibility of selecting the better endowed persons for admissions into citizenship—and even the right of having offspring." This was written in 1927. If it was stated today, Spearman would be attacked for his ignorance, elitism, and lack of sensitivity. Even though Spearman-type comments are now out of place, intelligence testing and scores continue to be widely used and are a topic of debates. The roots and the full debates surrounding intelligence testing and scoring are beyond the scope of this book. We are interested, however, in discussing intelligence in general as it applies to the profiling of Einsteins.

Alfred Binet of France created the first practical test of intelligence in 1904. Along with a younger collaborator, he developed the Binet-Simon scale. This test continues to serve as a model for contemporary IQ testing. The test today is referred to as the Stanford-Binet Intelligence Scale.

The original Binet-Simon test measures intelligence according to the most difficult items the test taker can perform. The highest level performed is equivalent to a child's mental age. For example, a five-year-old who performs tasks that most eight-year-olds perform is said to have a mental age of eight.

The Binet-Simon scale was slanted toward verbal and language skills. In 1916, Lewis Terman of Stanford University Americanized the original Binet-Simon scale. Terman predicted that the intelligence test could unambiguously confirm any deficiencies in a person. Terman graded one's intelligence according to an intelligence quotient classification as follows:

---

IQ above 140—near genius or genius

120–140—very superior intelligence

110–120—superior intelligence

90–110—normal or average intelligence

80–90—dullness

70–80—borderline deficiency, sometimes referred to as feeble or mindlessness

Below 70—feeble mindedness

---

Advocates of the power of intelligence to predict career success point to the research studies that have been able to stratify occupations by average intelligence level. (There are also available studies that show no ability to predict success.) One study of 10,000 people found that accountants had average IQs of 128, the IQ of mechanics averaged 106, and those of teamsters averaged 88. At the time of this study in the 1940s, Einsteins were not even thought about. Does this kind of research perpetuate the view that higher-status occupations are filled with the most intelligent individuals? Or is the strong association between IQ and status, in fact, an artifact of the credentialing and gatekeeping role higher education plays in the occupational structure?

---

### Black Hole

Intelligence test scores have been misused, misinterpreted, and misstated. There is a key lesson to be learned about an IQ test score: to measure intelligence is not to derive anything about its causes. *Measurement* is only a description—*explanation* is another task altogether.

---

We have no universally accepted set of studies showing conclusively that Einsteins are super smart. We do, however, propose that with regard to technology, computer literacy, systems integration, logic, problem solving, and creativity, Einsteins are exceptionally intelligent compared to non-Einsteins. However, Howard Gardner, a Harvard University professor, warns us about narrowly defining intelligence. When Vince Carter of the NBA Toronto Rafters performs an extraordinary dunk or Luciano Pavarotti reaches a miraculous high C from his vocal cords, we are in awe. We do not think intelligence, but we do think genius. Gardner proposes that kinesthetic intelligence and musical intelligence are what Carter and Pavarotti display. Gardner believes that Standford-Binet type measures of intelligence rule out other types of intelligence.

Besides the physical and musical types, Gardner proposes spatial (visual), interpersonal (understanding others), intrapersonal (knowing yourself), naturalist (making distinctions in the natural world), logic, and linguistics to make up his view of multiple human intelligences. Gardner proposes that children who do not excel in Stanford-Binet intelligence may not receive the nurturing and support they need. Many of these children seek out other forms of intelligence to pursue and develop.

Using Gardner's multiple intelligence description would suggest that Einsteins excel in logic, logistics, and spatial categories. There are not a lot of Einsteins dunking basketballs in the NBA or singing operas in Rome. In terms of the other Gardner intelligence types, let's just leave it at the level of needing further debate and study. Einsteins do not have the reputation of being interpersonally wise and smooth or preparing to climb the highest mountain peaks. They also have an image of not being very emotionally intelligent.

Daniel Goleman created a stir in management circles with the publication of his book *Emotional Intelligence*. Like Gardner, he believes that the standard IQ concept of intelligence is too narrow. Emotional intelligence is the ability to motivate oneself and persist in the face of frustrations, being able to control impulse and delay gratification and to regulate one's moods, being sensitive to others' feelings and concerns, and keeping distress from draining the ability to think.

## Super Smart Role Models

We are not talking about dunking basketball intelligence (kinesthetic) or empathizing (emotional intelligence) with the plight of others when discussing Einsteins. These forms of intelligence serve a purpose in life and are important in some occupations. On the other hand, we are talking about logic, creativity, curiosity, and the problem solving smarts displayed by Bill Gates, Paul Allen, Michael Dell, Bill Hewlett, and Gordon Moore. These are super smart Einsteins who have become part of the business, management, entrepreneurship, and computer literature. They are recognized names who serve as examples of or role models for Einsteins.

Do you qualify or fit the super smart label? Try these three questions (the answers will follow):

1. Why are manhole covers round?

2. How many piano tuners are there in the world?

3. Given a gold bar that can be cut exactly twice and a contractor who must be paid one-seventh of a gold bar a day for seven days, what would you do?

Terms used to describe Einsteins, in addition to intelligent/smart, include driven, passionate, committed, results-oriented. When job candidates seek employment at Microsoft, they had better get ready for a difficult journey. At Microsoft the "interview rounds" involve a grueling ritual in which candidates are grilled for hours. Microsoft (before any Department of Justice intervention) employed 39,000 people. The company prides itself on attracting, hiring, and retaining super smart people. The super smart mystique at Microsoft is worn with pride. The company is described by employees as a magic garden, a "country," and a permanent home. Almost all of Microsoft's employees have their own offices (not cubicles), and it has an eerie quiet atmosphere dominated by e-mails and no telephones ringing.

Another Microsoft ingredient expected of their Einsteins is the concept that "work is life." Microsofters live to work, instead of working to live. Ten hours a day, even twenty-hour workdays, are common among some employees. Although, the eighty-hour work week has yielded to the sixty- to seventy-hour work week, the work ethic is powerful.

Microsoft presents only one view of an Einstein dominant company and the value it places on intelligence and other attributes. A number of principles to focus on when defining or profiling what constitutes Einsteins are sharpened by examining Microsoft's 39,000 employee army, as well as Einsteins in other firms around the world. These principles are:

- *Curiosity*   Always searching for answers. Remember Einstein and his compass needle?
- *Work ethic*   Willingness to work long hours, sleep on the floor, and live on flight-fueled caffeine-loaded drinks.

- *Logical*  Try to examine the sequence or linkages in words, formulas, reports, data, and statistics.
- *Tolerance for ambiguity and uncertainty*  Being open to the unknown and a willingness to take a risk and suffer failure.
- *Passion for results*  You can talk through the night, philosophize about any subject, but what are the results? Did you ship a software program, install a new system, or produce enough routers to meet growing demand?

If Albert Einstein, Leonardo da Vinci, and Galileo were alive today and were working as Einsteins at Microsoft, Motorola, Dell Computer, Cisco Systems, or Intel, what would they say to aspiring Einsteins? Be curious, work hard, use your logic, take risks and experiment, and make sure everything works well and safely.

How did you do on the three questions on page 15?

---

### Einstein Answers

*Why are manhole covers round?*
A square manhole cover could be tilted on its side and placed diagonally over the hole. The result is, it would fall into the hole.

*How many piano tuners are there in the world?*
This depends on how many pianos there are, how often you believe they need to be tuned, and how much it costs to tune pianos. (This question is used to determine how thorough the job candidate is in searching for answers).

*Given a gold bar that can be cut exactly twice and a contractor who must be paid one-seventh of a gold bar every day for seven days, what would you do?*
First, cut the bar at the one-seventh and three-seventh marks. The result is three pieces: 1/7, 2/7, and 4/7. The first day pay the contractor the 1/7 bar size. The second day pay the contractor with the 2/7 bar and receive the 1/7 bar back as change (contractor now has 2/7 bar). The third day pay with the 1/7 bar. On the fourth day pay with the 4/7 bar and receive 3/7 back in change (2/7 + 1/7 bars). Continue until the contractor is fully paid on the seventh day.

Source: Mark Gimein, "Smart Is Not Enough, *Fortune*, January 8, 2001, 124–134

---

## Cognitive Styles and Einsteins

A reoccurring attribute when discussing or constructing an Einstein profile in addition to intelligence is problem solving. Swiss psychiatrist Carl Jung proposed that the population is made up of two types: extroverted and introverted. The extrovert is outgoing, gregarious, publicly expressive, and speaks before he or she thinks. The introvert is reserved, concentrates, thinks before speaking, and is reflective. Some claim that in the U.S. population over 60 percent of the people would be considered extroverts. Jung identified two types of perception (sensing and intuiting) and two types of judgment (thinking and feeling). Perception involves gathering and separating information, and judgment describes how decisions are made. A mother-daughter team of Katherine Briggs and Isabell Briggs Myers developed the Myers-Briggs Type Indicator (MBTI) to measure Jung's theory of problem solving type. Since its origination, the MBTI has been completed by millions of people around the world.

Classifying Einsteins into one of Jung's cognitive styles reveals that systems analysts, programmers, network administrators, and engineers come in many shapes, types, and packages. There is, however, a research stream indicating that Einsteins tend to be more introverted. At least, the stereotype and some research findings support this viewpoint.

Introverts like to take time to think things through clearly. They are open to information. Introverts and extroverts are equal in terms of standard intelligence test scores. However, introverts are predominant in earning the highest college-degree levels. This may be due to the fact that introverts can adjust to the isolation of study more easily than extroverts. Introverts tend to work passionately on problem solving for long periods of time. They pursue an issue in depth. Because of their passion and work ethic, introverts get upset when their ideas, suggestions, and recommendations are rejected or doubted.

The intuitive type (N) enjoys ambiguous problems, regularly floats new ideas, gets bored with routine, likes complexity, and has creative vision and insight. The thinking type (T) tries to establish objective decision criteria, likes analysis, is work-oriented, and can be viewed as cold and aloof. The perceiver type (I) enjoys searching and finding, tolerates ambiguity, is open-minded and curious, and is concerned with knowledge.

Although, as is the case with intelligence, a perfect cognitive style profile of Einsteins is not possible, it seems reasonable to conclude:

- Einsteins fall into each of the personality and style types.
- The majority (though not a vast majority) of Einsteins are likely introverts.
- The N (intuitive), T (thinking) type that prefers to define problems and opportunities, identify objectives, establish criteria for success, desire independence, and is conceptual and analytical best describes Einsteins.

## The Einstein Profile: A Summary

We are convinced that Einsteins come in every size, shape, form, color, nationality, age, personality, and IQ level (though at least above 110). The stereotypical tattooed, Twinkie-eating, twenty-something with a bungee-jumping attitude is fun to describe, but it doesn't fit the Einstein population well. Einstein managers and leaders who are responsible for the work flow, results, and protection of the firm's assets need a better handle on identifying, attracting, retaining, and leading Einsteins than resorting to "nerd" and "geek" descriptors. After all, there are over 40 million of these invaluable human assets walking on earth, and playing by a new set of management and leadership rules is imperative.

All that we can offer in this attempt to profile Einsteins is a general guide that has some merit. We do not have the perfect Einstein detector or map for managers to implement. Caution in using our profile is needed. This caution should be exercised because few Einsteins will fit exactly the main points in the profile. There is also caution needed because not every Einstein job, work assignment, or project is exciting, stimulating, and held in the highest esteem. Take the job of a "porn sifter" for a filtering company. This work involves tracking down new adult sites and blocking them out so kids or library patrons or goof off employees can't get to them. The "porn sifter" has to be intelligent and morally upstanding. However, the individual has to also think like a lecher and pervert to locate pornographic sites. This job requires a person to find pornographic sites that people may inadvertently unearth by typing the wrong letters into the URL command bar. Is this type of Einstein work exciting, stimulating, and prestigious?

These cautions are expressed before anyone starts to reach final, definitive conclusions about Einsteins in general and the work performed by them. The Einstein Profile (EP) is offered to managers and leaders as only a starting point in considering the best way to work with these unique and needed people in the new digital economy. The main characteristics in the profile that describe Einsteins are:

*Intelligent*, in terms of logic, spatial relationships, systems, mathematics, and problem solving.

*Computer literate*, that is, have knowledge about computer, programs, software and hardware.

*Work ethic directed*, which means working until the problem is solved, the product shipped, the service completed. Passionate about doing what they are challenged by, and will periodically work a 24/7 schedule if necessary.

*Curious*, emplified by always experimenting, tinkering, fixing, adapting. Would like answers to easy and difficult issues, phenomena, situations. Fascinated with technology and how it works.

*Introvert/Extrovert*, tending to be more introverted. Can work alone, but enjoys the give and take with other Einsteins.

*Reflective/Thinker*, thinks before speaking and mulls over the situation, problem, and situation at hand.

These Einstein characteristics can be reversed to fit the managers who are charged with leading organizational assets, including human assets. Managers must be intelligent about how to utilize the gifts of their Einsteins. They must possess computer literacy to the point of knowing what computers can and cannot provide in terms of added value. Managers must constantly strive (work ethic) to aggregate (challenge) the Einstein team by use of fair, firm, and tactful managerial principles. The independence of Einsteins is not well-suited for a close, hovering, and demanding managerial style. Also, managers must be curious to experiment with different approaches, at various times, with an array of Einstein clans and individuals.

The manager must also be quiet with some Einsteins and more gregarious and open with other Einsteins. Flexibility in terms of introversion and extroversion will be required. Managers must also be excellent communicators. They must be able to clearly explain and carefully listen.

Einstein once wrote, "All the valuable things, material, spiritual, and moral which we receive from society can be traced back through countless generations to certain creative individuals." He was talking about what we refer to here as "Einsteins." Why does one caveman carve a dagger from flint, while his fellow cavemen use sticks? Geneticists have long sought a "genius gene" that might explain the differences in cavemen, managers, workers, men, and women. The secret of genius is still unclear and mystifying. There are, however, patterns of intelligence, thoughts, style, and emotion that separate humans. We call the smart people who form the key assets of the modern workplace "Einsteins." Managing them effectively can be achieved by understanding their character, their desires, and their dreams.

# Managing Einsteins: Challenges and Actions

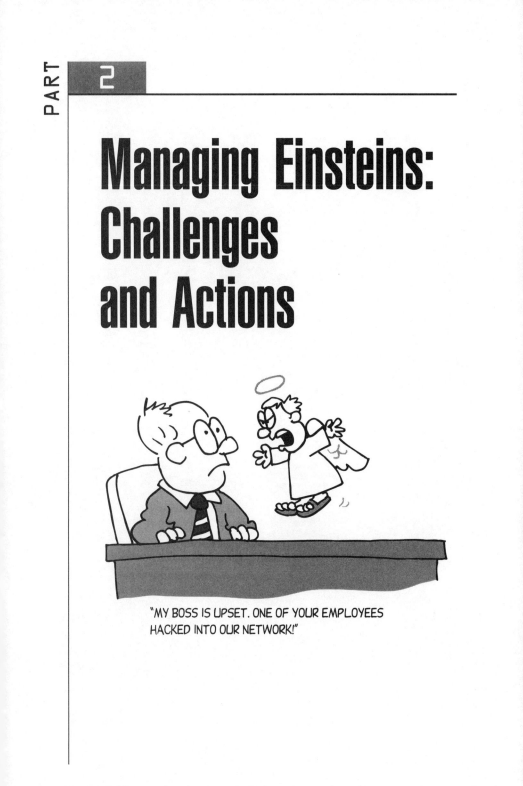

"MY BOSS IS UPSET. ONE OF YOUR EMPLOYEES HACKED INTO OUR NETWORK!"

## CHAPTER 2

# Recruiting Einsteins

## Preview Einstein Story

### A Sample of Einstein Jobs

The rapid spread of computers and information technology has generated a need for Einsteins to perform many different jobs. Einsteins design and develop new hardware and software systems, incorporate new technologies, integrate systems, work on special projects, engage in product quality testing, design websites, and conduct engineering analyses. There are hundreds of Einstein jobs that require intelligence, logic, curiosity, openness, and a willingness to experiment. One of the more publicized Einstein jobs is that of systems analyst. Einsteins develop new computer systems, including hardware and software. Most systems analysts work with a specific type of system. Analysts use techniques such as structured analysis, data modeling, information engineering, mathematical model building, sampling, and cost accounting to play the system.

Analysts, who do in-depth testing of products, are referred to as software quality assurance analysts. In addition to running tests, these analysts diagnose problems, recommend solutions, and determine if program requirements have been met.

Einsteins are also programmer analysts who design and update the software that runs a computer. Because they are responsible for both programming and systems analysis, these Einsteins are skilled and knowledgeable in both areas.

Another Einstein group is computer engineers who work with the hardware and software aspects of systems design and development. They usually apply the theories and principles of science and mathematics to design hardware, software, networks, and processes, and to solve technical problems.

*Continued*

The computer scientist title is applied to a variety of Einsteins who usually design computers and the software that runs them, develop information technologies, and develop and adapt principles for applying computers to new uses. These Einsteins work in jobs distinguished by a high level of theoretical expertise and innovations.

These few samples of Einstein work are used simply to illustrate that Einsteins are performing work that is expected to be among the fastest-growing occupations through 2008. Growth is driven by rapid growth in computer and data processing services. Falling prices in hardware and software are likely to induce more organizations to expand computerized operations and integrate new technologies. This means a demand for more Einsteins. Managers must keep a sharp eye on intelligent problem solvers who have a passion to work on challenging situations, technologies, and systems.

In October 2000, President Clinton signed into law the American Competitiveness in the Twenty-first Century Act, which increases the annual cap of H1-B for skilled foreign workers. The cap was increased from 115,000 to 195,000 for each of the next three years. The new law states that once an H1-B holder's green card application has been pending for 181 days, the worker can work for any U.S. employer without jeopardizing the process. One consequence of this act is that more international Einsteins will be allowed to work and stay in American firms (see Chapter 13).

The Information Technology Association of America's latest study of the labor market found that 850,000 jobs were unfilled as of April 2000. The number of unfilled jobs increased to 1.6 million by April 2001.

Visa cap increases and position vacancies indicate that recruitment and staffing of Einsteins is going to be difficult for most organizations. Staffing is the process by which the individual and the organization become matched to form an employment relationship. Staffing is not a onetime event, such as "we hired two Einsteins last Friday." Rather, it is a process composed of a series of interrelated activities including recruitment, selection, decision making, and offers. The hiring of an Einstein is the culmination of the staffing process.

# The Vital Role of Staffing

Staffing is a vital activity from the perspective of organizational strategy. Strategically, managers use staffing to anticipate and fulfill the organization's needs for Einsteins and non-Einsteins in ways that enable the firm to survive, accomplish its mission, and achieve objectives. Firms must have sufficient numbers of Einsteins and other employees aboard so the firm can function. Labor shortages, such as the type suggested by the Information Technology Association of America, would disrupt and jeopardize the success of organizations. Hiring non-Einsteins (underqualified) to fill Einstein-type positions would require special training, close supervision, and major adjustments in work assignments.

## Person/Work Match

At the core of staffing is the person/work match. This match seeks to align the knowledge, skills, and abilities of individuals and work requirements in ways that will result in desired outcomes, exceptional performance, high morale, retention of human resources, and work satisfaction.

Einsteins are characterized by their level of knowledge, skills, and abilities (KSA). Matching work requirements with individual characteristics are reflected in the diagram displayed in Exhibit 2.1.

---

### Black Hole

Too many managers are fixated about the amount of time Einsteins put into doing the work. Our advice is to move away from "time put in" to "results achieved." Managing, leading, and facilitating "time worked" is not productive or worth the effort. Results achieved should be your priority.

---

## Person/Organization Match

Often an organization attempts to determine not only how well the person fits with the work, but also whether there is a fit with the organization. Likewise, individuals also attempt to determine their own work preference and organization fit. Organizational values and culture are norms of desirable attitudes and behaviors for an organization's employees. Honesty, integrity, work ethic, fairness and justice,

**Exhibit 2.1**
Person/Work Match

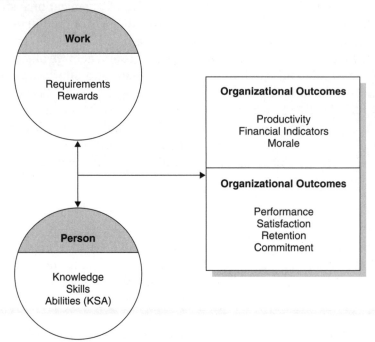

concern about customers, and trust are part of the valued culture mix that individuals attempt to gauge before joining a firm and even after becoming a part of the firm.

This search for a person/organization match is not a perfect science. Einsteins attempt to take stock of the fit before taking the plunge. The match, search, and ritual occur for Einsteins every time they look for a new firm, new work, or new position. Einsteins have had the luxury of constantly looking for the "new" situation because of the attractiveness of their KSA package, which is in high demand.

## Staffing Strategy

Einstein managers must develop a staffing strategy that explains and outlines how they will acquire and deploy Einsteins. For example, a software development organization may have as its mission "to develop and apply for individuals and families a time and cost efficient electronic approach to manage all finances and records." This mission drives the development of goals that capture the product development approach, sales growth, and competitive advantages achieved through the firm's electronic product and customer service. These objectives are linked to assumptions about the number of Einsteins needed, when, and how they will be rewarded.

The staffing strategy may suggest a range of possibilities, including (a) hiring the bulk of Einsteins from other software companies, (b) hiring Einsteins freshly out of college, (c) building a new training facility that will result in internally identifying employees who are potential Einsteins and immersing them in training, (d) developing compensation packages significantly above market averages to attract Einsteins, or (e) using a combination of the a, b, c, and d options.

Forecasting the number of Einsteins needed is a form of planning. Thus, it becomes a reflection of the firm's projections of sales, technological change, and productivity goals. Many specific techniques are available to conduct forecasts, including making estimates, studying labor market trends, hiring consultants, using mathematical models, and using statistical approaches. There is no shortage of forecasting tools that can be found in books, articles, and on the Internet.

Exhibit 2.2 presents a straightforward example of how a firm with ten current projects forecasts its demand for Einsteins three years into the future, when they expect to be operating fifteen projects. The firm

## Exhibit 2.2
### Predicting Demand for Einsteins

| Einstein Positions | A<br>Number<br>Currently | B<br>Ratio of<br>Einsteins/10<br>Projects | C<br>Projected Einstein<br>Needs for 15<br>Projects<br>B × 15 |
|---|---|---|---|
| Network Administrator | 4 | .40 | 6 |
| Programmers | 32 | 3.20 | 48 |
| Engineer: Design | 30 | 3.00 | 45 |
| Engineer: Hardware | 12 | 1.20 | 18 |
| Software Developer | 20 | 2.00 | 30 |
| Telecommunications Engineer | 6 | .60 | 9 |
| Project Manager | 10 | 1.00 | 15 |
| Systems Analyst | 16 | 1.60 | 24 |
|  | 130 |  | 195 |

**Exhibit 2.3**
Projected Developers Needed

| A Developers Quit (3-year record) | B Present Developers | C Turnover | D Developers Remaining | E Developers Needed by Third Year (EXH. 2.2) | F Projected Developers Hired by Year 3 [E-D] |
|---|---|---|---|---|---|
| 30 | 20 | 6 | 14 | 30 | 16 |

expects all fifteen projects to be operating by the end of the third year. The current Einstein staff of 130 will have to increase by 65, within three years, to a total of 195. There will also be some turnover considerations over the course of three years. Assuming there is a history of turnover, the firm could use calculations that incorporate this factor into the forecast. Assume that thirty developers left the firm in the previous three-year period.

Since there are now twenty developers, it is forecasted that three years in the future, six developers will have departed the firm (.30 × 20 = 6). This is shown in column C. This means that three years from now fourteen developers will still be working. Since thirty developers are needed, sixteen new developers will have to be hired.

Einstein managers must engage in their own supply and demand calculations. Putting off these calculations or ignoring this work is likely to result in scrambling for talent, being understaffed, and overworking the present Einstein team. A word of caution is needed. In the present era of increased startups and uncertainty, it is difficult for any manager to predict the future with a high degree of accuracy by using history. In many cases there may not be any history, which makes supply and demand calculations extremely difficult.

---

### Influence Tip

A manager who wants to be a leader has to think in terms of multiple staffing options. Einsteins can be hired as full-timers, part-timers, flextimers, telecommuters, independent contractors, temps, and whatever else it takes to get the work done. Staffing must be viewed as coming in many different shapes, varieties, and time packages. Do not limit yourself to a single staffing approach.

# Hiring Einsteins

Once an organization determines its current and future staffing needs, it needs to hire the best Einsteins available. This process involves recruitment, selection, and socialization.

*Recruitment* refers to organizational activities that generate a pool of Einsteins for specific work, jobs, roles, or projects. *Selection* is the process of making a "hire" or "no hire" decision regarding the Einstein being considered for the position. This process involves determining the characteristics required to perform the work and then measuring Einstein applicants on those characteristics.

**Organizational policies and practices.**　In some organizations, policies and practices affect recruiting and who is recruited. One of the most significant of these is promotion from within. For all practical purposes, this policy means that many organizations recruit from outside the organization only at the initial hiring level. Most employees favor this approach. They feel this is fair to the currently employed Einsteins and assures them of a secure future and a fair chance at promotion. Some employers also feel this practice helps protect trade secrets. The techniques used for internal recruiting will be discussed later in this chapter.

"FOR THE FIRST PART OF YOUR INTERVIEW, WE WILL DROP YOU IN A JUNKYARD. YOU WILL THEN MAKE A NUCLEAR FISSION GENERATOR OUT OF SPARE PARTS."

Is promotion of Einsteins from within a good policy? Not always. An organization may become so stable and lazy that it is set in its ways. In such cases, promotion from within may be detrimental, and new employees from outside might be helpful.

Other policies can also affect recruiting. Certain organizations have always hired more than their fair share of the disabled, veterans, or previously retired Einsteins, for example, and they may look to these sources first. Others may favor nepotism and hire relatives. All these policies affect who is recruited.

**Organizational image.**  The image of the employer generally held by the public can affect recruitment. All else being equal, it should be easier for an organization with a positive corporate image to attract and retain Einsteins than an organization with a negative image. Thus, for those organizations that reach the top of *Fortune* magazine's "most admired" list, such as ITT or the most recent two-time winner, General Electric, the time and effort needed to recruit high-quality Einsteins may be less than for competitors who rank poorly. Recruitment should also be somewhat easier for companies that exude a strong community presence or positive name recognition.

## An Einstein View of Recruiting

The Einstein applicant's abilities, attitudes, and preferences are a part of their portfolios. These factors affect recruits in two ways: how they set their work role preferences, and how they go about seeking positions. Understanding these is vital to effective recruiting.

**Preferences of Einsteins.**  Just as organizations have ideal specifications for recruits, so do Einsteins have a set of preferences for work characteristics. From an Einstein's point of view, choosing a position involves at least two major steps. First, he or she chooses an occupation—perhaps in high school or early in college. Then she or he chooses the organization to work for within that broader occupation.

A survey conducted by the National Association of Colleges and Employers found that occupational choice is most heavily influenced by parents, followed by teachers, career counselors, friends, and relatives. As previously mentioned, choice of an organization might be influenced by corporate image. The communication process in recruitment is critical to attracting applicants. In reality, however, this decision isn't always purely rational; it is also affected by unconscious processes, chance, and luck.

**Searching.** Einsteins who are successful at finding the "right work" tend to follow similar research processes. It is not always enough to simply be in the right place at the right time. The effective Einstein creates opportunities in a systematic way. An effective search involves several steps, including self-assessment, information gathering, networking, targeting specific jobs, and successful self-presentation.

The search is a process that begins with self-assessment. The purpose of self-assessments is for Einsteins to recognize their career goals and their strengths and weaknesses, interests and values, and preferred lifestyles. This information is used later in the search to help the Einstein assess whether there is a fit with a particular offer. The assessment is similar to what Einstein managers are doing, but from the perspective of the Einstein.

Information gathering and networking are methods for generating lists of potential employers and positions. Sources of information include newspapers, trade publications, college recruitment offices, and organizational "insiders."

Einsteins ask questions such as:

1. Company size preference: small, medium, or large, or no particular size?

2. Sector preference: private, not for profit, or public sector?

3. What kinds of industries interest me? This question is usually based on interests in products or services. Do I prefer working with mechanical objects or counseling people? This is a crucial question.

4. Have I checked to make sure that the sector, product, or service has a good future and will lead to growth and opportunity?

Einstein managers need to be aware of these questions so they are prepared to help Einsteins properly assess a position and the firm. Research suggests that recruiters want to see a résumé and cover letter that has been personally typed and is truthful.

Unfortunately for Einstein managers, not all job seekers provide truthful résumés. A survey conducted by Reid Psychological Systems found that as many as 95 percent of college students are willing to be less than truthful about themselves when they are searching for a job. And with the use of résumé databases constantly increasing as an initial screening tool, the temptation to embellish one's own qualifications might be difficult to ignore.

# Methods of Recruiting

Once an organization has decided it needs additional or replacement Einsteins, it is faced with the decision of how to generate applications. The organization can look to sources internal to the company and, if necessary, to sources external to the company. Most organizations have to use both internal and external sources to generate a sufficient number of applicants. Whenever there is an inadequate supply of Einsteins inside the organization, it must effectively "get its message across" to external candidates. It is here that the organization's choice of a particular method of recruitment can make all the difference in the success of the recruiting efforts.

## *Internal Recruiting*

**Posting.** Organizations can make effective use of skills inventories for identifying internal Einsteins for vacancies. It is difficult, however, for Einstein managers to be aware of all current employees who might be interested in the vacancy. To help with this problem, they use an approach called *posting and bidding*.

In the past, posting was little more than the use of bulletin boards and company publications for advertising job openings. Today, however, posting has become one of the more innovative recruiting techniques being used by organizations. Many companies now see it as an integrated component of an effective career management system.

Amoco's career management system includes a posting program. Openings in this organization are posted on a worldwide electronic system. If an employee applies for a transfer to a posted position and is turned down, then the person who posted the job is required to send the "applicant" specific feedback about why he or she was not selected.

**Inside moonlighting and employees' friends.** If there is a short-term shortage, or if no great amount of additional work is necessary, the organization can use *inside moonlighting*. It could offer to pay bonuses of various types to people not on a time payroll to entice workers into wanting to take on a "second" job. Nationally, it is estimated that approximately 6 percent of all employed people have held more than one job at the same time. Thus, some persons will clearly be motivated to accept the additional work if they are fairly compensated.

## External Recruiting

A number of methods are available for external recruiting. Media advertising, employment databases, employment agencies, executive search firms, special events recruiting, and summer internships are among them.

**Media advertisements.** Organizations advertise to acquire Einsteins. Various media are used, the most common being help wanted ads in daily newspapers. Organizations also advertise for people in trade and professional publications. Other media used are billboards, subway and bus cards, radio, telephone, and television. Some Einstein managers do a reverse twist—they advertise for a situation wanted and reward anyone who tips them off about a position.

**The Internet.** Perhaps no method has ever had as revolutionary an effect on organizational recruitment practices as the Internet. According to Forrester Research of Cambridge, Massachusetts, there are more than 2.5 million individual résumés posted on the Internet and approximately 30,000 different websites devoted in some manner to job posting activities. Quite obviously, the Internet has become one of the most prominent of all worldwide recruiting methods for recruiting Einsteins. Current estimates are that over 95 percent of all U.S. companies now utilize the Internet for some or all of their recruitment-related activities.

There are many reasons for the popularity of the Internet as a method of recruitment. From the Einstein manager's perspective, it is a relatively inexpensive way to attract qualified applicants. For example, using an executive search firm might cost an organization as much as one-third of a position's first-year salary as a commission. A large, multicolored advertisement in a professional journal can easily cost $10,000 or more. Compare these figures with membership fees of about $4,000 for an online employment site such as the *Online Career Center* (*www.occ.com*), which provides rapid access to literally thousands of prospective applicants.

From the Einstein manager's perspective, the Internet allows for searches over a broader array of geographic and company postings than was ever before possible. As of July 1, 2001, there were more than 430,000 job postings at *www.monster.com*, the nation's largest website devoted to recruitment, and over 8,000 employers who regularly use *www.dice.com* to find Einsteins. Computers allow the Einstein to search through these thousands of jobs by searching for location, specialization, type of work, and starting salary.

There are other online services, such as *CareerPath.Com (www.careerpath.com)*, which catalogs more than 100,000 traditional newspaper recruiting ads from large newspapers across the United States in one easily searchable database. There are many other, more specialized online sites that focus on jobs in particular areas, such as health care, higher education, and federal employment.

Organizations are also beginning to see that having their own Human Resources Web page on the Internet can be an effective addition to their overall recruitment strategy. A typical organizational home page will provide background information about the company, its products and services, and employment opportunities and application procedures. Many also include online résumé templates that can be completed and sent via the Internet.

**Employment agencies and executive search firms.**  Although similar in purpose, employment agencies and executive search firms differ in many important ways. Search firms tend to concentrate their efforts on higher-level managerial positions with salaries in excess of $50,000, while agencies deal primarily with middle-level management or below. Most search firms are on retainer, which means that the organization pays them a fee whether or not their efforts are successful. In contrast, agencies are usually paid only when they have actually provided new hire. Finally, search firms usually charge higher fees for their services. One of the reasons that organizations are willing to pay these higher fees to find Einsteins is that search firms frequently engage in their recruiting efforts while maintaining the confidentiality of both the recruiting organization and the person being recruited.

**Special-events recruiting.**  When the supply of Einsteins available is not large, or when the organization is new or not well-known, some organizations have successfully used special events to attract potential employees. They may stage open houses, schedule visits to headquarters, provide literature, and advertise these events in appropriate media.

One of the most interesting approaches is to provide job fairs: a group of firms sponsors a meeting or exhibition at which each has a booth to publicize jobs available. This technique is especially useful for smaller, less well-known employers. It appeals to job seekers who wish to locate in a particular area and those who want to minimize travel and interview time. For example, a recent job fair held in Virginia was able to generate 4,000 job candidates in a little under four hours of operation. And, yes, here as well there is an Internet site to help the recruit. CareerExpo, located at *www.eos.net/careerex*, provides current listings of when and where job fairs will be held in the United States.

**College recruiting.** There is a growing gap between Einstein skills that organizations will need over the next several years and those currently possessed by potential Einsteins. Also, although the number of jobs requiring a college degree is expected to increase rapidly, the Department of Labor predicts that there will be 18 million college graduates competing for the 14 million college-level jobs available in the year 2005. College recruiting of Einsteins is extremely difficult, time-consuming, and expensive for the organization. Nonetheless, recruiters generally believe that college recruiting is one of the most effective ways of identifying talented Einsteins. All this suggests that college recruiting will continue to play an important role in organizations' overall recruitment strategies but that organizations will be careful about controlling expenses.

## Realistic Job Previews

Einstein managers involved in recruiting must know how to provide realistic expectations about the work. When they do so, there is significantly lower turnover of new Einsteins, and the same number of people apply. Researchers have found that most recruiters give general, glowing descriptions of the company rather than a balanced or truthful presentation.

Research suggests that recruitment can be made more effective through the use of *realistic work previews*. A RWP provides the prospective Einstein with pertinent information about the work without distortion or exaggeration. In traditional work previews, the work is presented as attractive, interesting, and stimulating. Some work is all of these things. However, most work assignments have some unattractive features. The RWP presents the full picture, warts and all, as suggested in Exhibit 2.4.

**Exhibit 2.4**
Realistic Work Preview Procedures

REALISTIC PREVIEW
↓
Firm sets work expectations and articulates.
↓
Work may or may not be attractive, depending on individual's needs.
↓
Some Einsteins accept, some reject work offer.
↓
Einsteins' previous work experience confirms expectations.
↓
Einsteins' satisfaction; needs matched to work.
↓
Work attachment, satisfaction, and infrequent thoughts of quitting.

## Selection

Selection is the process by which an organization chooses from a list of Einsteins the person or persons who best meet the selection criteria for the position available, considering current environmental conditions. Although this definition emphasizes the effectiveness of selection, decisions about whom to hire must also be made efficiently and within the boundaries set forth in equal employment opportunity legislation. Thus, there are actually multiple goals associated with an organization's selection process.

At a basic level, all selection programs attempt to identify Einsteins who have the highest chance of meeting or exceeding the organization's standards of performance. Compounding the problem of developing an effective selection system is the fact that the goal isn't always to find Einsteins who have the most of a given quality. Rather, selection is the search for an optimal match between the work and the amount of any particular characteristic that an applicant may possess. For example, depending on the work, more intelligence isn't always better than less. Or it is possible for an Einstein to be too socially skilled if the work doesn't require high levels of such skills. Thus, it is highly unlikely that a selection system can effectively cope with all possible objectives. As a result, one of the initial tasks involved in developing and implementing an effective selection process is for the organization to identify which objectives are most important for its circumstances.

## Reliability and Validity

Once an Einstein manager has decided upon a set of selection criteria, a technique for assessing each of these must be chosen. The alternatives are numerous: application blanks and biodata forms, interviews, psychological tests of aptitude and personality, work sample tests of present skills, physical and medical testing, and checks of previous experience through references. Regardless of the method chosen for collecting information about applicants, the organization must be certain that the information is both *reliable* and *valid*.

**Reliability.** To be useful a measurement must be stable or repeatable over a variety of testing conditions. As a simple example, imagine that you tried to use a tape measure to determine how tall an applicant for a job as a firefighter was, because there are both minimum and maximum height restrictions for the job. If you measured a given applicant three successive times and obtained values of 6 feet, 6 feet ½ inch, and 5 feet 11½ inches, you may not know the applicant's exact height, but you would have a fairly good idea. On the other hand, imagine that your three attempts yielded values of 6 feet, 6 feet 6 inches, and 5 feet 4 inches. In this latter case, you would have virtually no idea how tall the applicant actually was. The point is that although reliability is rarely perfect, a measuring tool can still be useful if it is only somewhat unreliable. Once the measurements become too inconsistent, however, they become meaningless.

**Validity.** For a selection tool to be useful, it is not sufficient for it to be repeatable or stable. Both legally and organizationally, the measures that it yields must also be valid. There are many ways of assessing validity, but all of them focus on two issues. Validity addresses the questions of what a test measures and how well it has measured it. In selection, the primary concern is whether the assessment technique results in accurate predictions about the future success or failure of an applicant.

## The Selection Process

The selection decision is usually perceived as a series of steps through which Einsteins pass. At each step, more Einsteins are screened out

**Exhibit 2.5**
Typical Selection Decision Process

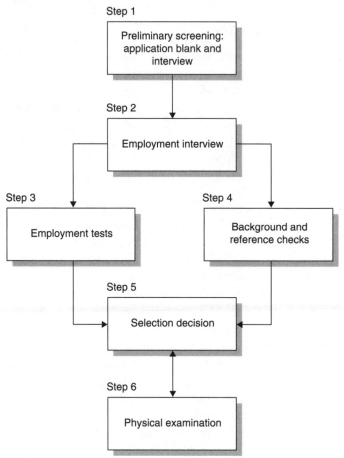

by the organization, or more applicants accept other job offers and drop form the list of applicants. Exhibit 2.5 illustrates a typical series of steps for the selection process.

Few organizations use all steps, since they can be time-consuming and expensive; and some steps, such as 3 and 4, may be performed concurrently or at about the same time. Generally speaking, the more important the Einstein work, the more each step is likely to be used formally.

**Step 1: Preliminary screening.** The most common first step in any selection process usually involves asking an applicant to complete an application form. *Application blanks*, as these are typically called, vary in length and sophistication. Nearly all application blanks ask for enough information to determine whether the individual is minimally qualified for the position.

Although application blanks can be very useful tools, Einstein managers must never forget that they are subject to the same legal standards as any other selection method. Thus, care must be taken that the application blank does not directly or indirectly violate federal or state laws related to employment discrimination. The application blank should not be designed in a way that forces applicants to reveal irrelevant information about themselves, especially information related to sex, race, religion, color, natural origin, age, or disabilities.

**Step 2: Employment interview.** This is the selection technique most often encountered by Einsteins applying for a job. Because interviews are so widely used to select new employees, they must maximize their potential for identifying qualified Einsteins. Two strategies for making the most out of an interview are (1) structuring the interview to be reliable and valid, and (2) training managers to use the best available interviewing techniques.

**Step 3: Employment tests.** There are literally hundreds of published tests from which to choose, and some of the more useful test cost as little as a dollar per applicant. Anyone interested in selecting a test for use in personnel selection can begin with the *Mental Measurements Yearbook*, which summarizes many of the tests and includes a brief evaluation of their effectiveness.

Various kinds of tests can be used for selecting Einsteins. The type that is ultimately used will depend on a number of factors, including the budgetary constraints of the organization, the complexity and difficulty of the job, the size and quality of applicant populations, and of course the knowledge, skills, abilities, and other characteristics required by the job.

**Step 4: Reference checks and recommendations.** If you have ever applied for a vacancy, you were probably asked to provide a list of people whom the organization could contact to get information about you. These references might have been work-related (such as a former supervisor or coworkers), or they might have been personal (such as friends, clergy, or family members). Rarely, when given the opportunity, does someone knowingly include the name of a reference that will give a negative impression to the new organization.

That built-in bias in favor of the Einstein is precisely the reason that, generally, references have often been criticized. Many argue that they will seldom provide an organization with meaningful information about applicants. Equally important, however, are genuine concerns over the legality of asking for and providing such information. Giving out confidential information about a former employee could be construed as a violation of the employee's right to privacy, and giving a negative recommendation opens the reference up to a defamation lawsuit.

Some Einstein managers refuse to provide references for former Einstein employees. The trend in this direction has also caused organizations to include explicit statements in their employee handbooks about corporate policies on checking references. Rather than risk a lawsuit, managers are instructed to give out only verifiable kinds of information such as dates of employment and job title. Under these circumstances, it is almost certain that references will be of little or no value to the hiring organization except as a check on the accuracy of information contained on the application blank.

---

### Einstein Wisdom

Einstein wanted an academic appointment at a prestigious school and needed a letter of recommendation (called a reference letter today) from his professors. A number of them refused to provide him with a recommendation. The result was devastating. He took a lowly job in a Swiss patent office and worked on his problem solving, study of physics, and playing the violin. He stated that "I am enough of an artist to draw freely upon my imagination. Imagination is more important than knowledge. Imagination encircles the world."

---

**Step 6: Physical examinations.**   Careful adherence to the Americans with Disabilities Act indicates that physical examinations can be used to screen out Einsteins but generally should be required only after a conditional offer of employment has been made. However, if an organization is going to use such examinations, all individuals who are conditionally offered employment should be required to have one. These requirements do not mean that an organization must hire an individual with a disability if that person cannot perform the job. They do, however, help to protect the rights of individuals with disabilities who are qualified.

## Socialization

The Einstein staffing process isn't complete until socialization occurs. The socialization process actually begins with the realistic work preview discussed earlier and outlined in Exhibit 2.4, earlier in this chapter. The realistic work preview occurs at what is called the anticipatory stage of socialization. All of the activities prior to the Einstein entering the organization or taking a different position in the same firm are anticipatory. The purpose of these activities is to acquire information about the firm and/or the work. What is working in the firm really like? Do I fit this firm's culture?

The second stage of socialization occurs when an Einstein becomes a member of the firm. This is called the *accommodation socialization* stage. Four major activities comprise this stage. They are (1) establishing new interpersonal relationships with coworkers (typically other Einsteins) and managers, (2) learning the tasks required to perform the work, (3) clarifying the Einstein's role in the firm and in informal groups, and (4) evaluating the progress the Einstein is making to satisfy personal needs, demands of the work, and role expectations.

Managers can help the accommodation stage go more smoothly by being aware of these four major activities. Making Einsteins feel accepted and a part of the team can minimize anxiety and enable them to optimize performance more quickly.

The role management stage evolves after accommodations have occurred. Conflicts between work expectations, managerial requests, personal goals, and home life can emerge. Einstein managers can support and coach Einsteins to get through these potential conflicting pressures is worth the effort. Coaching upon request, sharing viewpoints, listening effectively, and answering questions posed by Einsteins are some of the techniques used to enable them to better manage their roles. Also, Einstein mentoring programs in which a respected Einstein serves as an adviser may help reduce the role conflicts being wrestled with by the employee.

The socialization process has little chance of successfully integrating Einsteins if managers do not work at being supportive during the accommodation and role management stages. Some suggested supportive techniques include being available to listen, recognizing, praising, and calling attention to positive Einstein achievements, periodically expressing confidence in the Einstein's progress (if progress is displayed) and sharing your own socialization experiences to help members feel like part of the team.

## Putting It Together

Every manager must be concerned with ensuring that the organization has the right number of Einsteins available to accomplish its mission and objectives. The availability of Einsteins is limited and is expected to remain so in the future.

The challenges faced by managers include staffing strategy development, attracting a pool of Einsteins through recruitment, selecting the best Einsteins available, securing through acceptance of job offers the best Einsteins available, and socializing the Einsteins by being knowledgeable and supportive. This is a daunting list of challenges.

A carefully constructed staffing, recruitment, selection, and socialization program will provide the most consistent stream of Einsteins available. Note that the word *availability* is emphasized. Sometimes because of geographic reasons, resource availability, organization image, or a host of other factors, managers need to hire good but not the very best Einsteins. This is a challenge since the good Einsteins, under the guidance and support of managers, may have to be developed to become the best.

There is also the challenge of operating within the boundaries of legal requirements when hiring Einsteins. Several legal issues govern staffing practices. The Civil Rights Act, the Age Discrimination Act, and the American With Disabilities Act all prohibit various forms of discrimination. Einstein managers should know the law and take every step necessary to staff, recruit, select, and socialize within its boundaries. Being ignorant of the law and violating legal requirements is not a sufficient excuse for making errors. Managers have a responsibility and a duty to protect themselves and their organization from negligent hiring litigation.

Hiring Einsteins is a journey with many steps and processes. If the manager plans, organizes, controls, and directs the journey from the outset, the consequences are likely to be positive. Being disorganized, haphazard, and sloppy in hiring Einsteins will make the other managerial and leadership tasks difficult and in some instances impossible.

## CHAPTER 3

# Motivating Einsteins

## Preview Einstein Story
### Taking Care of Einsteins

USAA, the San Antonio–based insurance and financial services company, demonstrates the value of motivating employees with impressive corporate facilities. "Anywhere you go in town, if you tell someone you work for USAA, they're impressed," says one employee.

The amenities at USAA begin with an on-site child-care center. The facility can handle 300 kids, and there's car-seat storage for families where one parent drops a child off and the other picks them up.

If you don't drive to work, the company sponsors a van pool. If you ruin your hose, you can pick up a pair at the on-site store. There's a dry cleaning service, a bank, and several ATMs. Even the cafeteria food is tasty enough that employees demanded a service that provides dinner to go.

There are also athletic facilities. The company's three gyms are indistinguishable from those at many upscale health clubs, and one is open twenty-four hours. Outside, employees compete in intramural leagues on basketball and tennis courts, and softball and soccer fields. If you want to work on your golf swing, there's a driving range too.

Amenities like these cost the company a lot, but they buy a lot too. Says one USAA employee, "It makes me feel good to work for a company that other people want to work for, but it also means that I have to produce in order to earn the right to stay here."

Ronald B. Lieber, "100 Best Companies to Work for in America," *Fortune*, January 12, 1998, 72

Motivating Einsteins is a challenge that will require understanding and applying new interpersonal skills. Most management training on motivation introduces managers to motivational approaches that apply to everyone throughout the organization. This is useful. In order to motivate and influence people, general assumptions must be made about a common "human nature." Most managers know, for example, that it is generally effective to praise publicly and to discipline privately. They also know that most people, Einsteins included, respond to workplace incentives, financial and otherwise.

## The Einstein Motivation Model

To develop a motivation model for Einsteins, we wanted to base it on two principles:

1. Einsteins are very much like everyone else.
2. Einsteins are unique.

These apparently contradictory principles have guided us in forming our model. We want to convey to Einstein managers that in many ways their Einsteins are like anyone else they have managed. They have many of the same needs, desires, fears, and hopes of individuals of more common talent. In response to this guiding principle we have borrowed from the works of Maslow and Herzberg.

The second guiding principle, that Einsteins are unique, must also contribute to an effective model for motivating Einsteins. Thus, to craft motivational approaches that are designed to affect the uniqueness of Einsteins requires that managers appeal to their special talents and gifts. The concept of "flow" as developed by Csikszentmihalyi seems uniquely suited to Einsteins and their tendency to prefer focused intellectual work and projects.

Thus, we have developed a three-pronged model based on the work of Maslow, Herzberg, and Csikszentmihalyi:

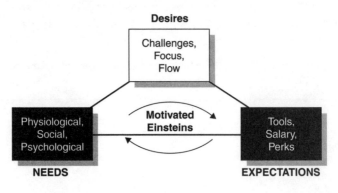

In this model, Einsteins are conceived to be motivated on three levels, need satisfaction, want satisfaction, and intellectual satisfaction. Maslow's hierarchy needs explains very well how people progress through need satisfaction and put themselves in position to achieve what Maslow called "self-actualization." Herzberg helps managers understand that employees *expect* certain things to be a part of their work environment. It's imperative that managers meet employee expectations by providing them with the basic tools and resources to do their jobs. Once basic needs and expectations are met, managers can turn their attention to employee *desires* for challenge, excitement, and (dare we say it?) happiness.

Before we begin that discussion, however, we want to provide you with a simple equation that you can keep in mind to help you motivate your Einsteins on a day-to-day basis. As a general rule, you should keep the following equation in mind for motivating Einsteins:

$$E = MC^2$$

You've probably seen this famous equation before. To Albert Einstein it meant that energy (E) is equal to mass (M) times the speed of light (C) squared. In our interpretation, effort (E) is equal to a proper amount of management (M) times communication (C) squared. Simply, Einsteins require less direct management and require more open communication than other employees. A light managerial touch with a liberal dose of honest communication can tap into an Einstein's vast reserve of personal motivation, leading to high levels of effort (E).

## What Is Motivation?

*Motivation* is a general term used to describe the process of starting, directing, and maintaining physical and cognitive activities. It is a broad concept that embraces such internal mechanisms as (1) preferences for one activity over another, (2) enthusiasm and vigor of a person's responses, and (3) persistence of organized action toward relevant goals. The word comes from the Latin *movere*, "to move."

Managers can't "see" motivation, just as no manager has ever seen thinking, perceiving, or learning. All that a manager sees is behaviors—talking, work on a team, a debate. To explain or justify these observed behaviors, managers make inferences about underlying psychological processes. Thus, motivation is defined as all those inner striving conditions described as needs, drives, desires, motives, and so forth. It is an inner state that activates or moves.

With the increasing diversity of the workplace, many researchers have turned their attention to subtle differences in motivation across groups. Fascinating analyses have been conducted of variations in motivation across cultures. For example, results indicate that people from Eastern cultures are motivated strongly by a desire to fit in and conform to workplace norms. For them, innovation, entrepreneurship, risk taking, and challenging authority—some things common to people from Western cultures—are frightening and unsettling. New research has also demonstrated differences between men and women. Top-selling books such as *Men Are from Mars, Women Are from Venus* have resonated because they highlight basic differences that most people have known about but were unwilling or unable to discuss.

To motivate Einsteins requires that we isolate them as a group and attempt to discover whether there are unique approaches to motivating them. To illustrate the uniqueness of the mind-set of Einsteins, consider the unique mind-set of another, more widely recognized group: Generation X.

Marketers have created campaigns that are uniquely designed to *motivate* Xers to buy their clients' products. Marketers undertake meticulous research to understand what messages, symbols, and incentives motivate Generation X. We accept this. We accept that there is a unique group among us that has unique forms of motivation.

Generation Xers have little fear of technology and, in the context of most older employees, are seen as early adopters and technophiles. This perception has only served to heighten Generation Xers interest in and reverence for novelty. Generation Xers are not content with the traditional sport and leisure of previous generations. They tend to crave novelty and thrill seeking. They have invented new, daring sports such as bungee jumping, snowboarding, rock climbing, and base jumping.

Just as we accept Generation X as a distinct group with unique motivation, so must we accept Einsteins as a distinct group that will respond to new forms of motivation. Many Einsteins are part of Generation X and share some of the qualities, characteristics, and attitudes of that group. However, Einsteins come in all ages, ethnic backgrounds, and personality types.

## Maslow's Hierarchy of Needs

Most behavioral scientists generally agree that human beings are motivated by the desire to satisfy many needs, but there is a wide difference of opinion as to what those needs and their relative importance are. Abraham Maslow, a clinical psychologist, developed an influential theory of motivation called the *Hierarchy of Needs.*

Maslow's Hierarchy of Needs is widely accepted today in management theory and practice because it seems to make sense and is easy to understand. This theory of motivation is based on two important assumptions:

1. Each person's needs depend on what he or she already has. Only needs not yet satisfied can influence behavior. A satisfied need cannot influence behavior.

2. Needs are arranged in a hierarchy of importance. Once one need is satisfied, another emerges and demands satisfaction.

Maslow believed five levels of needs exist. These levels are (1) physiological, (2) safety, (3) social, (4) esteem, and (5) self-actualization. His framework for these needs is presented in Exhibit 3.1.

Maslow stated that if all of a person's needs are unsatisfied at a particular time, the most basic needs will be more pressing than the others. Needs at a lower level must be satisfied before higher-level

**Exhibit 3.1**
Maslow's Hierarchy of Needs

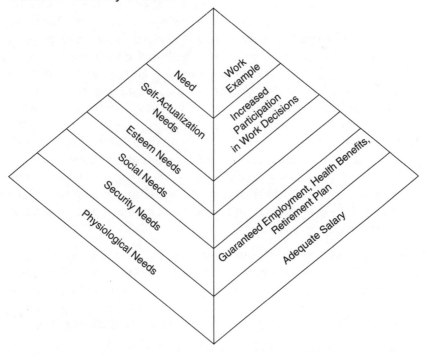

needs come into play, and only when they are sufficiently satisfied do the next needs in line become significant. Let us briefly examine each need level.

**Physiological needs**. This category consists of the basic needs of the human body, such as food, water, and sex. Physiological needs will dominate when all needs are unsatisfied. In such a case, no other needs will serve as a basis for motivation. Organizational factors that might satisfy physiological needs include enough pay to permit an employee to survive and working conditions that permit a healthy environment.

**Safety needs**. Safety needs include protection from physical harm, ill health, economic disaster, and the unexpected. From a managerial standpoint, safety needs manifest themselves in attempts to ensure job security and to move toward greater financial support.

**Social needs**. Social needs are related to the social nature of people and to their need for companionship. This level in the hierarchy is the point of departure from the physical needs of the two previous levels. Organizational conditions that help to satisfy these needs include encouraging team building, providing supportive supervision practices, and permitting coworkers the opportunity to interact socially on the job.

**Esteem needs**. Esteem needs comprise both the awareness of one's importance to others (self-esteem) and the actual esteem of others. The satisfaction of esteem needs leads to self-confidence and prestige. Organizations can support the satisfaction of these needs by recognizing good performance and permitting employees to work autonomously to complete challenging and meaningful job tasks.

**Self-actualization needs**. Maslow defines these needs as the "desire to become more and more what one is, to become everything one is capable of becoming." The satisfaction of self-actualization needs enables the individual to realize fully the potentialities of his talents and capabilities. Organizations can help employees satisfy self-actualization needs by encouraging creativity, allowing risk-taking decision making, and supporting workers in their efforts to develop their skills.

Maslow's Hierarchy of Needs does a good job of helping managers understand the fundamental needs of every employee. The needs Maslow identified are common to most people, and the broad definitions used by Maslow are comprehensive. You'd be hard pressed to come up with needs that don't fit somewhere on Maslow's model.

# Herzberg's Two-Factor Theory

Frederick Herzberg has developed a well-known theory of motivation based on a study of need satisfactions and on the reported motivational effects of those satisfactions. His approach is termed the *Two-Factor Theory of Motivation*.

Herzberg asked the subjects of his study to think of times when they felt especially good and especially bad about their jobs. Each subject was then asked to describe the conditions that caused those feelings. Significantly, the subjects *identified different work conditions for each of the feelings*. For example, if managerial recognition for doing an excellent job led to good feelings about the job, the lack of managerial recognition was seldom indicated as a cause of bad feelings.

Based on this research, Herzberg realized that there are two classes of factors that affect employee motivation: Maintenance factors and motivational factors.

## *Maintenance Factors*

Although employees are dissatisfied by the absence of some job conditions, the presence of those conditions does not cause strong motivation. Herzberg called such conditions *maintenance factors*, since they are necessary to maintain a minimum level of satisfaction. He also noted that maintenance factors have often been perceived by managers as factors that can motivate subordinates, but that they are, in fact, more potent as demotivators when they are absent. In other words, maintenance factors are those things employees expect to find in the workplace. Herzberg found that there were ten such maintenance factors:

- Company policy and administration
- Technical supervision
- Interpersonal relations with supervisor
- Interpersonal relations with peers
- Interpersonal relations with subordinates
- Salary
- Job security
- Personal life
- Work conditions
- Status

## Motivational Factors

Some job factors, which Herzberg calls *motivators*, cause high levels of motivation and job satisfaction when present. In contrast to maintenance factors, the absence of these factors does not prove highly demotivating. Herzberg described six of these motivational factors:

- Achievement
- Recognition
- Advancement
- The work itself
- The possibility of personal growth
- Responsibility

Prior to Herzberg's research, managers viewed job satisfaction and dissatisfaction at opposite ends of the same continuum, as shown in Exhibit 3.2. Herzberg's research findings introduced the notion of two continuums. If employees are not satisfied, they indicate no satisfaction, not dissatisfaction.

Motivational factors are job centered. They relate directly to the job itself; that is, the individual's job performance, the job responsibilities, and the growth and recognition obtained from the job. Maintenance factors are peripheral to the job and are more related to the external environment of work.

**Exhibit 3.2**
Contrasting Views of Satisfaction-Dissatisfaction

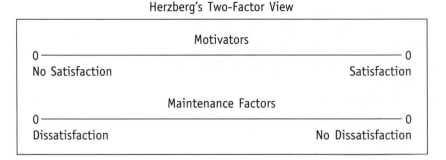

Traditional View

| 0 ——————————————————————————————— 0 |
| Satisfaction                                                   Dissatisfaction |

Herzberg's Two-Factor View

Motivators

| 0 ——————————————————————————————— 0 |
| No Satisfaction                                                     Satisfaction |

Maintenance Factors

| 0 ——————————————————————————————— 0 |
| Dissatisfaction                                                 No Dissatisfaction |

Despite some criticisms, Herzberg's theory of motivation has stimulated discussion and further research into motivation. Herzberg has looked at and discussed motivation in terms that managers understand. He has done so without loading his discussion with the psychological terminology that managers typically gloss over and ignore.

## Maslow and Herzberg Combined

There are similarities between Herzberg's and Maslow's models. A close examination of Herzberg's ideas indicates that what he actually was saying is that some employees may have achieved a level of social and economic progress in our society such that the higher-level needs of Maslow (esteem and self-actualization) are the primary motivators. However, these employees still expect to be able to satisfy their lower-level needs. Herzberg's model adds to the need hierarchy model because it distinguishes between the two groups of motivational and maintenance factors and points out that the motivational factors often are derived from the job itself. Exhibit 3.3 compares the two models.

**Exhibit 3.3**
Comparison of the Maslow and Herzberg Models

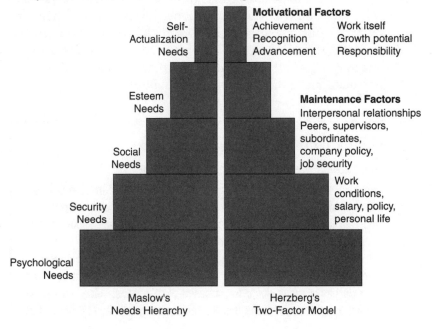

## Self-Actualizing Einsteins

Maslow didn't have Einsteins in mind when he crafted his famous needs hierarchy. The data he used to develop his theory came primarily from his clinical patients. Maslow as a clinical psychologist did not imagine that his theory would be universally used to interpret workplace motivation. He also did not foresee the dramatic increase in service and industrial organizations searching for and needing Einsteins.

Einsteins are far less concerned with some of Maslow's basic needs, such as physiological, safety, social, and esteem. While no one is immune from safety, social, and esteem needs, Einsteins do not focus on fulfilling their needs. They don't want to spend much time on trivial pursuits that don't apply to personal self-actualization.

Applying the concepts of Maslow and Herzberg to motivating Einsteins is a useful beginning. In general, Einsteins attempt to minimize the role played by the lower levels of Maslow's hierarchy. They prefer to spend their time, energy, and talent pursuing self-actualizing activities.

Today, most Einsteins require a computer, high-speed Internet access, flexible work hours, exceptional colleagues, a learning environment, advanced training, and other opportunities to develop their craft. Things that until a few years ago may have been motivational factors are now maintenance factors. Einsteins expect that their employers will demonstrate appreciation for their craft and will provide them with opportunities to learn and grow. Many Einsteins also expect firms to recognize their mobility and to be unconcerned that the skills they build make them even more mobile.

---

### Einstein Wisdom

*Some Einsteins Prefer Part-Time Employment*

Your firm may be able to benefit from Einsteins who wish part-time yet permanent assignments. Many firms don't like the idea of a flexible workforce. Most move in the exact opposite direction, jamming additional responsibilities and assignments on their already overworked employees.

Einsteins can be motivated by actually reducing the clutter of additional titles, responsibilities, and assignments. Permanent, part-time, project-centered work can be highly motivational for stressed-out Einsteins. Research by the Families and Work Institute found that 33 percent of women and 28 percent of men would prefer part-time work. The research also found that part-time Einsteins can be very productive workers.

Sue Shellenbarger, "Employees Are Seeking Fewer Hours: Maybe Bosses Should Listen," *Wall Street Journal*, February 21, 2001, B1

As many former motivational factors have now become maintenance factors, new motivational factors have taken their place. Many new approaches to motivation have been tried as firms compete to attract, retain, and develop Einsteins. One of the more common approaches used by small or startup companies is to provide Einsteins with significant equity stakes in the firm. This can be achieved through stock option programs (see Chapter 5). In large companies, the granting of stock options has less motivational value because of the dilutive effects of the large firm's greater number of outstanding shares. To make up for this, large firms have 401(k) and bonus programs to provide financial incentives.

Unfortunately, financial incentives are easy to match and not important to Einsteins beyond a certain point. These financial incentives are only somewhat useful in motivating your Einsteins. Instead, many firms have focused on the *workplace environment* as a source of Einstein motivation and inspiration. Innovative new office layouts centered on community and esprit de corps have emerged. Many firms have "game rooms" where Einsteins can go to relax, think, have fun, and interact creatively with others. These innovations are useful and, indeed, motivational. However, as in all things with Einsteins, they are ineffective if they don't change from time to time. Einsteins crave novelty. A game room that provides the same old stuff year after year is no longer worth visiting.

## Black Hole

*Dogs at Work? Doesn't Work*

During the heyday of the dot-com revolution, some firms were able to attract Einsteins by allowing them to bring their pets to the office. Up and down Silicon Valley you could find firms that allowed employees to bring their fish, birds, dogs, and cats to work.

Guess what? The bring-your-pets-to-work idea bombed. Where some Einsteins are motivated by having their pets near them, others decidedly are not. Besides the noise issues this presents, many firms learned that a great many people have pet allergies and/or fears and find the presence of animals in the workplace positively demotivating.

"DO I TAKE CARE OF YOU GUYS OR WHAT? I MANAGED
TO WRESTLE THE JACUZZI AWAY FROM THE
ACCOUNTING DEPARTMENT!"

## Einsteins and Flow

In a modern look at human motivation and happiness, scholar Mihalyi Csikszentmihalyi described a state of supreme satisfaction that people get when they are immersed in a project. Csikszentmihalyi called this state *flow*. Flow is reported by individuals as a satisfying state they reach when they are completely absorbed in challenging yet achievable projects. Csikszentmihalyi studied thousands of individuals in his research into flow. Although the individuals studied varied widely in background and profession, there are a few characteristics of the flow state that were similar across each of those who reported experiencing it:

1. They were involved in a challenging project.

2. They were making full use of their skills.

3. They received regular feedback on the state of their project relative to their goals.

4. They had no sense of "self" during the pursuit of their goals.

5. The project or goal was self-chosen.

Notice these elements of flow. They closely resemble the state of self-actualization described by Maslow. Csikszentmihalyi went further, however, in defining flow as a state where the sense of "self" is dissolved into the pursuit of the goal. You'll find this in Einsteins. They crave the loss of self-consciousness in the project. That's one of the reasons they often appear "self-conscious" and "out of sorts" when they are pulled off the project and asked to attend a social function, for example. Many Einsteins don't even own the formal attire that's required at such an event. If they do, they often appear as if they've dressed in the dark—ties that don't match, shirttail sticking out, the wrong shoes, funny glasses. Not only might their clothes appear awkward, but *they* appear awkward in their awkward clothes. You know the look—like a deer in headlights.

---

### Influence Tips

Duke University has an extensive IT department that has received recognition for its innovative approaches to managing employees. In exchange for talent and commitment, Duke's IT department provides employees:

- Opportunities to participate on a variety of projects, world-class technologies, and types of work.

- Involvement in assignments that challenge team members to higher levels of critical thinking and performance.

- Involvement in assignments that have meaningful impact across the Duke organization, the community, and/or industry.

- An environment that fosters the development and recognition of individual capabilities.

- A collegial, diverse, and professional environment in a pleasant social setting for a nationally respected organization.

- Competitive total compensation package (pay and benefits).

---

## The Fifth Element and Flow

Einsteins in general have reconfigured self-actualization in terms of the state of flow. You've probably experienced flow yourself. It's an exhilarating feeling of being completely immersed in a project. We pointed out in the last chapter that Einsteins prefer to work on projects rather than jobs. Managers must create interesting, challenging projects for Einsteins to work on. Once managers have identified challenging, engaging projects, they must pay close attention to the fifth element of flow: the project must be self-chosen. If projects are *im-*

*posed* from the outside, flow will not be attained. Instead, projects imposed from external sources lead to a state of *stress*. In order to achieve flow, the project being worked on must seem *optional*. It must be a project the Einstein has decided is important and thus worth investing all of his or her self. This complete *investment* of the self is what leads to the *loss* of the sense of self.

Motivating Einsteins, helping them achieve the highest level of individual performance possible, means helping them choose goals important to them and to the organization. Einstein managers must be prepared to work with Einsteins in a manner that persuades them to *choose* workplace projects and goals as if they were their own. Managers must also be prepared, once the projects have been chosen, to support those projects with the resources necessary for their successful completion. Finally, Einstein managers must be prepared to *step back* while the projects are ongoing, allowing Einsteins to make their own mistakes along the way. Einstein managers should intervene only to prevent an obviously impending disaster. Otherwise, managers should focus on providing regular feedback on the status of the project vis-à-vis the project's goals.

## $E = MC^2$

Once again, think about Albert Einstein's famous equation. This equation has been used to serve as a memory device that can be applied to motivating Einsteins. Let's review this version of the equation again:

$$E = MC^2$$

For Einstein motivation purposes, E is for "effort." This refers to the level of effort exerted by Einsteins on challenging, self-chosen projects they are working on. This level of effort will be directly proportional to the amount of proper management (M) times the level of direct communication (C) squared.

Of course, there's no precision in this equation. It is used here primarily as a mnemonic device to help managers stay out of the way of projects and tasks performed by Einsteins. Einsteins are hired because they're smart and know how to make decisions. It would be inappropriate not only to the reason Einsteins are hired, but also counter to their nature, for managers to exert a lot of direct or close management on them.

What's far more important than direct intervention is communication of key information and corporate data that helps in making decisions about what to do next on a project. Einstein managers must learn what amount of managing, leading, and facilitating works best in terms of motivation. In light of what managers determine through observation, practice, and applications, they can make adjustments. Thinking in terms of $E = MC^2$ will help managers stay focused on maintaining a light managerial touch once projects have been staffed with Einsteins and are under way.

## Motivating Einstein Teams

Motivating Einsteins must take advantage of their strong predilection for self-initiated activities. Einsteins are among the most self-motivated class of workers that has ever existed. During the twentieth century's industrial revolution, managers conspired among themselves to develop numerous novel motivational techniques. Some of these techniques were based on reward, others on threat of punishment. Workers, principally modestly educated, blue-collar labor, responded to these "motivational" techniques the way one might expect. They learned to "use the system" to maximize their personal returns and minimize their personal pain. The "game," sometimes called "blue-collar bingo," resulted in a stable rate of productivity, but not ultrahigh levels of performance.

During the latter part of the twentieth century, new motivational tactics were introduced into the workplace as both workers and organizations began to mature. Especially since the mid-1970s, with the introduction of Total Quality Management to U.S. companies, firms have been emphasizing teams and teamwork. Total Quality Management was the culminating managerial event in a line of changes that had been pushing power and authority down the chain of command. The command and control structure of the "bureaucracies" of the first half of the century were replaced by flexible, boundaryless organizations. This move toward greater worker self-control and autonomy over their own work activities was met with great resistance during the early days of TQM. Managerial thinking had to be changed. Managerial structures that had been in place for years had to be "reengineered." Gradually, managers learned to "let go" as workers demonstrated their ability to make good decisions and perform at high levels without constant supervision.

Rigid, oppressive, unexplainable rules are losing their hold. The modern organization has come a long way toward creating structures, cultures, and systems that enable today's educated, motivated worker to excel. However, when it comes to effectively managing and motivating Einsteins, most organizations have not gone far enough. Einsteins are unique and have strong negotiating power because of the shortage of their numbers and their talent in the labor market. The modern workplace is a "legacy system" that was designed to meet the needs and desires of a previous era in which mass production plants and industrial systems were dominant and in which labor was plentiful. Command and control systems remain in place. Rigid job categories, job descriptions, and pay scales still prevail in too many organizations.

In order to allow the organization to relax more of its structural tendencies, managers must learn to have faith in the ability of Einsteins to self-organize. Recent research has revealed that people do enjoy and perform at high levels in self-organizing teams. To most traditional managers, the notion of a self-organizing team is an oxymoron. After all, most of the groups that we know of as teams (e.g., sports teams) have been explicitly organized. Whoever heard of a baseball team that self-organized? Doesn't happen. However, remarkable things do happen when human groups are left on their own. Teams do form when people with a common interest are brought together. For example, you don't need a general manager or a league commissioner to make decisions on how to organize teams of children on the playground.

Einsteins continue to possess and apply what can be viewed as childlike teaming ability in adulthood. Like children, they check their egos at the door for the sake of enjoying the purity of the activity. They don't squabble about who is going to be the "leader." That's decided by who is best at which activity. Like children, they are aware of who's good at what based on demonstrated skill. There's no "political correctness," no false deference to "authority." If you're good, you're good. If you're not, you're not.

Managers who want to "organize" Einsteins into self-organizing teams need to recognize their childlike propensity to be good team members. Einsteins will contribute to the team project according to their skills. They will be compelled by internal psychological forces to perform at the highest level. They will learn from other team members.

There are a very few simple steps managers need to follow to create high-performing, self-organizing teams of Einsteins.

1. Develop a priority list of clearly defined projects.

2. Communicate the projects to your Einsteins.

3. Allow your Einsteins to decide among themselves who will work on which project.

4. In consultation with the teams that have formed, establish relevant milestones.

5. Monitor progress, provide support, and stay out of the way.

6. Start all over again.

Einstein managers will receive exceptional benefits in the achievements that will result from using this approach to motivate teams of Einsteins. Allowing Einsteins to choose their own teams and participating with them in the establishment of milestones ensures a balance between autonomy and control.

## A Final Comment

Einsteins have naturally high levels of self-motivation. They don't require the same management handling as other employees. Nevertheless, Einstein managers can take certain actions to ensure that Einsteins are able to work at a steady pace and have opportunities to attain the coveted state of flow.

Einstein managers should pay attention to the work environment as a starting point for motivating Einsteins. The manager's job is to enrich the environment with challenging projects, opportunities for learning, and the latest high-tech tools. This type of enriched atmosphere is motivation for Einsteins.

# CHAPTER 4

# Retaining and Rewarding Einsteins

## Preview Einstein Story

### Chubb & Sons Restructures Jobs to Retain Einsteins

Higher salaries, stock options, and better perks are weapons in the battle for top talent.

At Chubb, the annual turnover rate in CIO Chuck McCaig's department is a comfortable 9 percent—about half the industry standard. That is down from 22 percent in 1997, but it took a near complete overhaul to stop the bleeding. "We knew we couldn't afford to compete with the startups on compensation," McCaig says. "But we could create a different lifestyle here, one that's more attractive."

That process began by splitting the 1,100 worker department into smaller groups, each aligned with a major business unit such as claims or commercial insurance, in order to build a shared sense of accountability for reaching business goals. In 1999 these groups began reporting directly to the head of the business unit, rather than to McCaig.

In addition, Chubb established an "internal consulting pool" of up to 50 employees to allow them greater choices in their career paths and to secure talented candidates who may not fit a particular opening. The pool serves as a central resource from which any of the five IT divisions can draw. Says McCaig, "It's a neat way for people in one area to get skilled and move on to another—a Cobol person, for instance, who wants to move over to the Web team."

After managers have gone through all of the trouble of recruiting, screening, and hiring their Einsteins, they need to make sure the talent is retained. Einsteins are, even with some recent economic downturns, mobile. Their technical skills have placed them in very high demand. Their primary loyalty is to their profession and their skill base, not always to their employer.

Nonetheless, there are things that managers can do to retain their Einsteins. A beginning involves understanding the unique character, needs, and aspirations of Einsteins. Once an understanding is achieved, it will become obvious that retaining Einsteins will involve a wide range of novel retention techniques. For example, one traditional retention technique centers on creating the right type of job to match an individual's skills, knowledge, and abilities. This is called the "fit." Einsteins are less interested in having and retaining a "position" than other employees. Their lives revolve around "projects." To Einsteins, the work environment consists of a never-ending stream of discrete projects. Einsteins are rarely ever "finished." Nor do they believe in traditional notions of "career paths."

Einsteins have also changed the focus of rewards. Rather than being interested in "annual raises" or "sick days," they prefer to participate in the financial progress of the company through stock options and performance-based bonuses. The following Influence Tip discusses how one company uses such incentives to prevent its Einsteins from fleeing to more lucrative opportunities.

---

### Influence Tip

Even in the wake of dot-com layoffs, some offline companies are still scared their best people will leave them for the siren song of an online startup. To minimize this from happening, accounting firm Armanino McKenna, based in San Leandro, California, is enticing its employees with cold, hard cash. In July 2000, CEO Andy Armanino rolled out a plan to loan managers $50,000 each for a down payment on a new house. Armanino says he developed the idea after witnessing the decline of qualified workers in the finance industry. Hoping to lure people to his firm—and keep them there—the loan is intended to help managers find a home in the same zip code as the office. New or promoted managers who take the loan at its 6 percent interest rate must repay it over a seven-year period, or can opt to pay it through their annual bonuses.

---

Let's begin our look at retaining Einsteins by exploring how the idea of "work" has changed over the past decade.

# Managing Work Design

Managers should not encourage their Einsteins to think in terms of having jobs. The era of the rigid job description is considered outdated. Job descriptions are limiting, bureaucratic, and suited for assembly line, clerical, and repetitive tasks.

Einsteins are engaged in work that is nonroutine, involves making quick, independent decisions, and has few tightly defined responsibilities. Consequently, Einsteins derive intrinsic satisfaction from the scope of their work, the range of duties, and the empowerment bestowed on them by managers. The changes in the type of work performed have resulted in managers building into the duties and tasks a number of characteristics, including meaningfulness, autonomy, and feedback. Einstein work possessing these characteristics is said to have achieved a state of enrichment.

## *Enriching Work*

Doing enriched work requires more skills, feedback, and managerial support than repetitive, routine, and narrow jobs. Managers must permit Einsteins to exercise freedom and the judgment to take risks, experiment with new approaches, and make mistakes, which could occasionally result in failure, increased expenses, and lost opportunities. Einsteins must be in control if the benefits of enriched work are to come to fruition. Allowing Einsteins this high level of autonomy requires exceptional restraint. Managers who possess the self-confidence, sense of security, and expertise that enables them to show such restraint and to optimize the intelligence, talents, and skills of Einsteins will be more effective in retaining Einsteins than those who must always be in control.

The principles of enriching work are captured in Exhibit 4.1. Managers are advised to follow as closely as possible these five principles in designing work for Einsteins. The notion of Einsteins being in control (not in every detail) is necessary when implementing these principles.

Although Einsteins increase their commitment to the organization through enrichment, managers still have formal responsibility and accountability. The manager's role, however, becomes more focused on coaching, supporting, and facilitating, and is less command and control oriented. Einstein managers have the responsibility to achieve results and are accountable in the structural design and hierarchy of the organization.

## Exhibit 4.1
### Work Enrichment Principles

| Principle | Anticipated Impact on Einsteins |
|---|---|
| 1. Removal of controls, constant checking, close managerial oversight | More responsibility, sense of personal achievement |
| 2. Increased accountability for work | Recognition, more responsibility, pride |
| 3. Designing work as whole project unit (as opposed to only doing specific tasks) | Sense of completion, control, recognition, and meaningfulness |
| 4. Introducing in step ladder fashion more difficult work as each step is mastered | Growth, development, increased stature |
| 5. Giving Einstein say in work flow, pace, schedule, and amount | Increased control, stature, recognition |

The work designs under which Einsteins can grow and develop in terms of skill and competencies are:

1. *Experienced meaningfulness.* The Einstein perceives the work as important and vital.

2. *Experienced responsibility.* The Einstein believes that he or she personally is accountable (responsible for) the work effort being expended.

3. *Knowledge of results.* Einsteins receive periodic feedback from other Einsteins, and their Einstein managers provide some feedback on whether their work is satisfactory, below average, or excellent.

These three vital psychological states generate what is referred to as an internal (within the Einstein) state of motivation. If any of these three states is shortchanged, the Einstein's internal motivation regarding his or her work is diminished.

## The Manager's Role

Managers in their role of work designer for Einsteins can play a significant part in the process. By understanding how to cultivate the three psychological states through the proper design of a few core dimensions of work, managers can help Einsteins achieve a healthy internal state of motivation. Managers should understand that there are three specific core work dimensions that impact experienced meaningfulness. They are:

1. *Skill Variety*. The extent to which the work of an Einstein requires him or her to perform a variety of tasks that utilize different skills and ability.

2. *Task Identity*. The extent to which the work requires a complete or completely identifiable piece of work. A beginning-to-end effort results in a sense of completing a project.

3. *Task Significance*. The extent to which the work effects the lives of others within the Einstein team, in other organizational units or outside the firm.

4. *Autonomy*. The extent to which the Einstein's work allows him or her to experience decision making discretion in how and when the work is done.

5. *Feedback*. The extent to which Einsteins receive direct, clear, and timely information on how they are performing.

Through observation, discussion, and experience managers can assess these five core work dimensions as they apply to each Einstein working with them. Judging from the potential internal motivational impact of the five core dimensions, managers can reach a conclusion on how to proceed, where to intervene, and when to discuss their viewpoints with Einsteins.

Before any interventions are considered, managers should diagnose the situation. Understanding the five work enrichment principles and the five core work dimensions is where the diagnosis should begin. In essence, Einstein managers have to consider that:

$$\text{Motivating Potential of Einsteins' Work} = \frac{\text{Skill Variety} + \text{Task Identity} + \text{Task Significance}}{3} \times \text{Autonomy} \times \text{Feedback}$$

This straightforward equation is the center of how psychological states and core work dimensions interact.

Einstein managers will realize that work design approaches are not a cure-all for all their Einstein retention and reward needs. If Einstein managers can come close to helping, facilitating, and guiding Einsteins to do the work they like, with the people they enjoy, and in an atmosphere they prefer, the challenging task of designing work will be rewarding.

## The Human Capital Approach

Many companies that successfully retain their Einsteins have adopted what is known as "the human capital approach." This approach considers the human resources of the firm as an asset. Optimizing human capital is the ultimate goal and focus of this approach, which recognizes that human capital needs three things to be effective:

1. Knowledge

2. Motivation

3. Opportunity

Investing in knowledge development means that the firm will put the appropriate forms of education, training, coaching, and performance feedback mechanisms in place to enhance each employee's natural abilities. When managed effectively, investing in knowledge ensures that the organization will create the skills and abilities that help it become successful.

Investment in motivation refers to the financial and nonfinancial reward system the firm has created. These include salary, cash incentives (such as bonuses), stock options, and other things. Einsteins appreciate motivational investment just like anyone else. However, Einsteins are especially interested in investments that are clearly tied to performance. They don't fool easily. They understand the risk/reward nature of a free market economy. They don't mind living with risk, as long as appropriate rewards are available when they succeed.

Investments in opportunity are those that create a work environment that inspires innovation and creativity. Einsteins will provide dedicated hours of tedious and focused labor on technical projects. Using them solely for their characteristic work ethic, however, would leave their creative skills untapped. In fact, opportunity to create can, for Einsteins, be used as a nonfinancial reward. Many firms use the concept of a "skunk works" to enable the free exchange of ideas and new product development. Some of these skunk works have no pressure at all to produce commercial products. Others have constraints and are clearly focused on commercialization of new ideas and concepts. Einstein managers may want to encourage and support a form of skunk works where Einsteins are free to pursue new ideas and investigate their commercial viability. Such a team would require that each new idea be accompanied by a full-blown business plan with key milestones and financial projections.

## Other Retention Strategies

In addition to creating a project-rich workplace with adequate rewards, there are a number of other new strategies firms can use to retain Einsteins. These include:

1. Training

2. Cultural artifacts

3. Novelty

### *Training*

Einsteins love to learn. Most have significant formal education. More important, most are very active in informal education—reading broadly, attending conferences, and participating in chat rooms. This thirst for continuing education finds expression somewhere. Einsteins not only want to learn, they have an absolute hunger for it. If the workplace doesn't provide it, they may seek and find this hunger satisfied in another firm.

Einsteins want continuing education, but not just garden variety stuff. They want, first and foremost, education that enables them to develop skills in their craft. If they are programmers, they want courses in programming. It's even better if those courses provide some type of reputable certification. Building better, more current skills in their craft is the primary continuing education interest of Einsteins, but their interest in continuing education is broader. It's those broader interests that can be tapped into in order to help retain Einsteins.

Einsteins deplore "mandatory" training on mundane topics such as company policies, compensation packages, etc. To the extent that Einstein managers can avoid or minimize these types of training sessions, they should do so. There are strategies for enabling Einsteins to "check the box" on mandatory training that don't require undue expenditures of their time and energy. For example, many e-learning companies offer basic courses in 401(k) plans, office safety, and other areas that help employers comply with federal laws and minimize exposure to liability. Einsteins are more apt to find economically sound learning value in less time using some form of e-learning for mandatory courses than with a traditional classroom-based instructor.

In the previous chapter, Herzberg's Two-Factor Theory of Motivation was discussed. Recall the category that is called the "maintenance" factor. This means, simply, that employees expect the workplace to have certain things, such as a paycheck. Telling people they will be getting a paycheck is not motivational—it is *expected*. For Einsteins, continuing education in their craft is a maintenance factor—they *expect* the firm to offer this.

The other factor in the Herzberg model is the motivational factor. You'll recall that motivational factors are not *expected* in the workplace but help make life and work more enjoyable. For Einsteins, continuing education in noncraft, nonmandatory, typical areas can be motivational if handled correctly. Effectively using continuing education as a motivational retention tool requires several key strategies:

- Determine the preferred training topic through discussions with Einsteins.
- Link training to workplace projects and rewards.
- Encourage Einsteins to share their knowledge with others.

It should not come as a surprise that one strategy is to include Einsteins in the training content decision. After all, they're the ones getting trained—they know what they want. This strategy should be followed, but not slavishly. Einstein managers should make decisions about continuing education based *in part* on discussions with Einsteins and *in part* on the goals of the firm.

In determining continuing education, Einstein managers should also carefully listen in their discussions with Einsteins. One great way to make your company a "cool" place to work is to surprise Einsteins every now and then with a compelling guest speaker or send them to a leading-edge conference. Guest speakers Einsteins admire are those people who are considered to be at the top of their craft. Einsteins hold deep reverence and admiration for such people. Identify who they are. If possible, bring them in to address your troops. Your Einsteins will be thrilled. They'll all agree that the company is investing in their development. This is considered a reward by Einsteins.

Ultimately, all training should be linked back to workplace projects and the internal reward system. While Einsteins love to learn and will greatly appreciate efforts managers make to provide continuing education, they will quickly grow weary of it if it is not tied to project and work performance. Einsteins cannot shake their goal-oriented nature. If training events are apparently *not* relevant, they become a distraction. Worse, Einsteins may begin to believe that the company is wasting money, and they may begin to look around for alternative employment.

A great way to link training to rewards is to conclude any special training event with a discussion about how the lessons of the day apply to current issues. All training events should be followed up with such informal discussions. Einsteins love to analyze and talk about ways in which their new knowledge can apply to the workplace.

About a decade ago, Peter Senge coined the term "learning organization." Ten years later, many companies are still trying to figure out what it is. They are engaging in knowledge management, data mining, training, and myriad other strategies to get people to learn. What Senge did not talk about—and what none of the so-called learning organizations realized—is that there is no better way to learn than to teach. What is really needed is the "learning-teaching organization." All employees become learners and teachers alike. Imagine the dynamics and impact on performance. *Everyone* becomes fully engaged in the knowledge creation and transmission process.

## Cultural Artifacts

By "cultural artifacts" we mean those physical items that help the group define itself and thrive. In anthropological terms, a cultural artifact is a useful instrument that helps the group thrive, or a symbolic instrument that helps the group define itself. An effective manager of Einsteins ensures that both types of cultural artifacts are present in the work environment.

To Einsteins, useful artifacts include all those items that we described earlier to be a part of Herzberg's maintenance factors, such as computers, multifunction telephones, handheld and/or wireless devices, printers, etc. This is not as mundane as it sounds. Einsteins will be far more loyal to companies that are on the cutting edge of useful artifacts. Einsteins want to be on the cusp of technological innovation. It gives them and their tribe a sense of pride to be "ahead" of other tribes in terms of technological innovation and adoption.

Symbolic artifacts in the work environment are common in the high-tech companies of Silicon Valley. Paeans to great geek leaders and thinkers abound. Pictures of Leonardo da Vinci, Jaron Lanier, and even Albert Einstein adorn cubicles and lunchrooms. Images of outer space, nanoscale robots, and other futuristic fantasies festoon

Einstein workspaces. These symbolic artifacts help define the vision and dreams of the tribe.

For Einsteins, their vision is rarely confined to the prosaic vision of the organization. Rather, it is often cosmic in extent, almost metaphysical. It reflects the inner thoughts of the Einstein tribe. These inner thoughts often center on large questions about the place of humans in the universe and the role of the individual. The constrained expression of these thoughts through nonobtrusive posters, screen savers, paper weights, or other symbolic artifacts should be tolerated, even encouraged. It would damage the tribe's ability to define itself if all such expression were prohibited. Of course, it's possible for Einsteins to carry these things too far. If symbolic artifacts become blatantly offensive, dangerous, or distracting, they should be eliminated. At the same time, it would be inappropriate to institute a "policy" about what type of symbolic artifacts the firm will allow. By definition, symbolic artifacts are spontaneous expressions of tribal emotion. They cannot be legislated or regulated.

## Novelty

Einsteins love novelty. Perhaps more than anything else, they appreciate intellectual surprises. Einsteins become bored with routine. Effective management of Einsteins introduces novelty in appropriate ways and at appropriate times.

Above all, Einsteins are puzzle solvers. They enjoy applying their intellect to abstract and complex problems. As we pointed out, they also like entering a state of flow, immersing themselves completely in their project or problem until they have resolved it. This creates a dilemma for managers in timing the introduction of novelty. Einsteins abhor novelty when they are immersed in an engaging project. Taking them out of their flow will disrupt and disturb them, and they will find it difficult to reengage with the project. This is bad for them and for the organization.

Managers need to be careful in the way they introduce novelty to Einsteins. New product innovation, new organizational projects, or new strategies should be presented as future opportunities long before Einsteins are requested to work on them. An effective approach is to have a weekly staff meeting where managers introduce potential new projects and their targeted starting dates. With this approach, Einsteins can begin to position themselves to participate in the upcoming projects. In addition, they will be motivated and encouraged by the fact that the firm is continuing to move forward and invent new and innovative projects.

> ## Black Hole
>
> Managers should be very cautious *not* to introduce projects that have a low likelihood of getting started. Einsteins abhor routine and crave novel projects. But they abhor being misled and crave honest leadership all the more. In staff meetings, when managers talk about upcoming projects, they should attach a probability of launch along with the projected launch date. The common term for this is "managing expectations."

## Work Satisfaction

Einsteins as a group will tend to prefer challenging work that is in line with their self-concept. Work satisfaction will be directly related to the following three factors:

1. Opportunity for learning

2. Opportunity for focused work

3. Opportunity for social bonding

Einsteins require a work environment that includes far less formal structure than the typical workplace. In the place of rule-based structure, they favor learning-based structure. They see constant learning at work as an extension of their out-of-work lives. The structure that learning provides is more like a path than a box (or cage). Non-Einsteins often require a structure where the rules are well-defined and the boundaries between work and nonwork are clear. Einsteins want their work lives to be continuous to their nonwork lives.

While allowing Einsteins to pursue their interests on their individual learning paths through the workplace, managers must ensure that the appropriate physical space is also provided. Einsteins work well for long periods. They prefer intense, focused effort as opposed to disjointed, highly fragmented work. They want their time on task to be uninterrupted. They prefer to work under the pressure of deadlines. They also prefer to be autonomous in how the work gets done. No need for formalities—they know the score and *want* to be recognized for making valuable contributions.

Einsteins will not achieve work satisfaction if only the first two factors are fulfilled. In addition to a learning-based structure and opportunity to focus and work intensely, they also need opportunities for social bonding. In general, Einsteins want to bond with other Einsteins. Einstein managers should encourage and nurture this need.

However, the little known truth about Einsteins is that they also want to be recognized, appreciated, and praised by the non-Einsteins around them.

## Rewarding Einsteins

Everyone likes to be rewarded for a job well done. One of the most powerful ways to influence behavior is to clearly link rewards to outcomes. In order to make that effective, the rewards must be desirable and the outcomes must be measurable. No Einstein wants a poke in the eye for hitting their target, and few want false rewards for unreal achievements. Rewarding Einsteins is a matter of appealing to two of their strongest characteristics:

1. Their desire for growth within their craft

2. Their project-oriented approach to work.

Most Einsteins will prefer to have a base salary that enables them to take care of their fundamental needs: food, shelter, security. They will not respond well to a commission-only pay structure that is more appropriate for sales professionals. An effective reward system for Einsteins, thus, will begin with a rational and competitive salary structure that provides a healthy living standard and that is regularly adjusted to keep pace with changes in the cost of living.

The base salary structure should also include gradations depending upon job responsibilities and authority. However, don't expect the salary gradation to be motivational for Einsteins to "climb" the traditional "corporate ladder." In general, they are not interested in this. The gradations in salary will legitimize different levels of authority. Einsteins want order and rationality in the organizational structure, and salary gradations are an expected part of this.

As stated, Einsteins will not be motivated to high levels of performance by the salary increments within the organization. We have also stated that Einsteins will not work well under a pure commission structure. The best approach for Einstein managers is to tie performance to clear organizational financial performance targets. Several techniques can be used to link financial outcome to individual rewards, including:

- Employee stock option programs (ESOPs)
- Open-book management
- Pay for performance

## *ESOPs*

Employee stock option programs, or ESOPs, are effective, well-known means for linking rewards to organizational outcomes. During the dot-com heyday of the late 1990s, this became a popular and lucrative way to reward employees. Stories abound about young Einsteins who received stock options in some dot-com startup and rocketed to instant wealth at the initial public offering of their company. During those wild times it wasn't unusual to be able to attract and retain high-performing Einsteins with a reward package heavily weighted to stock options. Now hear this: those days are over. Along with the great dot-com crash of 2000–2001 came a change in the perception of the value of stock options. While not considered worthless, they are now seen as far riskier than other types of rewards.

The perceived value of stock options has changed. Does that mean they should no longer play a role in the reward structure for Einsteins? Not at all. In fact, the contrary is true. Einsteins still want to have an opportunity to participate in the value appreciation of the company they join. There is no better way to do this than through stock options. But Einstein managers should communicate that stock options don't translate into real money until they are sold. During the dot-com craze, the time between the issuance of options and cash-out was exceedingly short. Some startups went from garage to IPO in a matter of months. That is not likely anymore. Today, turning options into cash takes far longer. Thus, the motivational value of the option has been proportionally diminished.

## *Open-Book Management*

Open-book management is an approach to organizational information sharing that has had mixed results. Briefly, this approach advocates sharing operating results with employees. In theory, if employees are kept informed about the operating results of the firm—preferably on a daily basis—they will have a better understanding of how their individual contribution affects those results.

Open-book management has been used in all types of firms—from manufacturing to service to hospitality. Even some nonprofit and governmental organizations have utilized this approach. It's fair to say that no two organizations practice open-book management in the same way. Some will share *all* financial information with employees. Others will show only filtered information.

Einsteins respond well to an open-book management approach. They want to know the operating results of the company, and they want to know how their performance affects those results. To make open-book management effective for Einsteins, however, requires a more subtle approach than has been commonly utilized.

### Pay for Performance

Einsteins want pay for performance. In itself, this is not terribly unique. Many types of workers, from piece-rate laborers on the factory floor to the well-dressed pharmaceutical salesperson, are rewarded for their performance. What makes Einsteins unique is their desire to have it both ways—they want to contribute to the firm's overall performance and be proportionately rewarded, and they want to be rewarded for their day-to-day individual productivity. Einsteins are as interested in long-term value creation as they are in short-term individual gain.

Einsteins have a longer time horizon than other types of workers. As we stated, they are interested in short-term cash rewards, but the motivational value of such rewards is limited. Einsteins want to be informed about their firm's long-term financial goals. They want to participate in those long-term financial goals, both from the perspective of equity participant and a highly valued, talented employee.

## A Balancing Act

The key to designing a reward system for Einsteins is *balance*. Einsteins will be motivated to high performance if they participate both

"NO NEED TO THANK ME. WORLD DOMINATION THROUGH OUR PRODUCT IS ITS OWN REWARD."

in short-term gains and long-term value appreciation. This means that an effective reward system for Einsteins will provide:

1. A stable income that provides them with assurance that basic needs will be met.

2. Equity participation in the long-term value creation of the firm.

3. Performance-based financial incentives that are based on individual contribution.

4. Information sharing on a regular basis that reveals the financial condition of the firm and, importantly, demonstrates the firm is effectively balancing points number 2 and 3, above.

Designing a reward system for Einsteins is not difficult, but it does require more systematic feedback than traditionally has been commonplace in organizations. The most effective reward programs use corporate intranets to display key financial indicators on a daily, even hourly, basis. Researchers at Virginia Tech University have determined that employees who are informed about their personal financial situation are more productive than employees who are not.

If the organization doesn't have an intranet or is not interested in installing one, an alternative approach is to use a regularly scheduled employee newsletter to report key information. The newsletter is not as personal as an intranet can be, but it can contain key corporate information.

A third means of communicating corporate financial information to Einsteins is through an e-zine. An e-zine is an e-mail-delivered version of the company's newsletter. Einsteins are familiar and comfortable with this technology. Again, these will be most effective if they are distributed regularly (say, monthly) and if they contain understandable, useful financial information.

Einsteins are unusually self-motivated workers. When making judgments about the adequacy of their reward they consider these things:

1. Their financial need

2. Their role in the firm

3. Their long-term prospects

If any of these three elements is out of balance, Einsteins will be dissatisfied. As long as Einstein managers are able to keep these in balance—and, of course, this requires a great deal of information sharing—the reward system has a good chance to be effective.

## CHAPTER 5

# Communicating with Einsteins

## Preview Einstein Story

### New CEO Opens Communication at Altera

Altera Corporation's president and chief executive, John Daane, had a challenge on his hands when he took office on November 30, 2000. The maker of programmable chips was in need of organizational reprogramming. According to one observer, all decisions were dictated from the executive suite. Employees had little discretion or flexibility. Now that Daane is on the job, his biggest challenge is to create a more open culture.

Former employees and industry observers describe the company before Daane as a place where new ideas were routinely shot down. One of those critics is twenty-year industry veteran Farzad Zarrinfar. He was named to the position of vice president of product marketing for Altera six months before Daane's arrival. Three months after taking the post, however, Zarrinfar left for another company. He left because it was difficult to make changes in the prevailing culture. He said, "In the programmable logic device industry, there are cultures that have been built at companies for years and years and years. Once that culture is built, it's very difficult to change it."

Daane agrees that changes are needed at Altera. One of Daane's first moves was to hire a new director of corporate communications. He also hired a number of field service engineers to make the company friendlier with customers. Some observers have given Daane high marks on the changes he has brought about at Altera.

From: James DeTar, "Altera Deals with Culture Clash," *Investor's Business Daily*, February 16, 2001, A5

Workplace communications is a challenge for Einstein managers. It is nearly a law of nature that all organizations have less communication than they actually need to function at peak capacity. Despite the myriad new communication opportunities available today—e-mail, intranets, voice mail, newsletters, etc.—one of the most oft-heard complaints at the water cooler is, "Nobody told *me!*"

## Basics of Communication

Communicating with Einsteins is daunting—many managers even find it perplexing. Einsteins are intelligent, and they often speak a language only they understand. No manager wants to appear stupid. Many adopt an attitude of feigned indifference, pretending they don't have time to learn technology and taking comfort that they have this young geek to take care of all that stuff; sort of like having a trained monkey. That act doesn't fool anyone. It's no use trying to discount the value of Einsteins' technical knowledge. They have it, managers often don't. That doesn't make Einsteins more powerful than managers, but they are smarter, at least in that technical sense.

The first lesson, then, in communicating with Einsteins is to avoid silly posturing. Don't make your Einsteins feel like trained monkeys. They are tired of that act. They don't like it. They won't tell. That's not their style. But rest assured, they prefer that you have the courage to recognize where their expertise exceeds your own.

The basic communication model shown in Exhibit 5.1 is useful for Einstein managers to review.

Briefly review each component of this model. The first stage of communication is the originator or sender (e.g., Einstein manager, the

**Exhibit 5.1**
The Communication Process

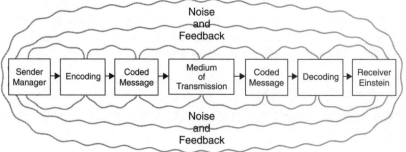

organization, customers). Messages must be encoded for transmission. People are familiar with several types of encoding schemes, including words, graphics, facial expressions, and emoticons (icons some people use to express emotion in e-mail).

The message is the sum total of encoded symbols delivered through a medium. Many Einstein managers are unaware of the actual messages they send despite the fact that they were in full control of the encoding process. The medium is simply the channel for transmission of the message. Choosing the appropriate channel for the various messages Einstein managers need to send every day has become increasingly challenging.

At the other end of the communication channel is the receiver who is responsible for decoding the message. The receiver may or may not have received the message in pure form. Often, noise enters into the message channel no matter how hard Einstein managers try to avoid it. Noise could be anything from static on the phone line to rumors that arrive to the receiver before your message.

The last link in the communication chain is feedback. Many Einstein managers either miss or ignore this important final step. Senders tend to assume that the message they encoded and delivered is the one that was received. However, more often than not this is not what happens. Differences between the encoding and decoding process, noise in the system, and even imperfections in ability to decode can lead to vast differences in the message that was assumed to have been sent and the one that was received. Getting feedback on the message that was received can help overcome communication breakdowns.

## Einsteins Speak

Looking at the communication model in Exhibit 5.1, it's easy to see where the challenges lie in communicating with Einsteins. The technical background of Einsteins means that they have an encoding system that may be quite different than Einstein managers. Anyone privy to a conversation between Einsteins on their favorite technical topic witnesses a communication unlike any other. Einsteins tend to speak in rapid bursts, laced with unknown terms. They tend to not be concerned about an observer's lack of understanding, preferring to stay "locked in" with the discussion partner who does understand them. Einsteins tend to face and speak with one another, probing each other's depth of knowledge in a manner not unlike the programmed sparring among males in many animal species as they determine dominance.

"WOULD YOU BE MORE COMFORTABLE IF I
SPEAK TO YOU IN 'BINARY CODE?'"

Einsteins will generally not see Einstein managers as part of their tribe and, thus, will not enter into dominance-determining behavior. Rather, Einstein managers will be regarded with deference at best, annoyance at worst. The best an Einstein manager can hope to achieve is deference. It would be a mistake to attempt to become a part of the tribe's communication, rituals, and discussion issues.

## Careful Questioning

Einstein managers can often mistake the deferential attitude displayed by Einsteins as weakness, meekness, or shyness. While that occasionally may be true, it is a trap Einstein managers should avoid. Einstein deference is real, but it is not based on meekness. Einsteins defer primarily because they are impatient. They want to *get back to work*, and they believe the quickest way to do so is to defer and not confront managers directly, even if they disagree.

This can be a source of serious problems. If Einsteins disagree with their managers, but managers don't realize it, the results obtained may not be what are expected. Einsteins often live by the adage, "It's better to ask forgiveness than ask permission." In their rush to get back to work, to get back to the concentrated effort that gives them the satisfying sense of flow, they will say one thing and do another. They do this not out of a sense of spite or direct mischief, rather, they do it out of impatience.

To avoid this potential communication breakdown, managers need to use *careful questioning* skills to determine what Einsteins are thinking and how they feel about what they've been requested to do. Careful questioning is a delicate art that conveys a sincere willingness to understand, avoiding all defensiveness and/or irritability. This is not easy. Coaxing Einsteins out of their deference means standing in the way of their desire to get to work. Careful questioning conveys that the manager wants to understand. It conveys that the Einstein manager doesn't mind being wrong or even uninformed.

---

### Einstein Wisdom

You may recall the famous character "Stuart" from the Ameritrade commercials that aired during 2000. In one spot Stuart, the quintessential Einstein, is teaching his boss, Mr. C, to trade online with Ameritrade. Stuart is thrilled that Mr. C has learned something new from him, breaking into a funky dance when Mr. C executes a trade. In fact, Stuart is so thrilled to have taught Mr. C this skill, he invites him to a party at his house on Saturday night. Mr. C, unfortunately, reverts back to insincere bureauspeak, however, telling Stuart "I'm going to try to make it." Yeah, right.

---

## Communication Events

There is a wide range of communication transactions that managers should perform with Einsteins. These "communication events" include:

- Requesting/Ordering
- Coaching
- Praising/Thanking
- Disciplining
- Teaching

### Requesting/Ordering

Making a request or giving an order to get something done is something every manager must do. In most organizations the chain of command and the reward/discipline system is the basis for determining who can give orders to whom, and how those orders will be enforced. Einsteins know about the organization's chain of command and will defer to it, but they do not respond as other employees might. Giving a direct order to Einsteins should only be done in extreme or crisis situations, when time is of the essence. In nearly all other circumstances, managers are far more likely to get the results desired by using *request* language (wording) and behavior rather than *ordering* language and behavior.

## Coaching

Einsteins are smart, but they don't know everything. Einsteins will often require coaching to perform at higher levels. This must be handled delicately, almost as delicately as a therapist handles a client in counseling. Einsteins would generally rather avoid situations in which they feel uncomfortable. One of the reasons that Einsteins are often squirreled away in the bowels of the company making its systems run is because that's where they're comfortable. Recognizing when Einsteins desire to be coached is a challenge confronting managers. Usually, Einsteins require time to warm up to the offer. They are receptive to good coaching—they love to learn—but they will require unconditional acceptance of progress. Einsteins prefer any form of coaching to be unrelated to their overall performance assessment.

---

### Influence Tip

*Effective Communication Aids Retention*

People don't usually leave their jobs out of the blue. "In spite of what you might hear in an exit interview, most people do not arbitrarily leave a place where they are happy," says Mary Ellen Brantley and Chris Coleman, authors of *Winning the Technology Talent War*.

There are things managers can do to detect warning signs of unhappy Einsteins and avoid the hassles of turnover. According to Brantley and Coleman, these include:

- Keep an ear to the ground and actively communicate with Einsteins.

- Explain company and departmental strategies as much as possible.

- Include staff in making changes and decisions.

- Provide support and compassion in times of personal transition.

- Reward extra training.

- Improve your own leadership abilities.

From: Amy Reynolds Alexander, "Using Radar to Overturn Turnover," *Investor's Business Daily*, January 23, 2001, A4

---

## *Praising/Thanking*

Everyone responds to gratefulness, praise, and recognition. Einsteins are no exception. Einsteins respond well to praise, but it must be handled in a subtle way. They do not want to be singled out in front of their tribe by managers. Einsteins prefer thanks or praise (recognition) to be accorded first to the team. If they are to be singled out, they prefer that it be recognition bestowed by the team. Einstein managers who want to single out a MVP—most valuable programmer—should elicit that distinction from within the team. Einsteins know who the MVP is, and an award of thanks or praise that is generated in this manner will be seen as a true prize by the recipient. It signifies not only a high level of perfection of their craft, but also solidifies the individual's place among his or her peers (tribe).

## *Disciplining*

Disciplining Einsteins should be a private affair. In general, managers should avoid any public discipline of Einsteins. Einsteins will not lose their deference toward an overbearing manager for such an outburst, but they will lose respect.

Einsteins observe very well structured behavioral rituals within their tribe. These rituals establish an informal but powerful dominance hierarchy. If managers enter this environment and upset the tacit hierarchy that exists by dressing down an Einstein publicly, it upsets the entire team. Not only will that manager's position with the hierarchy be cast into question, but also lingering resentment will be a part of future interactions. Once done, this cannot be undone, even through apology.

## *Teaching*

Teaching Einsteins must be done correctly to be effective. Don't make them sit still for instructions unless you have the following in place:

1. A clear lesson

2. A lesson that concerns their craft

3. A technique for measuring effectiveness

Linking the lesson to the craft is the most important element of teaching Einsteins. A second simple truth about them is, again, that their first loyalty is to their craft. Einsteins are a bit fanatical about this. They have little time, patience, or understanding for things external to the craft. In some ways they resemble the grizzled old cowboy Curly from the "City Slickers" movies. Curly (played by Jack Palance) told one of the city slicker cowboys (played by Billy Crystal) what the meaning of life is. It is *one* thing, he said. Everything else "doesn't mean squat." When asked what that one thing is, Curly replied, "That's what you've got to find out." He meant that every person has to find that single most important thing for himself or herself. For Einsteins it's clear. The craft is number one.

In reality, Curly's philosophy closely resembles the common philosophy of Einsteins. They have very little concern for work-related gossip, issues, or situations outside the perfection of their craft. Some things Einstein managers can do to link the lesson to the craft include:

- Testimonials from others within the tribe regarding the value of the lesson
- Providing formal certification or other notification of the training that can be recognized within the world of the craft
- Holding a contest or entering a national competition that pits Einsteins against other Einsteins.

One effective approach used by many organizations today is e-learning or Web-based training. This mode of delivery uses an interface familiar to Einsteins—the computer. It can be taken in bits and bites rather that all at once, and it minimizes the time Einsteins are away from their craft. Some examples of e-learning firms that provide this type of training are:

- SkillSoft
- Click2Learn
- SmartForce
- Element K

## The Communication Equation

Einsteins not only need *more* communication than other employees, they require communication of a *different sort*. We have already used Albert Einstein's famous equation, $E = MC^2$, to explain how to motivate Einsteins. As we defined it in Chapter 4, E = Effort, M = Managerial intervention, and C = Communication. In short, to generate a high level of effort from Einsteins (E), managers must balance their managerial intervention (M) by an exponentially larger factor of communication (C). The amount of communication that is directed to Einsteins, in turn, is a function not only of quantity, but also of quality.

## Quantity of Communication

Einsteins are deeply enamored of the new communication tools. They are early adopters, with an abiding belief that technology is the key to communication, productivity, and staying connected. You'll often find Einsteins outfitted with multiple communication devices strapped to their belt. Some of the gadgets give them a swashbuckling appearance of the cowboys in the B-movies. In fact, that may be part of the appeal of the new cell phones and pagers of the modern day hero. Einsteins enjoy wearing their communication devices even more when they are *ringing*. A ringing cell phone, vibrating pager, or blinking e-mail receiver indicates engagement, connectedness, importance. It tells the world that "I am a person other people need."

Managers can take advantage of this early adopter, modern-day-hero psyche common among Einsteins. Smart managers encourage use of the new communication tools. Let's just pause a moment to review some that have emerged in the past decade:

1. *E-mail.* The "killer application," e-mail has become as commonplace as the telephone. Imagine getting a business card without an e-mail address.

2. *Cell phones.* Like it or not, cell phones are here to stay. Despite questions about their safe use while driving, the seeming lack of etiquette displayed by many users, and even questions about possible health effects, this technology is now part of modern life.

3. *Pagers.* These began as simple devices that alerted users to the fact that someone was trying to reach them. Pagers now offer much more than phone alerts. Capable of receiving text messages of nearly any type, the modern pager is a must-have utility for most Einsteins.

4. *Intranets.* The World Wide Web (Internet) is great for many things. The number of pages of information on the Web continues to grow exponentially. Corporate intranets are a fast-growing communication tool now used by over 80 percent of Global 2000 companies. Intranets, sometimes called "corporate portals," allow companies to "push" select information to individual desktops, while at the same time including user-guided access to select information repositories.

5. *Personal digital assistants*. These devices, also called PDAs, are the most must-have, cool technology. Still in the nascent stage of development, PDAs provide windows access to text messages, voice messages, the Internet, and the corporate intranet. Nirvana. An Einstein's dream device. If you go to Einstein hangouts, you may find them comparing their PDAs.

There's always the telephone, and don't forget about radio, TV, and print-based communication tools. In fact, most organizational communication is still paper-based, although e-mail has pulled up to a close second.

Effective communication with Einsteins uses multiple channels to provide *quantity*. There is a danger, however. It's called "information overload." Einsteins are great at processing information rapidly, but even they can be overloaded. To minimize or prevent this from becoming debilitating, managers must ensure that the information delivered is of high quality.

## *Quality of Communication*

As we stated, there is little difficulty today for most organizations to deliver a high quantity of information to employees. What *has* become very difficult is delivering information quality. The vast data and information "warehouses" that most organizations possess must be organized and arranged to create quality. Imagine going to a bookstore where there were thousands of books, but no orderly arrangement. The only way to find the book you want is by browsing. You would agree that this bookstore provided a great quantity of information but that there is no quality.

During a large part of the twentieth century, managers and executives of North American businesses believed that information about the business was useful to and should only be provided to top management. It was widely believed that most employees did not want access to company information and wouldn't know what to do with it. Worse, many managers believed that access to company information would be counterproductive for most employees. The thinking was that most employees were not intelligent enough to interpret the information. This state of affairs was called the "information blackout."

Not many organizations today still use the information blackout approach. Most recognize that the modern worker is better educated than the average worker of the early twentieth century. In addition, waves of changes in managerial thinking, such as the total quality management revolution, have encouraged "employee empowerment." This involves pushing information and decision making to the person executing the decision.

The next stage of evolution as the information blackout approach became dated is something we call "information dictatorship." This approach is characterized by select information access, determined by a few "elites" at the top of the organization. Information dictatorship was a natural first evolutionary step away from information blackout. Imagine the horror many managers must have felt as they loosened the reins they had held on corporate information. Not only were they concerned that the new recipients of the information might not be able to handle it, they were also concerned about their own role in the organization. What would be the source of privilege if not information? If formerly proprietary access to information is now available to everyone, what is the source of managerial elitism?

The information dictatorship helped answer these troubling questions. Managers were able to retain power within the organization by being the elites who determined what information any individual or group would gain access to. In this scenario, the manager is a gatekeeper. There is power in being a gatekeeper. The information dictatorship approach was a psychological way station—a necessary stage for managers to go through as they come to terms with a changing role in the organization. It may simply have been too much of a psychological shock to traverse from information blackout to complete companywide information access in one giant step.

We often refer to organizational intrigue as politics. To be sure, office politics concerns far more than access to information, but access to information is an unnecessary source of office politics. Unlike other resources, which may be the basis of organizational intrigue—such as capital—information is not a *scarce* resource. If I share my information with you, my stock of information has not been reduced. In fact, information quality is increased as more people are allowed to share.

The inventor of the Ethernet, Robert Metcalfe, discovered something that he called the "network effect." This simply means that the value of information, and the value of information by-products, such as the fax machine, expands exponentially as more people gain access. This powerful insight has come to be known as "Metcalfe's law." Metcalfe said that the value of a network varies with the square of the number of connected units.

Bernard Liautaud, founder of the consulting firm Business Objects has extrapolated Metcalfe's law of networks to apply to information sharing. Liautaud developed the following formula to capture the "network effect" of information sharing:

Value (information) = Users$^2$ × Business Areas

What this says, simply, is the value of information varies with the square of the number of users, and is multiplicative with the number of business areas that share in the information. (Business areas is defined as divisions or departments within the organization.)

Liautuad's extension of Metcalfe's law to information clearly argues for organizations to step beyond information dictatorship. It argues for increased sharing of information not only among individual employees but also across organizational boundaries. Liautaud says that organizations must move to information democracy: a setting where information access is *minimally* restrictive and *maximally* shared.

Einsteins thrive in an information democracy. They abhor organizational intrigue and detest the give-and-take of an information dictatorship. Einsteins have a deep belief that information is and should be free. Einsteins (not Al Gore) invented the Internet primarily as a tool for the free sharing of information. They took this belief with them when the commercial Internet revolution began in the mid-1990s. The Einsteins who founded many of the commercially oriented dot-coms actually tried to give away their products and services *for free*. Those heady days led to the subsequent euphoria of the dot-com bubble and the malaise of the crash.

## Imprinting

The first thing to remember about Einsteins is that organizational loyalty can be earned from two things: fairness and inclusiveness. Fairness has to do with the way they are treated in the company's overall system of rewards. Inclusiveness has to do with the quality of information the firm provides to them. We'll focus on this issue first.

You can think of Einsteins as having this "imprinting" instinct. Einsteins are tribal by nature. However, their tribal affiliations do not have rigid boundaries. In a way, Einsteins are a bit like baby ducks. When a baby duck hatches, the first large object it sees moving about is "Mother." If the large object happens to be a chicken or even a human, it doesn't matter. The baby duck has an "imprinting" instinct and will follow the object loyally throughout its adolescence. Einsteins are a little like that. They come into your organization without any preconceived notion of the boundaries of the tribe. Will it be just those people in the department? Will it be only those who share a room of cubicles? Will it be only those who dress and act like an Einstein?

Einsteins define their tribal loyalty mostly on communication criteria. Where the baby duck's criteria is something like "Mother = large moving object near nest," the Einstein's imprinting is something like "Tribe = entity that communicates honestly and openly."

Einsteins are incredibly honest. They don't have time for deception and intrigue. They believe that progress occurs through open and honest communication. The scientific method is their truth-finding technique. They don't feel a need to protect or preserve "sacred truths." Einsteins want data. They crave novel information that forces them to think in new and unexpected ways. They respect those around them who share their core values, which include:

- Truth evolves
- Progress comes from open communication
- There are no sacred cows

Einsteins will be loyal to the tribe that shares their open, forward-looking perspective. Thus, organizations as a whole can be seen as the tribe if they provide open, honest, frequent communication. Einsteins want to use their craft for the good of the tribe. As a manager, the quality of information you provide will establish the boundaries of the tribe.

Einsteins prefer to know the effects of their work. They want regular, fresh information on the day-to-day status of key indicators of progress. Managers who want Einsteins to define their tribe as the organization will share regular, bottom-line information on key indicators of the organization's progress. More, these indicators will be linked directly to the contributions—individual and team—of the Einsteins on staff. Many firms today use "digital dashboards" or "balanced scorecards" to provide minute-by-minute updates on a firm's bottom-line performance. Most Einsteins adapt well to these technology-based communication channels.

The key thing to remember if you use the digital dashboard or balanced scorecard approaches is they must be relevant. Many firms have found these techniques wanting, primarily because there is no direct link to the individual. If the indicators are too macro, they will not have a trickle-down effect on personal motivation. For example, Einsteins within IBM are interested in the firm's stock price. However, there is very little the individual can do to affect stock price.

Quality communication with Einsteins is built on defining the boundaries of the tribe, and it is based on the fundamental belief that truth evolves and progress comes from openness. To set the boundaries of the tribe, identify what critical variables Einsteins can influence on a daily basis. For example, if managers want a group of Einsteins to identify with the network administration department, provide data about the moment-to-moment performance of the network. Einsteins in network administration will jealously protect this data and will use it to define their personal success.

## The Communication Environment

Einsteins are like satellite dishes. They receive a wide range of incoming signals. The evolution of life on earth has produced carnivores, herbivores, and now informavores. Einsteins are informavores—they seek out, receive, and process information from a wide range of sources. Not all of this incoming information translates into behavioral effects. Einsteins will receive and process a lot of information, but they channel it to their core pursuit—building skill in their craft.

---

### Black Hole

*Ignoring Einsteins Is a Form of Humiliation*

One of the most effective methods of humiliation used by managers is the practice of ignoring an underling who is in or near the manager's office while the manager pursues seemingly unimportant tasks. This sends a message that the employee has no human presence. It is similar to changing clothes in front of the family pet; the animal is watching, but it couldn't possibly matter.

This tool of humiliation can be fine-tuned to any level simply by adjusting what activities are performed while the employee waits.

*Level of Humiliation*

- Taking phone calls: Not so bad

- Reading other things: Bad

- Flossing: Very bad

- Learning a foreign language: Very, very bad

From: Scott Adams, "Dilbert's Management Handbook," *Fortune*, May 13, 1996

---

Einstein's view the organization as an environment in which they are allowed and enabled to practice their craft. They are not *loyal* to the environment. The emotion they feel is more that of gratitude. They are grateful for the security they enjoy and, more important, for the tribal bonds they are allowed to build. Managers should strive to create and nurture the gratefulness, and not be as concerned about organizational loyalty.

In the past few years, there has been an explosion of new technologies that allow for regular and even instantaneous feedback to Einsteins on key organizational health parameters. Two of the more well known are:

1. Balanced Scorecards

2. Digital Dashboard

## Balanced Scorecard

The balanced scorecard is a tool that provides a snapshot of current operating performance and indicates the drivers of future performance. The balanced scorecard is primarily a *management* tool, but can be tailored to individual use. It combines "hard" financial data with "soft" data such as customer acquisition, retention and satisfaction, employee satisfaction, and organizational learning. Proponents of the balanced scorecard approach see it as a tool for implementing strategy, linking strategy to action, and for making strategy understandable to everyone in the organization.

The problem with the balanced scorecard, from an Einstein's perception, is that it is too strategy focused. Overall organizational strategy is interesting to Einsteins only as it impacts on their tribal strategy. They are not going to be interested in "the big picture"—how the company fits in the overall market or in the global economy. Of course, they want the organization to have such a fit, but they want someone else to worry about that. Einsteins want to keep their focus on their craft and build the skills they know will enable them and their tribe to survive.

## Digital Dashboard

A recent innovation that is based on Web technologies, the digital dashboard is usually delivered via a company's secure intranet, and integrates disparate data from the company's many databases. Digital dashboards typically have a user interface that conforms to their name—a dashboard. Like the dashboard in your car, the digital dashboard will contain an analog-appearing dial, bar charts, line charts, and news, sports, and weather updates.

The digital dashboard is fairly easy to set up and relatively inexpensive. Third-party providers abound, and most will assist with set up and integration with company databases. Many digital dashboards are provided as part of so-called corporate portals. Corporate portal providers are listed in the back of the book. Most so-called "back office" software companies, such as Oracle, SAP, and Microsoft, will also have digital dashboard technology.

## A Final Comment

Einsteins crave information and thrive in an information-rich, high-communication environment. Einstein managers should avoid efforts to try to one-up their Einsteins in technospeak. Their dedication to their specialized craft and tribe usually means they have adopted the latest jargon and slang long before the Einstein manager. Instead, the Einstein manager should focus on open and honest communication about the business, project, or task, goals, and the financial situation.

## CHAPTER 6

# Leading Einsteins

## Preview Einstein Story
### GE Creates Leaders from Within

Every spring, in a process mysteriously labeled "Session C," top executives at General Electric, spend about 160 hours combing through résumés, reviewing the management talent that will lead GE through the next century. But the promising candidates who glide across their radar screens aren't from outside the organization. They are already at GE. Execs prepare internal résumés listing their accomplishments, strengths, and ideal next moves. They discuss those expectations with their managers to get a sense of whether they are realistic. And then unit leaders recommend a select few who will attend the company's vaunted management training programs at its Crotonville campus in upstate New York. Only 360 professionals—six classes of 60—get selected.

A second program, for general management hopefuls, is held up to four times a year. Teams of students tackle some of GE's thorny business problems and later make a presentation to the corporate executive council. Yet another executive development course, held once a year for aspiring company officers, attacks "big business" issues facing the company and reports its findings at the annual officers' meeting in October.

GE thinks giving top people the chance to develop within the company will keep them around. The tactic doesn't always work, as many GE grads have left to head other companies—famous examples include Stanley Gault and Larry Bossidy, who ran Rubbermaid and AlliedSignal, and Glen Hiner and John Trani, now CEOs of Owens Corning and Stanley Works.

From: Nicholas Stein, "Winning the War to Keep Top Talent," *Fortune*, May 29, 2000, 42

*Leadership* is an important and necessary skill for achieving individual, group, and organizational performance in any context. Managers, whether they are chief executive officers or first-level supervisors, influence attitudes and expectations that encourage or discourage performance, secure or alienate employee commitment, reward or penalize achievement. Leading Einsteins requires many of the traditional leadership abilities—such as strong communications skills, vision, optimism—and several other abilities that are unique to this group. For example, leading Einsteins requires insight into their unique communication styles, tribal behavior, and motivational predilections. This chapter discusses the fundamentals of leadership and how these uniquely apply to the Einsteins on your workforce.

## Herding Cats

We've already talked about the principles of motivating Einsteins. A closely related yet important distinct function related to managing Einsteins is leadership. The concept of leadership is elusive and has attracted great attention from scholars, pundits, journalists, and others since the invention of writing, and probably long before that. We marvel at individuals who, following subtle unwavering inner lights, produce great works and elevate those who follow them to new levels of being. What is this "inner light"? How can you capture it?

Leadership is a will-o'-the-wisp that comes and goes within the lifetime of a single individual. There's nothing that enables anyone to predict when or where the next great leader will emerge. No one has figured out how to create, train, or develop leaders every single time such a practice is attempted. However, there are some things you can do to increase your effectiveness in leading Einsteins.

To effectively lead Einsteins, you must carefully cultivate those elements of leadership that appeal to the Einstein psyche. Like any other form of leadership, it must be bestowed from the followers—the Einsteins, in this case. Leadership that is taken from above is not really leadership at all—it's dictatorship. Einsteins want and will respect leadership; they abhor and will rebel against dictatorship.

---

### Black Hole

*Einsteins Abhor "Dictators"*

Leading Einsteins is like "herding cats"—you can guide them in a certain direction but you can't order them. Einsteins will react in a variety of ways to

> dictatorial leadership. The best you can hope for is lowered morale and foot-dragging. The worst is sabotage or exit. Einsteins are, typically, fiercely independent and do not respond well to dictator-style leadership. That doesn't mean that managers should avoid their leadership responsibilities. Rather, they should adopt a style that suits their Einsteins. In general, Einsteins will respond well to leaders that provoke and stimulate them. Good leaders will not try to be smarter than Einsteins. Instead, they will be comfortable with their inferior intellectual position, and will use their access to resources to create and fund interesting and challenging projects.

Managing Einsteins is one thing, leading them effectively is quite another. You've heard the old adage about leadership and management: Management is climbing the corporate ladder; leadership is making sure the ladder is leaning against the right wall. To be sure, organizations would prefer management and leadership to go together. The boundaries between the two are fuzzy at best. Nonetheless, someone can be a very effective manager without being an adequate leader. A person can be a great leader without being an effective manager.

## Winning Respect

Leading Einsteins is most effective if it is earned by example. Respect-based leadership is a powerful force that can help achieve great things through Einsteins. What do Einsteins respect? In a word: results.

Being friendly won't help. Being glib won't help. Being concerned won't help if no results are produced. Many managers make the mistake of thinking that respect comes from friendliness or concern. In fact, some popular books on leadership suggest that a person should be concerned with and friendly toward everyone. The standard line is that you don't know whether the mailroom helper or the janitor might turn out to have more influence than you ever realized. Best to be on good terms with everyone, just in case. Einsteins consider this fake and want nothing to do with phony friendliness. They want to know what a person has done on projects in term of results.

This dismissal of phony friendliness is not elevating brashness or aloofness to a preferred state. Certainly not. The message instead is that leading Einsteins will not be achieved through a reputation of friendliness. It's fine and comfortable to be friendly—we even recommend it. But this is not enough of a recipe to be considered an effective leader of Einsteins.

Einsteins are not hero worshipers. There are people whom they admire. They admire certain individuals for what they have done— their admiration is directed to those who inspire them to greater achievements. For example, Einsteins do not admire Bill Gates for what he stands for or for how much money he has. They admire him because he built the greatest software company in the world. Bill Gates, Andy Grove, Steve Jobs, and Scott McNealy are admired for what they have accomplished. They are admirably thought of as high-tech titans.

Applying what is learned in this chapter to leading Einsteins boils down to one simple truth: leaders must lead by example. The personal leadership power that you will be granted by Einsteins is the power that is earned. There's no easy way. You can't get your leadership through a fancy title. You can't get it by ordering it. And you can't get it from someone above you in the organization. Einsteins will have to *give* you leadership power.

## Influence: The Core of Leadership

*Leadership* is not an easy term to define precisely. We define it as the ability to influence the activities of others, individually or as a group, toward the accomplishment of worthwhile, meaningful, and challenging goals.

The exercise of influence is the essence of leadership behavior. The use of influence as a *primary* method of affecting the organization is perhaps the major difference between leaders and managers. Leaders use influence as their primary tool to move the organization toward its goals.

Seven influence strategies have been proposed as vital for practicing leadership roles:

1. *Reason.* Using facts and data to develop a logically sound argument

2. *Friendliness.* Using supportiveness, flattery, and the creation of goodwill

3. *Coalition building.* Mobilizing others in the organization

4. *Bargaining.* Negotiating through the use of benefits or favors

5. *Assertiveness.* Using a direct and forceful approach

6. *Higher authority*. Gaining the support of higher levels in the hierarchy to add weight to the request

7. *Sanctions*. Using rewards and punishment

Einsteins respond to these influence strategies differentially. The most powerful influences managers can apply to the Einsteins on their staff are *coalition building* and *bargaining*. Coalition building with Einsteins is the process of creating an esprit de corps, a team feeling in pursuit of a common goal. This can be exercised in a vast number of ways. The world's great team builders have all used the same basic principles to establish esprit de corps:

- Communicate a compelling vision
- Delegate responsibility
- Recognize and reward progress
- Identify and celebrate finality
- Start the process again

Effective leaders, when they reach a goal, pause, and then set out again. Einsteins abhor a project vacuum. Leaders must be prepared to fill that vacuum with compelling new projects once the old ones have been completed or are winding down. That means that leaders of Einsteins must constantly be looking ahead. To lead Einsteins on a team, a leader must be vigilant to beat them to the future. Leaders must get there ahead of Einsteins. Of course, this is no easy task, but there are specific steps that can be taken to stay at least one step ahead:

1. Read deeply in the area of your expertise.

2. Read broadly in areas that are in or on the fringes of your expertise.

3. Follow analyst research, especially from firms like Meta Group, Forrester, Gartner, Ernst & Young, and others.

4. Talk to people in your field at conferences, in online forums, and at professional societies.

5. Write about where you think your business is going and how you can help it get there. The act of writing your thoughts serves two functions: (1) it clears your mind of the day-to-day tactical stuff, and (2) it reveals to you thoughts you probably didn't know you had.

## Einstein Wisdom

Albert Einstein, like many scientists, inventors, and discovers, was captivated by the "Aha Experience." You know what that is. It's the moment of insight that you get when a problem over which you had been puzzling suddenly resolves itself in your mind. The "Aha" is partly joy in realizing that the answer emerged practically unbidden from your mind, and partly the relief from knowing you've solved the problem. "Aha experiences" are not mystical or mysterious. They are the result of the vast mechanism of your mind putting together all that is stored inside. Writing your thoughts on paper is a technique for urging the "Aha Experience" to occur. It clarifies your thinking and shows itself to your mind in a new form. Gary Player once said, "The more I practice, the luckier I get." This principle applies to your own insight into the future. The more you apply yourself to thinking and writing about the future, the luckier you'll get in beating everyone else to it.

# Leadership Styles

Leadership has been one of the most studied topics in management, yet the conclusions reached have been contradictory, exaggerated, and controversial. Part of the problem lies in the definitions, measurements, and theories used to study leadership. The three main approaches at the center of the debate surrounding leadership are:

*Trait theory of leadership.* Attributes performance differences among employees to the individual characteristics (traits) of leaders.

*Behavioral theory of leadership.* Attributes performance differences to the behaviors and style of leaders.

*Contingency theory of leadership.* Considers the leader's behavior and style in combination with situational factors as the key reasons for performance differences.

Over the years, these main approaches have been refined and various dimensions have been added, but they still remain the primary basis for leadership theory, research, and application discussions.

## Trait Theory of Leadership

We observe good leaders such as Gordon Bethune of Continental Airlines, Meg Whitman of eBay, and Lou Gerstner of IBM. So it's natural to ask whether the secret of leadership is to be found in the individual characteristics of leaders. Are there differences between leaders and nonleaders in terms of personality traits, physical characteristics, motives, needs? Many people believe that effective leadership has roots in a particular personality trait. Some even assume that unless one possesses that trait, he or she is doomed to failure as a leader.

The trait theory of leadership constitutes an important but somewhat controversial approach to understanding leadership. Not all effective leaders are tall, good-looking, or exceptionally smart. Not all effective leaders are charismatic or glib. In addition, there are cultural differences in the traits that are necessary for effective leadership. A good leader in an American company may not have the traits needed to be successful in, say, a Chinese corporation.

Although trait leadership theory has its problems, it can't be denied that leaders exhibit traits that followers admire. And some executives involved in the recruitment and selection of managers believe that the *trait theory* is valid.

The systematic study of the personal characteristics and traits of leaders began as a consequence of the need for military officers during World War I. Many business and governmental organizations also began researching the characteristics that distinguished their most effective from their less effective managers. The studies that attempt to identify these traits have produced a lengthy list. They are grouped into six categories:

- *Physical characteristics*—age, height, weight
- *Background characteristics*—education, social class or status, mobility, experience
- *Intelligence*—ability, judgment, knowledge
- *Personality*—aggressiveness, alertness, dominance, decisiveness, enthusiasm, extroversion, independence, self-confidence, authoritarianism
- *Task-related characteristics*—achievement need, responsibility, initiative, persistence
- *Social characteristics*—supervisory ability, cooperativeness, popularity, prestige, tact, diplomacy

The Center for Creative Leadership is a nonprofit research and educational institution located in Greensboro, North Carolina. Two of the center's researchers, Morgan McCall and Michael Lombardo, sought to compare traits of twenty-one derailed executives—successful people who were expected to be promoted but who reached a plateau, were fired, or were forced to retire early—with those of twenty "arrivers" who made it all the way to the top. The derailed executives' flaws merged into a list of ten traits:

1. Insensitive to others; abrasive; intimidating, bullying style

2. Cold, aloof, arrogant

3. Betrayal of trust

4. Overly ambitious, thinking of next job, playing politics

5. Specific performance problems with the business

6. Overmanaging, unable to delegate or build a team

7. Unable to staff effectively

8. Unable to think strategically

9. Unable to adapt to boss with different style

10. Overdependent on advocate or mentor

None of the derailed executives had all the trait flaws cited. The ar-rivers appeared to possess more ability to get along with all types of people. They either possessed or developed the skills required to be outspoken without offending people. They were seen as being direct and diplomatic.

The Center for Creative Leadership researchers suggest, however, that no one—the arrivers or the derailed executives—can possess every skill and trait needed to fit every situation. A leader is human, like everyone else, and therefore possesses strengths and weaknesses. But if there is one trait that seems to be associated with success, it is the ability to get along with people.

## Behavioral Theory of Leadership

The disappointing results of the search for common leadership traits have led to a somewhat different line of thought. Rather than focus-ing on the *characteristics* of effective leaders, an alternative is to fo-cus on their *behavior*. The question of behavioral leadership theories then becomes: What do effective leaders *do* that ineffective ones *do not do*? For example, are effective leaders democratic rather than au-tocratic, permissive rather than directive, person-oriented rather than task-oriented? Or are effective leaders characterized by some balance of these behaviors?

Terms such as *permissive-directive, democratic-autocratic,* and *person oriented/task oriented* refer to whether the leader's behavior reflects *primary* concern for the work or for the people who are doing the work. We noted earlier that the essence of leadership is getting work done through others. One point of view holds that the best way to lead is to be task oriented.

The key to working with Einsteins is to lead through persuasion and excitement. Einsteins are overachievers. Putting their energy into a task is not an issue. They don't need the standard bromides about hard work that might be useful for those of lesser ambition. Einsteins seek and enjoy hard, task-oriented work. The trick is, they must be led in a way that guides them to choose the tasks you want them to achieve.

There are many practical approaches to making this happen. For example, you might decide to list the tasks that need doing and have your Einsteins "volunteer." In this way, you may be offering nothing but poison, but at least your Einsteins will get to choose their poison. Don't underestimate the power of perceived freedom.

Another technique—perhaps more powerful—is to use a form of "open book" management with your Einsteins. If Einsteins are fully informed about the issues facing the company, they will dig in and do "whatever it takes" to make things work.

**Employee-centered leadership.** Rensis Likert is a pioneer in the development of the idea that the behaviors of the most effective leaders are person oriented. Likert and his associates at the University of Michigan have conducted studies in various organizational settings. These studies have led Likert to conclude that the most effective leaders focus on the human aspects of their groups. They attempt to build effective teamwork through supportive, considerate, and nonpunitive *employee-centered* behavior. Such leaders were found to be more effective than those who emphasized *task-centered* behavior; that is, leaders who specifically detailed the work of subordinates, closely supervised them, and rewarded them only with financial incentives.

Unfortunately, this approach is less powerful with Einsteins. Independent by nature, Einsteins are prone to distrust and even to dislike individuals who concern themselves excessively with personal issues.

It would seem that we are left with the choice that the effective leader is *either* task oriented or person oriented, *but not both.* And if this is the case, then aspiring leaders need only a narrow range of skills. If the most effective leaders are task oriented, then leaders need only be skilled in the technical aspects of planning and organizing the work of others. But if the most effective leaders are person oriented, then human relations and interpersonal skills are required. But what if both points of view are correct? Most believe that effective leaders are equally task and person oriented in their behavior toward Einsteins.

The idea that the one best way to lead effectively requires a balance between task-oriented and person-oriented behavior has considerable appeal. One approach to studying this is the *two-dimensional theory* of leadership.

**Two-dimensional leadership.** One of the most significant investigations of the behavior of leaders began immediately after World War II at Ohio State University. The researchers developed two key concepts in the two-dimensional theory: *initiating structure* and *consideration.* Initiating structure refers to task-oriented behavior in which the leader organizes and defines the relationships in the group, establishes patterns and channels of communications, and directs the work methods. Consideration refers to person-oriented behavior in which the leader exhibits friendship, trust, respect, and warmth toward subordinates.

The difference between managers high on initiating structure and on consideration is displayed in Exhibit 6.1.

Leading Einsteins will require both initiating structure and consideration. However, the notion of initiating structure is modified for Einsteins, since they want structure; they crave it and seek it out. With equal and opposite passion, however, they revile having structure imposed. Einsteins prefer to choose or create their own structure. While this may sound like a recipe for organizational anarchy, quite the opposite is true. Remember, Einsteins crave order and actively seek it

**Exhibit 6.1**
Two-Dimensional Leadership Theory

| Initiating Structure | Consideration |
| --- | --- |
| • Insist on rigid work methods<br>• Insist on being informed<br>• Push subordinates for increased effort<br>• Decide in detail on what to do and how to do it | • Express appreciation for jobs well done<br>• Stress importance of high morale<br>• Treat all employees as equals<br>• Be friendly and approachable |

out. Recent research has demonstrated that people, even more so than inanimate matter, have a tendency to self-organize. Effective leaders can control this process by establishing appropriate projects around which their Einsteins will naturally self-organize.

## Contingency Theory of Leadership

Some believe that the practice of leadership is too complex to be represented by unique traits *or* behaviors. Instead, their assumption is that effective leadership behavior is contingent upon the situation. But even this idea is not fully settled. One variation is that leaders must change behaviors to meet situational needs. A second variation is that leaders' behaviors are difficult to alter and that the situation itself must be changed to make it compatible with the leaders' behavior.

The contingency theory of leadership is considerably more complex than either the trait or the behavioral approach. As indicated in Exhibit 6.2, effective leadership depends on the interaction of the leader's personal characteristics, the leader's behavior, and factors in the leadership situation. In a sense, the situational approach is based on the idea that effective leadership cannot be defined by any one factor. This approach does not deny the importance of the leader's characteristics or behavior. Rather, it states that *both* must be taken into account and considered in the context of the situation.

**Leadership flexibility.** A recurring theme in leadership theory and practice is the concept of *participation* by subordinates in decision making. This theme originated in the writings of the behavioral

**Exhibit 6.2**
The Situational Approach to Effective Leadership

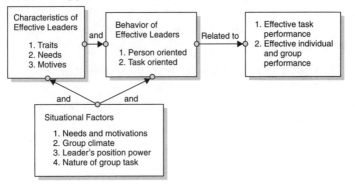

**Exhibit 6.3**

Continuum of Leadership Behavior

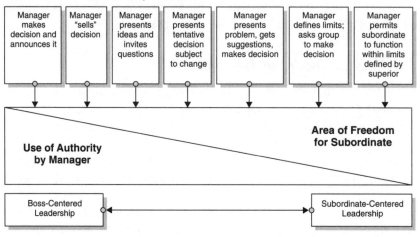

| Manager makes decision and announces it | Manager "sells" decision | Manager presents ideas and invites questions | Manager presents tentative decision subject to change | Manager presents problem, gets suggestions, makes decision | Manager defines limits; asks group to make decision | Manager permits subordinate to function within limits defined by superior |

**Use of Authority by Manager**

**Area of Freedom for Subordinate**

Boss-Centered Leadership ◄─────────────────► Subordinate-Centered Leadership

approach to management, and it has held a prominent place in the thinking of managers for the last forty years. The fundamental idea is shown in Exhibit 6.3.

At the extremes of this continuum are boss-centered leadership and subordinate-centered leadership. Between these extremes are five points representing various combinations of managerial authority and subordinate freedom. One of the extreme positions, boss-centered leadership, represents a manager who simply makes a decision and announces it. The subordinate-centered leader permits subordinates to participate fully in decision making. Within prescribed limits, the subordinates act as partners with the leader.

Whether a leader should make the decision and announce it (boss-centered) or share the problem with subordinates and seek group consensus (subordinate-centered) depends on the interaction of factors related to the problem and to the subordinates. Factors related to the *problem* are:

- The likelihood that one solution to the problem is more effective than another
- The extent to which the leader has sufficient information to make a high-quality decision
- The extent to which alternative solutions are known with some certainty

Factors related to *subordinates* are:

- The likelihood that effective implementation of the solution depends on subordinates accepting it as appropriate
- The likelihood that if the leader makes the decision, the subordinates will accept it
- The extent to which subordinates recognize and accept the organizational objectives to be attained by the solution
- The likelihood that conflict among subordinates will result if the preferred solution is adopted

In a practical sense, combining these seven factors creates different situations. At one extreme are situations for which a number of solutions exist, none of which require acceptance by subordinates for effective implementation. The manager should make the decision and announce it. On the other hand, participation is warranted to the extent that only one solution is likely and its consequences are not known with certainty, *and* subordinates have relevant information, *and* their acceptance is necessary for implementation. The effective leader changes style whenever the situation demands it. That is, the leader is flexible enough to be relatively task-centered or employee-centered as situations change.

Leadership scholar Jared Diamond has discussed what he calls the *Optimal Fragmentation Principle*. This principle states that organizations that have excessive unity of thought tend to have low levels of productivity and innovation. Similarly, firms that have an excessive level of diversity of thought also tend to have low levels of productivity and innovation. Diamond states that there is an optimal level of internal fragmentation that leads to high levels of innovation and productivity.

Lou Gerstner arrived at IBM during a period when Big Blue was suffering through softening sales, decreasing morale, and a lack of confidence. Gerstner took immediate steps to transform the organization from the insulated secretive groups that had dominated for years into a more Microsoftlike organization consisting of many small groups that freely communicate. This shift in organizational design was a stroke of genius and has revitalized IBM into a major global technology player.

Einsteins prefer an open environment where they are free to give and take ideas wherever they can find them. Leaders should use the Optimal Fragmentation Principle liberally with their Einsteins. Their natural predilection toward working in small teams and deriving optimal solutions through "open source" techniques is aligned with the Optimal Fragmentation Principle. Einsteins will feel comfortable working in such a fragmented organization and they will tend naturally to self-organize into optimal levels of fragmentation. Effective leaders will do well to guide the process with a light touch.

---

### A Case Study

The Principle of Optimal Fragmentation has evidence of its power in large and small scales alike. For example, in the fifteenth century the Chinese government decided to halt all shipbuilding throughout the country. Since China's neighbors were not seagoing, aspiring Chinese explorers had nowhere to turn to build the ships they needed. In contrast, Columbus made nine unsuccessful applications for support to various princes of Italy, France, Portugal, and Spain before Spain's king and queen finally granted him three ships. The fragmented political and exploratory aspirations of European leaders enabled Columbus to succeed where the unified outlook of Asian leaders severely restricted sea exploration.

More recently, the distinct cultures of Silicon Valley and Route 128 in Boston have been interesting. The companies in Silicon Valley compete fiercely with one another, yet there is also a generous sharing of ideas. In contrast, the companies of Route 128 in Boston have been more secretive and insulated. As a result, Silicon Valley has overtaken Route 128's early lead as the center of technology innovation.

Jared Diamond, "The Ideal Form of Organization," *Wall Street Journal*, December 12, 2000, A26

---

## Charismatic Leadership

Scott McNealy of Sun Microsystems and Michael Dell of Dell Computers are used as examples of leaders with charisma. A charismatic leader is a person who by force of his or her personal abilities and style is capable of having a profound and extraordinary effect on followers. The charismatic leadership view combines both traits and behaviors.

What McNealy and Dell are able to do because of their energy, self-confidence, and dominating personalities is to project a conviction in the rightness of their beliefs. Charismatic leaders generate excitement and increase the expectations of followers through their vision of the future. Research suggests that charismatic leadership is a function of what followers perceive. Some fortunate individuals are born with this gift, but most charismatic leaders apparently learn it and use it with great success.

Some theorists propose that charisma is distributed throughout the organization. We usually only read about world-class leaders. However, there are executives, middle-level managers, salespersons, and truck drivers who possess charisma.

Through interviews with ninety reputedly charismatic leaders, researchers identified a set of behavior strategies used by these individuals:

- *Focusing attention* on specific issues of concern; concentrating on analysis, problem solving, and action.
- *Communicating* with empathy and sensitivity.
- *Demonstrating consistency* and trustworthiness by one's behavior; being honest, sticking with a decision, and following through on decisions.
- *Expressing active concern for people,* including oneself, thus modeling self-regard, and reinforcing feelings of self-worth in others.

There may be no more effective way to lead Einsteins than charismatic leadership. Paradoxically, Einsteins are not hero worshipers. Yet, they have remarkable reverence for and deference toward those individuals who can help them excel in their chosen field. Einsteins are exceedingly self-aware and objective. They are neither afraid nor ashamed to admit their own weaknesses. They are objective about their skills and their place in the local "pecking order."

## Einsteins Leading Einsteins

Leadership involves other people; therefore, where there are leaders, there must be followers. Leadership can arise in any situation where people have combined their efforts to accomplish a task. Thus, leaders may or may not be managers. Within the organization, informal groups develop, and within those groups are people who influence the behavior of other group members. Such people are the "informal leaders." Individuals who influence the behavior of their assigned groups are the "formal leaders" of organizations. Most Einsteins avoid the mantle of leadership. They prefer the anonymity of their team over the public prominence of leadership. Nonetheless, informal leadership among Einsteins is an important component of their work satisfaction and, therefore, retention.

The savvy leader of Einsteins cultivates internal leadership. This can be done in a subtle and indirect way by recognizing the "natural leaders" on the Einstein teams. These are the individuals who distinguish themselves from the rest of the team. Individual Einsteins distinguish themselves as natural leaders in several remarkable ways that may make them candidates for informal leadership. These include:

1. *Outstanding technical skills.* Some Einsteins possess skills at a level so high they become "legendary" among the other Einsteins.

2. *Outstanding work habits.* Some Einsteins become informal leaders because they have exemplary or unusual work habits. Stories abound about Einsteins who "slept in the rafters" and lived on Coke and pizza to complete projects. This type of "yeoman" effort can create the respect and awe required for leadership.

3. *Been there, done that.* Some informal leaders can arise from the experiences they've had elsewhere with legendary individuals or companies. This form of "leadership by association" is less powerful than the first two.

4. *Project creator.* This is perhaps the most powerful source of leadership respect among Einsteins. Having the vision and creativity to invent interesting projects will win the respect of Einsteins.

"I SECURED EXTRA SUPPORT FOR YOUR PROJECT. FOR THOSE LATE NIGHTS, WE WILL SUPPLY YOU WITH ALL THE PIZZA YOU CAN EAT!"

Generating leaders from within Einstein tribes is an effective way of keeping projects moving forward. Internal leaders have natural respect, rather than the formal respect Einsteins will accord leaders by virtue of the corporate hierarchy. The key is to enlist the internal leaders as champions, people who will represent the interests of the firm in an Einsteinian way to Einsteins.

---

## Influence Tip

### Microsoft Looks to Seniors for New Talent

As part of its Skills 2000 program, Microsoft has partnered with Green Thumb, an Arlington, Virginia, nonprofit organization, to run three pilot programs to train people age fifty-five and older for entry-level jobs in network and database administration and technical support. About seventy people have completed the training.

One recent graduate is Warren Willard, fifty-eight, who had worked for several large resort chains in Hawaii before she returned to Sacramento and encountered difficulty finding another management position. She says completing programs like Green Thumb's "shows that we're willing at a later age to go out and be flexible, try new things, study and work hard." Willard completed an internship with Myriad Systems, a computer consulting firm in El Dorado Hills, California. There, she worked alongside the company's owner to set up networks, build new systems, upgrade and repair computers, and staff the help desk.

From: Kim Kiser, "Move Over Nerds," *Training*, January 1999, 54–58

---

# A Final Comment

Leading Einsteins requires establishing a guiding vision and converting the vision into challenging, rewarding projects that allow Einsteins to practice their craft. Autocratic or dictatorial leadership styles are not welcome among Einsteins. They prefer leaders who help them develop their personal skill base.

## CHAPTER 7

# Tribes and Teamwork

## Preview Einstein Story

### Learn Before a Team Is Built

How does an Einstein manager utilize the talents, skill, and idiosyncrasies of Einsteins? Carefully, is the answer. There are all kinds of Einsteins, and they have a tendency to be attracted to each other in organizations. Einsteins form into "tribes," and some of these aggregations evolve into teams. Engineer, programmer, systems analyst, IT specialist, and hundreds of other titles and positions are held by Einsteins. Before building or nuturing high performance teams of Einsteins, managers need to understand the background, desires, and styles of these superintelligent individuals.

One of many Einstein tribes is the "programmers." Unfortunately, managers think in stereotypes about teams of programmers or teams that include programmers. What follows is a programmer's description of life at work.

The stereotypical programmer is an introverted young man (the majority are male) who works long hours to coax the computer to work as he wants it to perform. He often works in twelve to sixteen hour blocks, at odd hours such as 10:00 p.m. to 11:00 a.m. He subsists on almost anything available. Pizza and high caffeine colas are part of the consumption. The programmer loves *Star Trek* trivia and watches Monty Python reruns. He is considered a genius one minute and an eccentric "geek" the next.

Many programmers appear to travel through a career path cycle. One programmer describes his journey as follows: "When I get the first small programs to compile and get rid of all the syntax errors, I'll have computer programming figured out. After the syntax errors stopped, some programs still didn't work. I then adopted a belief that once I get the

*Continued*

program debugged, I'll have computer programming figured out. This belief was good until I worked on larger programs and still had problems. I then thought once I figure out how to design effectively, I'll have software development figured out. I created some beautiful designs, but some of them had to be changed because the requirements kept changing. At that point I thought once I figure out how to get good requirements, I'll finally have software development figured out." This goes on and on and never ends.

Managers need to examine stereotypes, education, and the career path of Einsteins before teams of them are managed, led, or facilitated. What we have found is that the world of Einsteins consists of tribes or groups that have common characteristics. Before your attempt to build, learn about tribes and teams.

## Tribes and Teams: An Overview

Eric Schmidt, CEO of Novell, Inc., considers himself a card-carrying "geek" (we call him an Einstein). He was introduced in Chapter 2. A good deal of credit for Novell's return from the "dark side" of profitability is attributed to Schmidt's ability to manage his Einsteins. His experience and society's general view of Einsteins label them antisocial. Schmidt considers Einsteins to be quite social among themselves, especially when they are within their tribes. Yet, outside the "tribes" territory, antisocial or socially clumsy may be the best description. The tribes are arrayed into "mainframe-era" graybeards, Unix Einsteins, the new PC-plus-Web generation, and others. The tribes subdivide within their group, but don't fight each other. The tribes are at peace and get along with each other—because they fight non-Einsteins and ineffective, dishonest, pushy managers.

## Some Lessons About Tribes

A *tribe* is defined as a group of people who share unique attributes, which in many instances evolve from their experiences, knowledge skills, and values. An article in *Boston Magazine* discusses the twelve tribes of Boston, which explains how the city works because of tribal behavior. Included in the Boston tribe categories are the Irish tribe, the Black tribe, the Italian tribe, the Medical tribe, the techno tribe, and others. The current Boston techno tribe is dominated by software and Internet systems Einsteins that have perched and spread along Route 128 to parts of Waltham, Kendall Square in Cambridge, Newton, and Andover. A leading candidate for the Boston techno tribal chieftain is Bob Metcalfe, an MIT undergrad and Harvard Ph.D. who helped lay the groundwork for the ARPA net—the Internet predecessor—and invented Ethernet before starting Silicon Valley's 3COM Corporation.

Boston's techno tribes have their customs, hangouts, slang and lingo, dress code, and enemies. There are other cities in the world that have their own techno tribes that share common attributes and impact the life, flow, and values of their location. Tribes can have a major impact on their surroundings and on the individuals who do not become a part of the tribal membership.

Under U.S. law, the word *tribe* is a bureaucratic term. For a community of Native Americans to gain access to programs, and to enforce rights due to them under treaties and laws, they must be identified, recognized, and function as a tribe. For thousands of years before the coming of Europeans to North America, perhaps as many as 400,000 of the ancestors of the Seminole Indian tribes built towns, villages, and civilizations across large landmasses. Today the Seminole Indian tribe of Florida lives on five reservations and adheres to customs, rituals, celebrations, and values passed down over a long history.

Use and identification in organizations of Einstein tribes is only about three decades old, but they do exist and are recognized by astute managers. Like the Boston tribes and the Seminole Indian tribe, Einsteins stick together. They are attracted to each other because of common interests, language and slang, needs, and intelligence. The Einstein tribes have their knowledge base, beliefs, attitudes, customs, rituals, folklore, symbols, language, dress codes, social behaviors, and etiquette, which are unique to the membership. The Einstein tribes develop and flourish inside and outside the organization. Similar to other primates and most higher mammals, Einstein tribe members prefer to "hang" with those who think, look, act, dress, and talk like themselves. They are suspicious of those not like them, especially those in the manager tribes or the "suits." Many Einstein tribes like to reject so-called normal organizational practices, including formal dress codes, deference to people in higher positions, acceptance of what are considered rigid policies, and regular work hours (8:00 a.m. to 5:00 p.m.).

## What Are Self-Directed Teams?

A *self-directed team*, also referred to as a *self-organized team*, is a group of knowledgeable and skilled employees who are responsible for a "whole" work process or project. The team members work together to solve problems, plan, control, and direct work. In other words, the self-directed team is responsible for performing the work, but also informally managing themselves.

The distinguishing features of self-directed teams that appeal to Einsteins are:

- Being empowered to conduct the operation, task, project, as the members desire
- Planning, controlling, and managing their own process
- Working on the team's schedule at its own pace
- Setting their own goals and reviewing their own members' work performance
- Coordinating their work with other teams, groups, departments, or projects
- Acquiring any new training needed to improve
- Hiring their own replacements or bringing in their preferred new Einsteins
- Disciplining their own members

The increase in global competition, the expansion of and need for computer technology, the shortage of Einstein talent, and the recognition that people are attracted to others like themselves (tribes) have boosted the interest in teams. Teamwork is not a new idea that only fits Einsteins. Americans cheer for their teams in sports stadiums and have been emphasizing teamwork since the first ship full of pilgrims arrived.

Parents discuss teamwork with their young children for years. Yet, in the real world the individual is exhalted. Most organizations use individual reward systems, individual performance appraisal approaches, and individual goal setting. We celebrate the individual and how individualism has contributed to the nation's economic success. Unfortunately, the overemphasis on individuals has placed teams and their value, potential, and contribution in work organizations on the shelf, away from the limelight. We contend that individualism should definitely be celebrated in our free enterprise society. However, teamwork needs more attention, study, and consideration, especially when Einstein tribes are so obviously needed to contribute to economic and quality of life growth.

Building a team is a straightforward concept, especially when you recognize that teams are made up of individuals with diverse knowledge backgrounds, skills, talents, and aspirations. Each Einstein has a clearly defined skill set that needs to be optimally utilized. Organizations that are committed to building strong Einstein teams recognize the value of allowing a group of employees to evolve into a team to maximize their contributions. The difference between a group and a team is subtle but important. Teams are mature groups that can perform work effectively. They need a special type of management, leadership, and facilitative support. Many groups are immature aggregations of individuals that have difficulty getting along and performing. Leaders who accept, understand, and work with the team concept, as well as respect individualism, will be rewarded with powerful value-added contributions.

## Why Teams at Work?

Even today, most work in organizations is not attributed to the team concept. At the beginning of the twentieth century, work was organized into simple, repetitive tasks so the work could be closely managed. It was managers that did all the problem solving, decision making, and facilitating. The work was structured for poorly educated, nonquestioning, rather passive workers (often immigrants) who were happy to have a job that paid a wage.

The use of self-directed teams didn't really appear until the early 1970s, with a handful of firms such as Proctor & Gamble and the

"WHEN IT COMES TO TEAMWORK, THERE'S
NOTHING LIKE A CHALLENGING COMPUTER GAME

Topeka, Kansas, Gaines dog food plant setting the pace and providing examples for others to review, critique, and copy. Today, the team concept is well-suited for Einsteins, as more managers realize that empowered teams of creative and intelligent workers can effectively meet the needs of the firm.

## Empowering Einstein Teams

Einstein team empowerment and the energy that comes with feelings of ownership are powerful motivators. *Empowerment* means the passing of authority and responsibility to team members; an empowered Einstein team knows that the job, work, and project belongs to it. The Einsteins on the team decide how the work is done. They possess a sense of empowerment to complete the work as they see fit.

Exhibit 7.1 provides an Einstein team's range of empowerment. At Level I, about 20 percent, a relatively new team assumes some responsibility; while at Level IV, a fully functioning mature Einstein team is assuming significant responsibility and authority. A team at Level IV can be involved in budgeting, equipment decision, and reward decision making. There are still managers around, but a larger part of the responsibility and authority (80 percent) rests with the Einsteins themselves. Einstein managers even in self-managed teams are expected to be around to coordinate, support, coach, encourage, and control the work and progress of the members. The presence of teams does not mean the absence of Einstein managers. It does mean that managers must play more of a leadership and facilitator role.

Team empowerment can grow at various speeds. Typically, percentages or degrees of empowerment are not calculated. Such calculations would be guesses and probably considered pseudoscience. The use of percentages here is only an illustrative example with a partial list of Einstein responsibilities and authority. Becoming a self-directed Einstein team is evolutionary. Einsteins adapt over time to greater amounts of responsibility and authority.

---

### Influence Tip

Effective Einstein teams often have internal members emerge as informal leaders. When a particular Einstein possesses some needed expertise, he or she may be afforded leadership deference from other members. Einstein managers should expect informal leaders to rotate as the situation changes, expertise needs change, or membership changes.

**Exhibit 7.1**
Einstein Team Employment Amounts

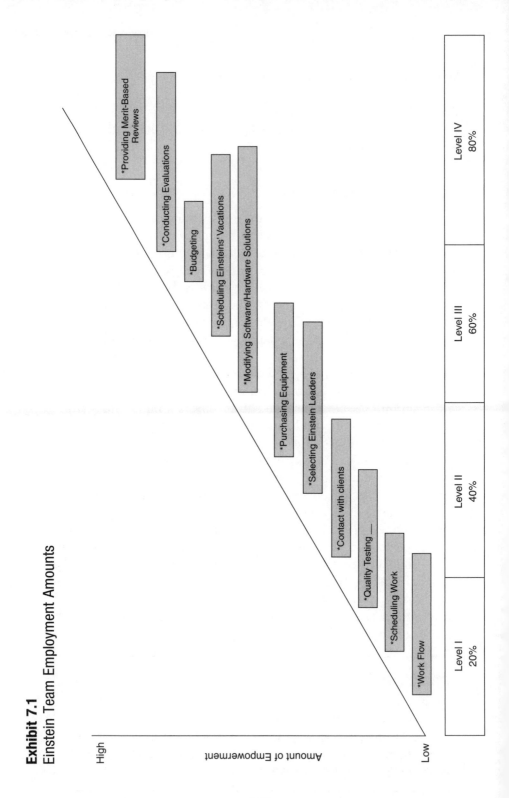

## The Einstein Manager/Leader

Even with self-directed Einstein teams, managerial representation, experience, and talent among Einstein managers is crucial. Some leadership and managerial responsibilities shift to the team, but the more organizationally linked responsibilities do not usually change.

As is the case in any organization or setting, Einstein teams undergo a learning curve in terms of transformation. When team members learn new responsibilities, they become more proficient. Many Einsteins, especially the younger and less organizationally experienced, have no history of being a part of a self-directed team. Goal setting, budgeting, evaluating, and working as a team must be learned. Managers sometimes are reluctant to help Einsteins learn these practices. However, the teaching role is a major responsibility of Einstein managers who are in place to guide the learning and practices of team members.

The Einstein managers may feel as if they are losing their authority, their power, as a team matures. In some sense they are, since the number of managers is typically reduced in a team-based system. The psychological impact of a "sense of loss" can be devastating to Einstein managers. Since most managers operate in a system in which they are the "boss" who directs others and makes requests, any type of empowered self-directed team is going to create a sense of "lost" power, control, and authority.

Can Einsteins in management positions learn to work as self-directed team resources and team facilitators? This is a difficult question to answer with an emphatic yes. Some can and will learn, and others will sabotage, quit, or leave the job. There is no certainty in categorizing which Einstein managers will or can adjust. In reality, everything is not going to work smoothly for every manager or every Einstein team.

# How Do Self-Directed Einstein Teams Operate?

There is no such thing as a plain, routine, or regular self-directed team. Different types of organizations have an array of Einsteins who become a team or form into multiple teams. A number of typical issues are addressed in this section, since they apply to diverse self-directed Einstein teams and not to any particular typical or ideal team.

## The Size Issue: How Many?

Research findings suggest a range of team sizes from six to twelve as the most preferred and the most effective. Keeping the Einstein team to a smaller size is better. Too many Einsteins spoil the mix and dynamics, slow the process, and have a tendency to become impersonal. There is also the difficulty of facilitating the various needs and wants of a large team. Another issue involves time available to closely coach Einsteins in any arena. Coaching well requires large chunks of time, patience, and effort. A large team precludes finding the needed time to properly coach and display intense concern about each Einstein's learning and progress.

## Is Multiskilling Important?

Yes, in small self-directed Einstein teams there are multiskilling needs. Members learn more than one task on the team. This provides flexibility, and the variety results in greater job challenges and a clearer understanding of the total process.

As the team matures, it is important to carefully select new members. The culture, norms, style, and performance of the team is of course membership-driven. This means that screening candidates and selecting members requires time, due diligence, and caution. A change of one member can turn a high performing, satisfied, and exciting Einstein self-directed team into a poor performing, unfulfilled, and conflicted team.

## Can the Team Reward and Discipline?

Yes, the handling of rewards and discipline can become a part of the team's empowerment responsibility and authority. Teams can even develop a progressive discipline program. The first discipline step may involve discussion, the second step could be a written reprimand, and so forth. The team can also play a role in providing input about member performance. The more empowered teams may even allocate rewards based on the evaluation the team generates for each member.

The Einstein manager can help team members learn how to plan, organize, and control. They can also be available to assist and facilitate when support and advice is needed. They serve as a buffer between top-level executives who might make incorrect assumptions about Einsteins because of a lack of contact and familiarity with them. The manager in closer proximity to Einstein teams has better insight about the preferences, likes, dislikes, strengths, and weaknesses of teams.

## The Maturity Cycle

Highly effective self-directed Einstein teams are comprised of committed individuals who trust each other, have a clear sense of their

**Exhibit 7.2**
Crucial Elements in Team Maturity

| Element | Example |
|---|---|
| Trust | Team members trust each other, maintain confidence, and support each other. |
| Commitment | Team members have a sense of belonging, being a part of team. Similar to feelings held by tribal members. |
| Communication | A lot of interpersonal, team communication. Not usually inclined to communicate with non-team members. |
| Goals | Solve problems. Overcome barriers. Use experience, knowledge, and collective wisdom to address issues. |
| Participation | Everyone on team has roles to perform. Everyone's participation is valued, respected, and appreciated. |
| Process Orientation | Process includes tools, customs, rituals, agendas, and methods of dealing with problems (e.g., software requirement, system bugs, and architecture). |

purpose and role, communicate clearly within the team, and follow a fast-paced process that helps them plan, organize, and control their work. The six factors in self-directed Einstein team maturity are displayed in Exhibit 7.2.

Important human needs include being loved and appreciated by others. In effectively building teams, the love and appreciation needs are translated through actions showing care for your Einsteins. When considering the concept of care and love of employees in organizations, Herb Kelleher of Southwest Airlines is at the top of a short list. If you look up Southwest Airlines on the New York Stock Exchange, you'll see the ticker symbol is LUV. Kelleher is a famous, unabashed sultan of "love." He says, "We are interested in people who internalize, who focus on other people, who are really motivated to help other people." What Kelleher strives for is trust, commitment, communication, goals, participation, and process. His team-building recipe fits Einstein teams as well as airline employees.

## Building Commitment

Caring and supporting are important, but inspiring Einsteins to care about each other is also crucial. Managers should observe the Einstein team and look for examples of teammates going out of their way to help each other. Demonstrating patience and concern, enjoying each other's success, showing compassion, and forgiving each other are signs of commitment. As a manager, keeping an eye and an ear for observing and hearing these behaviors is a start in building commitment. Managers can lead the way and show Einsteins by:

- Pointing out exceptional examples of caring within the team to other team members
- Not holding grudges
- Practicing the Golden Rule
- Telling and showing Einsteins you care about them, their needs, and their goals
- Exerting the energy to observe and listen

It takes time working as a unit to build commitment, trust, excellent communications; to achieve goals, increase participation, and generate a positive team culture. These events have to occur over a period of time before a team takes shape. Even Einsteins who work well, are intelligent, and are anti-authority take time to become effective. Teams evolve or mature over time until they reach a high level of maturity, though it should be noted that some teams never do reach this level.

The more mature teams are designated as Level IV in Exhibit 7.1. Mature Einstein teams will not tolerate autocratic, command managers. Actually, they require and thrive working with supportive manager facilitators. The supportive manager is a champion of empowerment, of coaching and learning, a continuous and open communicator, and shows care, concern, and compassion. What results from this type of managerial behavior and leadership influence is a fully functioning, pleasant, and productive Einstein team.

The fully committed self-directed Einstein team displays:

- Open trust and stability
- Communication on an as-needed basis
- Participation of all members, as a requirement
- Continuous improvement as part of the team culture and value system

If every Einstein team displayed these characteristics, managing would be a delightful job. The manager of the mature, self-directed team serves more in a leadership role operating at the boundaries or outside the team itself. As a leader, the person serves more as a coach, facilitator, counselor, and helper. In less mature self-directed Einstein teams, the manager performs the roles of authority, expert, experience, monitor, and "boss." The level of maturity of the team makes a big difference in the roles managers/leaders must play to achieve desired performance.

# Frequently Asked Questions

As usual, we are not able to provide a cookbook list of simple answers to what makes some self-directed Einstein teams tick and how Einstein managers can make them tick better. Later in the chapter we offer some suggested and proven action steps for managers to implement. However, at this juncture answering a few pressing questions will be helpful.

## What Is the Biggest Challenge Facing Managers?

Acceptance of self-directed teams after years of commanding, directing, and maybe even intimidating is difficult for managers. Doing something that has become almost routine for managers requires a lot of soul searching, hard work, and relearning. Einsteins are unique, and a hands-off or delicate approach with mature and high-performing teams is the recommended action for managers.

## What Einstein Team Roles Take Precedence?

Every Einstein team role is important. The ability of team members to assume different roles will lead to a better team culture and more success. One thing for certain is that Einstein team leaders will naturally emerge from within the team. These team leaders should be approached and listened to, and become a part of the manager's support, facilitation, and trust-building approach.

## Is Conflict Inevitable on a Team?

It is probably very likely. Some conflict indicates that creative problem solving is at work. Members challenging each other should be expected among Einsteins. Eliminating conflict is not possible and shouldn't be attempted.

## Do Einsteins Solve All Problems?

No. Einsteins may think they solved a problem, and in the future a barrier occurs or the problem reappears or a failure occurs. Every problem solving endeavor is an opportunity to learn, solve, debate, and improve. Why would Einsteins be expected to solve every problem correctly or in a timely fashion? Einsteins want to problem-solve, but occasionally they hit the wall or miss. Expect it and live with it because failure is going to take place. Helping Einsteins deal with failure in problem solving is part of a manager's support, teaching, and coaching roles in working with the team.

### Is Empowerment Out of Fashion?

No. It is overused, misused, and misinterpreted. It is a way of getting Einsteins involved in the operation of the organization at all levels. Einsteins, when empowered, can be efficient, effective, and highly motivated to utilize their talents, skills, and intelligence.

Remember that empowering Einsteins isn't like a vaccination shot. It doesn't work in twenty-four hours. As a manager, you have to work with Einsteins to make it work. It takes a lot of work, patience, and creativity to make empowerment pay off. Give it a chance to grow and be patient with your Einsteins.

### Why Are Communications Skills So Important Even in a Small Team?

To ensure trust and commitment to goals, each Einstein team member must feel comfortable working with other members. They must have a clear sense of each other. Communication is the way to be heard, listen, and observe what each member believes, feels, and thinks. Being a good communicator as a manager will provide in-the-team lessons on how to perform this critical task. Managers in communicating can be powerful role models for Einsteins on how to do something well.

### What Should a Manager Do with a Team's Successes?

Yell, recognize, jump up and down, and just plain celebrate successes. The rule is celebrate, praise, and recognize. Announce the team's success to others in the organization and even outsiders. Everyone likes to be recognized. It feels good. The celebration and recognition says that you know and care that the Einsteins have succeeded. Even if you are a manager, wearing a suit and clean-shaven, leading the "cheers" indicates compassion, pride, and happiness for the Einsteins. This sends a signal to them and builds pride in the team's culture.

Einsteins like to win. They like to be a part of a winning team. In sports, teams win trophies and medals. On Einstein teams, you win thank-you's, recognition, appreciation, and validation. These kinds of winning chits make work worthwhile, meaningful, and stimulating.

# Words of Caution

The lessons to this point have extolled the upside of self-directed Einstein teams. There are some possible negative consequences of teams. At least some knowledge of these negatives can help a manager cope with teams that unravel or do not live up to expectations.

## Pressure to Conform

Team members are sometimes pressured by more experienced or more forceful members. Harmless conformity includes such things as getting a tattoo or eating at a particular restaurant that a member dislikes. In other Einstein team situations, conformity is not so harmless. For instance, a design engineer in a group of eight may believe that a program will crash a client's system. After learning that the other seven team members believe everything is fine, the design engineer goes along with the majority and quits complaining. He keeps quiet because he doesn't want to offend team members.

Research has demonstrated that individuals conform to the majority because of social pressure and the fear of being ostracized or ridiculed. The conformity pressure can be harmless or it can be important, but it is a reality in Einstein teams.

## Social Facilitation

There is a tendency for individual team member output to improve in the presence of others. This can and even does occur when individuals are not a part of a team. The presence of others can result in the speed-up of work and a decrease in the quality of the work. When Einstein work is complex, requiring closer attention to details, the presence of others (team members) often results in performance of a poorer quality.

## Minimally Acceptable Solutions

Teams have a tendency to, or occasionally adopt, a minimally acceptable solution. They settle, in some instances, for a good enough solution. Instead of working harder to achieve the "very best possible," there may be perceived time, resource, and management pressure to reach an "okay" acceptable solution. In highly competitive situations this will eventually catch up to the Einstein team and result in problems. Minimally acceptable is not and should not be the "quality" standard of any team.

## Social Loafing: Taking a Ride

As the size of a team increases, the effort and/or performance of each member tends to decrease. This is called the "social loafing" or "free rider" effect. Some Einsteins may try to obtain benefits from team membership while not sharing in the work, effort, and commitment load of these benefits.

An undermotivated, "free-riding" Einstein can squeeze by without contributing his or her fair share of skills, abilities, and knowledge. When each Einstein's contribution is visible, when controls and monitoring are in place and a mature, self-policing team is observant, social loafing tends to be limited. Within mature Einstein teams, loafing is not accepted. The "free rider" is informed or reprimanded.

## Groupthink

Groupthink, which we'll refer to as "teamthink," occurs when the social concerns of a team and the motivation for agreement overrides the team's motivation to carefully evaluate the risks and alternatives of a particular decision. That is, Einstein team members decide that harmony within the team is preferred to an expression of doubts and resistance about a decision.

Teamthink can appear in mature Einstein teams where there is:

- A sense of invulnerability shared by the members: "We are the best and always make the most outstanding decision."
- High moral standards that the team believes it possesses. This can manifest as a disregard of moral and ethical considerations in the real world.
- Ignorance among non-Einsteins about an issue, concept, or situation.
- Unanimity that creates a feeling that everyone on the Einstein team agrees.
- The belief that silence is better than threatening the "we" feeling of the Einstein team.
- An association of disloyalty when dissent is presented to the team.

The costs of teamthink are a decrease in decision making quality; improper reality testing of ideas, suggestions, and recommendations; moralistic pontificating; and a feeling of superiority that can damage the team's decision making effectiveness.

---

### Black Hole

Teams that strive to be alike in thinking, style, and behavior, become locked into a groupthink mold. This type of rigidity results in too much member agreement without examining alternatives, a bias in collecting and evaluating information, and ignoring the risks of the team's preferred choice. Be on guard for groupthink.

---

### *Individual Dominance*

Sometimes a dominant Einstein controls and pressures other team members. Dominance by one member takes place when a person is charismatic, super intelligent, technically superior, respected, or a persuasive communicator. Guarding against dominators is in the best interest of teams. Unfortunately, dominators cannot see the lost efficiency of the team and need to be called out in private for a one-on-one manager and dominator Einstein discussion. These sessions may succeed, but there is no perfect script to assure that dominators will change their behaviors.

---

### Einstein Wisdom

- In order to be content, men must also have the possibility of developing their intellectual and artistic powers to whatever accords with their personal characteristics and abilities.

- The only source of knowledge is experience.

- In order to be an immaculate member of a flock of sheep, one must above all be a sheep oneself.

---

## To-Do Steps

Leaders must build, nurture, and recognize effective self-directed Einstein teams constantly. Weighing the negatives of teams and cautiously using experience, knowledge, and best-in-class examples can help managers become leaders and builders of high-performing teams. After all, the leader (manager) ultimately is responsible for building effective teams. An important requirement of leaders is to first ensure that the organization is competitively viable. Leaders must provide Einsteins what they need to succeed or achieve results. Without results, there is no need for Einstein teams or leaders (non-Einsteins). A modest set of "to-do" recommendations for managers of Einstein teams is provided.

## Act with Integrity

In addition to achieving results, leaders must act with integrity to build commitment, trust, and achieve goals. Einsteins often look for honesty in their non-Einstein leaders. A person's behavior is constantly reviewed to assess honesty. Leaders who act on what they say fare well in the assessment. Integrity requires alignment of values, words, and behavior. Leaders who change the story based on the audience are considered untrustworthy and will quickly lose their ability to influence or even to be referred to as leaders.

In a fast-paced world, there is plenty of pressure on bringing about proper alignment. Consider the following two examples:

> A product development team of Einsteins commits to a goal of delivering a new software program by the end of September (nine months from now). A competitor, however, comes out with a new software program that requires additional features or the Einstein team's effort will go nowhere from the start. The Einsteins make adjustments and add new features. The time to make the adjustments delays the completion date. The executive level of management reacts negatively to the delays and blames the Einsteins for failing to deliver the software when it was promised. The September date is badly missed. The executive perceives the team's failure as a lack of consistency in what was promised and the delay. The executives are questioning the Einstein team's integrity and honesty.

> A high-tech firm with a history and record of no layoffs notifies employees in June that the firm has to work harder to stifle competition. When the financial reports are complete in November, management lays off thirty Einsteins and fifty non-Einsteins. This constituted about 10 percent of the Einsteins and 5 percent of the total company. Everyone in the firm, Einsteins and non-Einsteins, feels that management lied and broke a promise.

These two examples illustrate the potential problems of appearing to favor bottom-line results over integrity. These are tricky situations to resolve, but it is necessary to work at eliminating such problems in the future.

In the software development case, the Einsteins did fail to meet the software delivery date, but they had to if a competitive product was going to emerge. At the least, the Einsteins should have kept everyone informed of their progress. They also should have confided in their non-Einstein manager that it was necessary to make adjustments. Operating internally, within the Einstein team, without communicating, extremely exacerbated the problem, especially at the more distant executive level.

In the high-tech firm case, management erred in committing to a policy that had to be discarded when financial conditions changed. They could have created a team of non-managers, Einsteins and non-Einsteins, to come up with solutions (e.g., part-time, job sharing) to address the problem. The task force, representing everyone, could have made a decision that would not have had such negative reactions.

## Show Concern for Einsteins

Einsteins need to feel that they are worthwhile and important. Without demonstrated concern on the part of managers, Einsteins often conclude that management is only focused on quarterly goals, financial targets, and market valuation. Managers must be aware of their influence on the motivation of Einsteins to accomplish common goals.

There is a tendency for managers to purposefully distance themselves from Einsteins. This is a mistake. Managers need contact, familiarity, and time to talk to Einsteins. Yes, Einsteins want autonomy, freedom, and room to problem-solve and tackle challenging tasks. However, they also want to feel like a part of the business and to make contributions that are helpful to the entire firm. Managers can serve as the conduit between Einsteins and the entire firm if they maintain contact.

## Build Trust

Managers seeking to build trust with Einsteins are probably better served by going at it indirectly. Managers who want to build a high-performing Einstein team have multiple goals. The major goal is to increase the likelihood of success by cultivating trust. Trust is a means of enhancing performance over time. Lessons from other firms show that trust between Einsteins and managers is often won or lost during periods of adversity. Hewlett-Packard created a reservoir of trust by using a temporary reduction in work hours across the board. For example, Einsteins and non-Einsteins, rather than going through permanent layoffs, were instructed to reduce their weekly work hours. By taking every other Friday off for six months, employees hung on to their jobs until conditions improved. This symbolic effort sent a signal that Hewlett-Packard was concerned about the entire workforce.

Managers seeking to improve trust should focus on the outcome that the firm or team must achieve. Trust functions most effectively in the background. Effective managers should model their behavior around the issues of integrity, concern, and results. Effectively, role modeling these factors will create or lead to a high trust culture. These three modeled behaviors say "Take care," "We are honest," and "We need results to survive."

Along with the three modeled management behaviors there are a number of important other actions needed. Managers need to seek out, recruit, and select superior talent. Having a pipeline of superb talent permits the replenishment of lost talent and the infusion of new ideas. Superior self-directed Einstein teams do not just appear. These teams need superb talent. Managers who are committed to excellence in talent are trusted and respected more.

## Implement Necessary Controls

Controls are also necessary in building high Einstein team trust. The word *controls* sends shivers down everyone's back. In reality, controls safeguard against abuses that can undermine the entire firm. Managers need a "few" vital performance measures of "how the team is doing." In the traditional hierarchically controlled firm, the emphasis is usually on "many" measures. The managers and the Einstein teams can agree on the "few."

Managers also need to informally review (control) the performance of Einsteins. The informal review could involve the team, all at once. Einsteins care a great deal about how their fellow Einsteins view their performance and contributions. The informal review is much different, but just as important as the old-fashioned performance review session. Managers need some assurance that performance targets will be met, and the informal review can provide them with a necessary snapshot view of how everything is progressing.

## Encourage Risk Taking

Action is what Einsteins prefer. The ability to make rapid decisions and move forward is a key in motivating them. Moving forward is preferred by results-oriented Einsteins. But moving quickly, acting decisively, and moving forward will occasionally result in mistakes. There are going to be failures, incorrect decisions, and sloppy actions. Managers have to tolerate this fallout and encourage Einsteins to learn from these mistakes. Giving Einsteins some freedom to fail and deal effectively with failure are worthwhile management techniques. One firm that has instituted risk is 3M. The firm has a culture that accepts and learns from "well-intentioned failures." Employees at 3M who fail are treated no differently than their risk taking colleagues who produce successful results.

The lessons learned from 3M and other innovative firms suggest that managers must not destructively attack, nag about, and criticize team failures. Killing Einsteins' initiatives and creativity to take future risks, after a failure, is the opposite of what management needs. Encourage action, rebound from failure, and learn from mistakes is what the manager has to instill in the culture through his or her behavior. A manager needs to remember to be on guard when communicating with Einsteins after a failure. Once a "failure bomb" has exploded, managers need to monitor what they say, the tone they use, the eye contact, and even the way they walk around. Managers are a walking billboard, signaling how they feel about a recent failed Einstein team project. Walk tall, smile, listen carefully, and project confidence. Remember, risk taking requires action, confidence, and a supportive management team.

# One Last Look at Tribes and Teams

Innovation, creativity, and performance are the ingredients of success. A firm can't outsource these important elements of the organizational recipe. The firm needs to nurture, cultivate, and effectively orchestrate its own talent. Team building, nurturing, support, and monitoring are needed. Einsteins are like the Seminole Indians of Florida: they have unique attributes that evolve from their experience, knowledge, skills, and values. Using this uniqueness by working with and building self-directed Einstein teams is a responsibility of and challenge for managers.

There is often a temptation to do too much to encourage the pride, spirit, and drive of Einsteins. These characteristics can't be imposed from outside a team. Einstein managers must have and display finesse to become familiar with their Einsteins, but should not smother them with support. Team enthusiasm, pride, and motivation come from within the unit working well together.

Displaying integrity, showing concern, building trust, building and implementing controls, and encouraging risk taking are some recommended managerial action steps. Smothering is not recommended. Einsteins will rebel against smothering, which is considered insincere.

There is no magical formula for building superior self-directed Einstein teams. Yet, what others have discovered is that if the power, talent, and intelligence of Einstein teams can be harnessed, organizations can soar to new performance heights. Einstein teams can be a key to success if they are managed properly.

## CHAPTER 8

# Dealing with and Disciplining Difficult Einsteins

### Preview Einstein Story

*EAPs for the Digital Age*

While many employers are now cutting employees in order to cut costs, others—like Agilent Technologies, a spinoff of Hewlett-Packard based in Palo Alto, California—are managing costs by keeping the employees they have productive and happy. Fifteen percent of Agilent's employees work alternatives to a traditional Monday-through-Friday work schedule, and all employees have access to services like dependent care resource and referral, and an employee assistance program (EAP) provided by Magellan Behavioral Health.

"We want to enable employees to focus on achieving business success while they juggle work and personal life responsibilities," says Lakiba Pittman, global diversity program manager at Agilent. The company's facilities also include fitness centers, on-site nurses who perform stress management counseling, and quiet rooms where employees can go to get away from their desks.

EAPs have traditionally been associated with alcohol addiction treatment—an association dating back to the post–World War II era when many GIs came home with alcohol problems, and employers were forced to deal with alcohol use at the work site. Today, EAPs take a broad approach to employees' mental health. The International Employee Assistance Professionals Association (IEPA) defines EAPs as programs
*Continued*

that help organizations address productivity issues by assisting employees in the resolution of personal concerns, including health, marital, family, financial, alcohol, drug, legal, emotional, stress, or other issues that may affect job performance.

According to Lynne Sarikas, director of sales and account management at Ceridian LifeWorks Services, a Minneapolis-based provider of workplace effectiveness services, there are five key points for assessing ROI (return on investment) in EAPs. The first is time savings. "If employees have an issue, [it] isn't going to go away just because they have a job. Normally, resolving these kinds of issues can only take place during normal working hours. If they have someone else helping, they're spending more time on the job." The other factors include enhanced productivity, reduced absenteeism, reduced disability costs, and increased employee retention. "That one is the most significant," said Sarikas. "It is so incredibly difficult, time consuming, and expensive to replace employees. Anything you can do to keep them on the job has significant value."

Adapted from: Emily Fitzloff, "Easing the Work/Life Continuum," *Business 2.0*, November 17, 2000

Working with Einsteins is not always pleasant. Although they are highly intelligent, motivated, and creative, they are occasionally a handful and a headache. In this chapter, we identify six types of difficult Einsteins and management techniques for dealing with them. Next, we will examine the more formidable challenge of dealing with difficult or rebellious teams of Einsteins. Finally, we look at the best techniques for disciplining Einsteins and for resolving difficulties that may arise.

## Einstein Wisdom

*Seven Habits of Highly Subversive Employees*

Here are some behaviors that have been exhibited by unhappy Einsteins:

1. Follow boss's instructions to the letter but ignore real goal

2. Be generous to the customer: give extra and undercharge.

3. Cc boss's absurd e-mails to others.

4. Proposition other employees using the boss's e-mail.

5. Screw up projects that reflect directly on the boss.

6. Withhold crucial data.

7. Set up a website about how your company stinks.

From: Carol Vinzant, "Messing with the Boss's Head," *Fortune*, May 1, 2000, 329

# Six Difficult Einsteins

Smart people can be very difficult. Sometimes they are difficult because they know they are smart and they have an overinflated view of their importance. Sometimes they are difficult because they have thought more deeply on a topic and they have points-of-view that are well-entrenched and very difficult to alter. And sometimes they are difficult because they don't have the patience to wait for anyone else to catch up to their Einstein-type thoughts.

It's often easier to deal with things if we are able to put a name or label on the difficulty. People with unknown maladies will often state that they were able to deal better with the problem once they knew what it was and were able to attach a name to their affliction. Our research has revealed six basic types of difficult Einsteins:

1. The Arrogant Einstein

2. The Know-It-All Einstein

3. The Impatient Einstein

4. The Eccentric Einstein

5. The Disorganized Einstein

6. The Withdrawn Einstein

This list of types is definitely not exhaustive. You may be able to identify others that aren't on this list, but these six types include some of the more challenging of the difficult Einsteins we've run across. We'll look at each in turn.

## The Arrogant Einstein

Einsteins are smart and they know it. They are not always formally educated. In fact, most of them will tell you that their nonformal education/learning is more important than their formal education.

Einsteins often receive praise and accolades for their intelligence. They stand out from the crowd in their ability to resolve life's puzzles. Some Einsteins begin to believe that their smartness gives them a special place in the world. Constant reinforcement of this theme in popular business periodicals abound. Glitzy business publications love to go on at length about our "new economy." The standard refrain of these publications is that the new economy is founded on the intelligence and wit of young, bright superstars who see the world "in a new way." As we are preparing this book, the bloom is off the rose. Layoffs have hit the Einstein world, and these new economy wizards are becoming a little more humble about the real world.

Is it any wonder that one of the more common types of difficult Einsteins is the Arrogant Einstein? They can't open a magazine or management book without reading about how important they are. Even this book has made the case that Einsteins are important to attract and retain.

Not all Einsteins are arrogant. In fact, most have learned to take their intelligence in stride. They recognize that people have different types of talent and that intelligence is just one type. A good way to deal with Arrogant Einsteins is to be "matter of fact" about their arrogance. Don't allow their arrogance to affect your responsibility to make sound business decisions. Don't allow their arrogance to become an intimidating factor in your decision making. Einstein managers may have to accept the fact that some of the Arrogant Einsteins will grumble about them. Tolerating a small amount of this allows people to "blow off steam." It can become troublesome, however, if the grumbling begins to affect the performance of others.

One very effective technique is to confront the Arrogant Einstein head-on and listen to the gripes. The very act of venting gripes can defuse potentially damaging behaviors. Of course, when Einsteins spend time talking, they expect more than lip service. They expect that their ideas will lead to action and change. It is actually counterproductive to listen to an Arrogant Einstein's gripes if you have no intention of doing anything about them. The best solution is to listen to the gripes and take some action in a few areas that you agree can be changed. This action will be welcomed by Arrogant Einsteins, even if you can't make all the changes they want.

### The Know-It-All Einstein

We distinguish the Know-It-All Einstein from the Arrogant Einstein. The Arrogant Einstein is a public know-it-all. At least you know where you stand with them. The Know-It-All Einstein is more insidious. This type believes they know best, and will do things their way regardless of what is requested or needed. This type of Einstein can be maddening. Their behavior is difficult to identify and very difficult to change. They have supreme confidence in their own judgment, have little regard for authority, and have little need for public approval.

Einstein managers won't spot a Know-It-All Einstein right away. Usually, this type of Einstein will be recognized over a period of time, when their behavior becomes a pattern. You recognize them because they will go off and work on projects they believe need doing. Occasionally, you won't know where to find them. They won't be malingering; they'll be honing their craft on a project they believe to be more important than you do.

You can deal with Know-It-All Einsteins best by indirect methods. Confronting them or sanctioning them only serves to reinforce their opinion that they know better. Indirect management of the Know-It-All Einstein involves keeping track of where they are and where they are applying their skills.

The know-it-all craves the extra attention. This indirect approach provides them with the attention they crave and keeps them focused on the projects the manager thinks are highest priority. In the best cases, managers can actually wear down the know-it-alls. Einsteins who eventually realize that they cannot hide and work on their own priorities, and that their skills are appreciated, may eventually require less maintenance.

## The Impatient Einstein

One of the more annoying traits commonly displayed by Einsteins is their impatience. All Einsteins are impatient. This is something that must be understood to manage them effectively. In its common form, Einstein impatience shows itself in darting eyes, tapping feet, and short, staccatolike conversations. This must be dealt with by Einstein managers. There is an extreme type, however, that we call the "Impatient Einstein."

The Impatient Einstein is difficult to manage. Often, in fact, the Impatient Einsteins are superstars of the team. They understand things quickly. They don't need to be told twice. They are usually extremely deferential and obedient. Impatient Einsteins are often this way because they know they will do exactly what you want them to do. They do not need extra time to plot how they will actually do things. In many ways the Impatient Einstein is a star employee. Einstein managers will have little need to explain any assignment twice. There is also little need to constantly check the Impatient Einstein's work. The greatest danger of the Impatient Einstein is losing them because they can not be adequately challenged at work.

What should the Einstein manager do with Impatient Einsteins? Let them do their work. They will dig into their assigned tasks with laser intensity. Managers must be careful that they are working and progressing in their craft. Impatient Einsteins are not likely to complain when they become bored. Instead, they will begin to look around for other options. Impatient Einsteins want to get back to practicing their craft as quickly as possible. They are not likely to confront managers who assign them projects to make that possible, or who help them continuously develop their skills. They are far more likely simply to leave.

## The Eccentric Einstein

Many Einsteins possess what is called an "addictive personality." That's not to say they are prone to drug or alcohol abuse. An addictive personality is one that enjoys pursuing hobby or leisure activity to an extreme. You may have seen or known people like them. They're the ones who dress up like Mr. Spock and travel halfway across the country to participate in *Star Trek* conventions. They're the ones who travel great distances around the world and live in hardships only to climb a challenging rock they've heard about.

Many Einsteins have eccentricities. Managers often find that Einsteins have leisure pursuits that are outside the mainstream. This is occasionally made known by posters on their cubicle or office walls, knickknacks or paraphernalia lying about, or T-shirts and clothing with logos and labels that announce their interests. Most of them are normal—even though they are "different."

Eccentric Einsteins have taken their outside interest to an extreme form. They may have their entire workplace dedicated to their off-work activities. Their daily speech, downtime, preoccupations, and tribal affiliations revolve entirely around their eccentricity.

Not all eccentricities are focused on off-work activities. Some concern work styles or patterns. Some Eccentric Einsteins are eccentric about work style. They want to create a legend for hard work, problem solving, pizza and Coke consumption, or continuous hours of work. A recent book, for example, talked about an Einstein who preferred to work during evening and dawn hours because he liked to work in the nude.

How do you manage Eccentric Einsteins? This is a delicate question. In the main, Eccentric Einsteins are not harmful. They enjoy their eccentricity partially for the diversion it provides and partially for the identity it provides them within the tribe. Forbidding or prohibiting all expressions of their eccentricity is probably, well, a bit eccentric. Managing eccentric Einsteins means allowing "healthy" expression of the eccentricity. Anything that doesn't interfere with work flow or with the professionalism of the office can and should be tolerated—even encouraged.

Einsteins, like everyone else, seek to express their individuality. Immersion in the tribe takes that away. Expressing an eccentricity gives it back. Einstein managers can assist in this self-actualization process by encouraging tasteful, nondisruptive expressions of eccentricity.

## The Disorganized Einstein

Have you ever walked into an Einstein's domain and felt disoriented by the clutter? Some Einsteins dwell in the nether regions of the company, surrounded by old computers, wires, components, and other artifacts of their work. They seem oblivious to their surroundings. Some even appear comfortable—like they *belong* there. To you it looks confusing and disorganized. However, if you ask the Einstein who resides there to find something for you, they will track it immediately. What appears to be disorganized "junk" to Einstein managers is ordered chaos to the Einstein.

Einsteins do not want to spend a lot of time filing, organizing, and arranging. They prefer to use loose organization principles that allow them to find needed articles using dead reckoning rather than clear landmarks, like file labels and so on. This is all right to a point, but their organized disorganization can easily cross the line to complete disorganization. When that happens, valuable assets get lost, costs are incurred, and valuable time is wasted searching for needed items.

How can their transition from organized disorganization to total disorganization be avoided? There are several steps managers can take to keep this from happening. One step is to assign an individual—preferably *not* an Einstein—to keep track of the firm's physical assets. This may involve regular inventory checks, online asset management software, and wireless asset tracking systems. It's now possible, for example, to tag all physical assets within a firm with a wireless transmitter. That tells a receiver what it is and where it is.

Another technique for preventing the transition to disorganization is to assign ownership of physical assets. When an asset is received by the organization, someone can be assigned ownership. Ownership can be transferred and traced until the asset is disposed of, donated, or sold.

## The Withdrawn Einstein

The Withdrawn Einstein is an asset that is suboptimized. Neither arrogant nor eccentric, the Withdrawn Einstein tends toward underachievement. There are often a host of factors that lie behind the behavioral characteristics of the Withdrawn Einstein. Some of these factors are intrinsic and cannot be changed—it's their nature. However, many Withdrawn Einsteins are this way due to environmental factors that have influenced their lives. Mostly, Einsteins are "different." They've been different since their youth. They are brighter, smarter, and prone to deeper analytic thoughts than their peers. Einsteins often adopt a withdrawing style to cope.

There are several techniques that managers can use to help release the potential of Withdrawn Einsteins. No matter the strategy adopted, however, it's important to recognize that changing their style takes time. There is no magic pill that will suddenly and miraculously change an introverted Einstein into an extrovert. Indeed, one of the difficulties you will need to overcome is that Withdrawn Einsteins usually *don't want* to change.

Effective managing of Withdrawn Einsteins means overcoming this resistance to change and providing support during the transformation process. You can begin the transformation process by meeting privately with your Withdrawn Einstein and telling him or her that you think they are capable of achieving at a higher level. This must be done with no hint that there is something wrong with their current performance. Usually, there is not. This is purely about self-actualization—achievement at a higher level. Your Withdrawn Einstein probably won't be surprised at your words. Most Withdrawn Einsteins have heard the "underachiever" label before. Your challenge will be actually to do something about it. The next step is to take action. Several effective techniques to help the Withdrawn Einstein emerge include:

- Request that they conduct a brief seminar on their craft for others in the firm
- Request that they attend national conferences or conventions in their craft and prepare a brief trip report to be presented to you and several other managers
- Request that they write a paper or article to be published in a widely circulated trade publication

- Request that they deliver a paper at a national conference or convention in their area

You'll notice several things about these techniques for transforming a Withdrawn Einstein into a self-starting, high achiever. First, they revolve around teaching. Requesting Einsteins to teach others about their craft is the least threatening way to get them in front of a group of their peers. It also provides the greatest assurance of an event that will provide positive feedback. Second, the challenges gradually become more difficult. In the therapeutic world, psychologists help patients overcome fears and phobias by gradually exposing patients to what they fear. If done correctly, this technique is nearly 100 percent effective.

The most important tactic that you *must* apply in helping change Withdrawn Einsteins is to not lose focus. They will be inclined to lose theirs—you can't lose yours. The process may take a year or more. You must stay with it. Stick to your action plan. Provide opportunities and encouragement. Gradually, the Einsteins will "take over" the transformation process when the benefits clearly outweigh the costs.

## Disciplining Einsteins

Einsteins, like any other employee within an organization, will occasionally require discipline. In general, the same rules of effective discipline that managers would apply to any other employee apply as well to Einsteins. Effective discipline can be boiled down to a few simple rules:

1. Make sure the Einstein is fully aware of company policies and procedures.

2. Document carefully each instance of transgression.

3. Clearly inform the offending Einstein of the policy violation and the consequences of the offense.

4. Apply discipline equally to all Einsteins.

5. Allow Einsteins the opportunity to respond to allegations of misconduct.

6. Use progressively severe consequences—with termination being the most severe—to deal with offensive behavior.

The most commonly used and perhaps most effective approach is what's known as "progressive discipline." This approach places increasingly severe consequences on employee behaviors that run afoul of standard policies and decorum. Managers who use the progressive

"YOUR E-MAIL VIRUS WIPED OUT THE INTERNET FOR THREE DAYS! THIS WILL LOOK BAD ON YOUR PERFORMANCE REVIEW!"

approach allow employees the opportunity to improve their behaviors before taking extreme measures such as suspension or termination. This has several advantages:

1. It allows firms to retain employees who may have made a mistake, were unaware of policies, or who have behaviors that can be corrected.

2. It protects the manager from possible liability by affording the employee in question due process and the opportunity to improve.

Einsteins respond well to progressive discipline. Their goal-oriented nature makes the process of behavior change a challenge they actually enjoy. Wise use of progressive discipline with Einsteins will take advantage of this unique component of their character.

Disciplining Einsteins in the early stages of progressive discipline should be focused on correcting an unacceptable behavior. After the first incident of *documented* behavioral problems, the manager should establish an action plan specific to the offending Einstein. The action plan should focus on developing the Einstein, and should avoid dwelling on the particular incident—although there should be no mistake that it is the reason for getting together in the first place. Of course, the severity of the incident will determine the action to be taken. The more severe the incident, the more direct should be the intervention. To be sure, some incidents, such as sabotage, violation of company security, or violence, must be dealt with harshly—possibly even by immediate termination.

---

## Black Hole

### *Don't Raise Your Voice*

The workplace can often provoke high levels of emotion. Managers and employees don't always see eye-to-eye on what is to be done or on how to do it. When the stakes are high, emotions can also run high, leading to anger, shouting, or other outbursts. Einsteins are not immune from these high emotions, but they generally don't respond well to them. Einsteins believe that intellect rather than emotion is better for solving problems. If they are confronted by an angry manager, they are not likely to respond well. Rather than influencing expanded effort, the angry, shouting manager is likely to effect resistance, retaliation, or reluctance. If an issue crops up with high stakes and high emotion, bring in your Einsteins and discuss the issue rationally. Wait for the emotion to cool before deciding what to do.

---

For those disciplinary violations that do not require immediate termination, the following action steps will help you get your Einstein back on the right track:

1. Set up a personal meeting with the offending Einstein.

2. To open the meeting, clearly state why you are getting together, the nature of the problem, and the correct behavior that you expect.

3. Establish an action plan that will help the Einstein achieve behavioral changes over a period of time.

4. Have the Einstein decide upon a reward that he will give himself/herself when goals laid out in the action plan are accomplished.

Note that the reward provided for achieving the behavioral change is actually granted by the Einstein. As an organization, you do not want to encourage negative behavior by providing rewards to those who run afoul of your discipline program. Nonetheless, effective, lasting behavior change requires a reward. Having the Einstein establish and provide the reward removes the organization from the unwanted position of rewarding the negative behavior, and places the Einstein in charge of the change process—a position that is preferable.

Effectively disciplining Einsteins takes advantage of their predisposition toward goal setting and autonomy. Pointing out where they have gone wrong and helping them establish a plan to change develops these predispositions. The clever Einstein manager will use this knowledge to motivate Einsteins to behave in ways consistent with company policies and procedures. Individual Einsteins will vary in their action plan. Einstein managers will need to make that assessment on a case-by-case basis. Nonetheless, the action plan and individual reward-setting approach should be an effective technique to correct unwanted behavior among the Einsteins on the staff.

## Terminating Einsteins

One of the most difficult tasks for any manager is terminating employees. There are usually high levels of emotion involved in termination. The manager is emotional because of a natural human concern for the individual being terminated, regardless of what they may have done. The terminated individual is emotional because they feel a sense of personal failure and concern about their future welfare.

Managers can defuse some of the anxiety surrounding terminating Einsteins by doing their homework ahead of time. The steps involved in the process of progressive discipline should also precede most terminations. We say "most" because there will be times when terminating employees is a matter of financial crisis rather than performance deficiency. These two types of termination are different in style and form. Below, we describe how each should be implemented by Einstein managers.

---

### Influence Tip

*I'm Fired!*

Sometimes the problem employee you need to deal with is yourself. As he drives to work each morning, Robert L. Bailey, CEO of PMC-Sierra, Inc., imagines that he's about to be pink-slipped. "I convince myself—I swear this is true—every day, that my job is hanging by a thread and I'm about to be fired. I ask myself what I need to do differently when I get to work to save my job."

From: Christopher Tyner, "Top 10 CEOs of 2000," *Investor's Business Daily*, January 2, 2001, B6

---

## Termination for Cause

Terminating Einsteins for cause should proceed in an orderly process. If you have done progressive discipline correctly, you will have accumulated a series of documents detailing the events leading up to termination. Recall that in progressive discipline the manager wants to keep records of each meeting and intervention with the Einstein. You want to record the incident that prompted the disciplinary action. You also want to record the actions that you take to intervene, and the standards the employee is to achieve to remain in good standing with the firm.

If an Einstein manager does progressive discipline correctly and carefully, documenting the interventions and their results, he or she is prepared for the terminating event. With Einsteins, the terminating event should proceed quickly and privately. It's best to handle it near the end of the workday, allowing the Einstein to clear out his or her desk and quietly move on. You do not want to create a situation where others in the terminated Einstein's tribe are distracted or disturbed by the termination. Einstein tribes are not overly protective of members. Those who have not been living within the rules of the environment are known to all. Tribal members who remain with the firm will not likely feel threatened by the sudden termination of one of their own. They will generally feel relief for the return to internal tribal harmony and for the terminated Einstein to go out and find a better fit.

## Termination for Crisis

Throughout 2000 and 2001 many previously high-flying technology companies were faced with something they never thought they'd encounter: layoffs. Despite the fast pace of the so-called new economy, the world has not freed itself from the inexorable business cycle. Economic booms come and go, and no sector of the economy is immune from periods of retrenchment. Occasionally, even the most successful firms must reduce the size of the workforce. Einsteins don't worry about layoffs. Their vaunted mobility ensures that they will land on their feet if they are laid off. At the same time, they don't like to be laid off, since it interrupts their work on projects and separates them from their tribes.

Many firms are in a state of denial when financial or other crises approach. They believe they can "hang on" somehow, and don't prepare the organization or its people for a possible crisis. This head-in-the-sand approach leaves them with few options when the crisis hits. There is no money left for severance or other benefits, and everything must be handled quickly and without proper sensitivity. Firms that are forced to handle layoffs in a hurried manner due to lack of foresight are unlikely to get their Einsteins back if and when things get better.

The far better strategy is to recognize the difficulties the firm is facing and communicate those difficulties to Einsteins. As we have been stating, Einsteins aren't typical employees. They aren't concerned about their jobs. Einsteins are mobile and they know it. Informing them about approaching train wrecks doesn't scare them. In fact, quite the contrary is true. Informing them of an approaching train wreck compels them to work even harder to help the firm succeed. This extra effort is not generated by fear, but by pride. Einsteins pride themselves on their ability to face adversity and win. They will actually enjoy the challenge of an impending crisis and will fight to help Einstein managers ward it off.

When the time comes to lay off Einsteins, you must break your normal, participatory management style and assume the role of the autocrat. You should not ask the tribe to select members for sacrificing to the RIF (reduction in force) gods. This is one of the few times that managers of Einsteins *must* be autocrats. You must make your selection of who will be laid off in private, and you must handle the layoff in private. Don't hand out envelopes containing pink slips in front of everyone. Firms that do this show a lack of human concern and are not likely to be places to which laid-off Einsteins prefer to return.

Prior to laying off Einsteins, develop as lucrative a set of severance benefits as you can afford. You may have to be creative here. At least two weeks of salary can be very helpful as the Einsteins look for new employment. Other possible benefits include:

- Outplacement services
- Job leads to partner, supplier, or client firms
- Project-related consulting assignments with the firm, or with clients, partners, or suppliers
- Continued use of company resources, such as e-mail, voice mail, and other services to help them in their quest for new work

At the least, if you want to leave the door open for departing Einsteins, you need to let them know how much they are valued and that the company would like them to return. Actually telling a laid-off Einstein that the company wants to get them back plants a very important seed. You can help the seed grow by staying in touch with your Einsteins and letting them contribute to projects on a consulting basis as conditions improve.

## A Final Comment

Einstein managers will eventually have to deal with difficult Einsteins. Being able to manage and control the work environment while at the same time deal with the arrogant, know-it-all, important, eccentric, disorganized, and withdrawn Einstein is a part of daily responsibilities. For a variety of reasons, Einsteins occasionally, or in some cases regularly, sing off key. By off key we mean stubborn, antagonistic, complaining, insecure, blunt, and in-your-face behavior. Don't get sucked in. The difficult Einstein probably knows that he or she is causing problems. The experienced manager pauses and reflects before knee jerk reacting. Try to understand the difficult Einstein by listening, observing, inquiring, and only then acting.

Another important lesson is to confront the difficult Einstein in private. When addressing difficult behavior, privacy is paramount. The confrontation should be about asking, not telling. From your perspective, tell the Einstein how you see the difficulty. Ask his or her perspective. After these steps are complete, move toward and implement a corrective action plan.

## CHAPTER 9

# Etiquette and Manners

## Einstein Preview Story

While Governor of Wisconsin, Tommy Thompson proclaimed May 1, 1998, Good Manners Day. Some say that good manners and proper etiquette have gone the way of the dinosaur. Governors have to encourage people to be nice to each other. Research suggests that rudeness and incivility at work is worsening. Surveys have shown that 12 percent of the people who regularly encountered rude behavior quit their jobs, and that men are seven times more likely than women to be rude or insensitive to subordinates than superiors. Unfortunately, today there is more in-your-face yelling, dressing down to go to work, and very few considerate acts displayed.

The increasing emphasis on gaining competitive advantage, competing in a global marketplace, and shortages of individuals possessing needed skills and talent has pushed etiquette and manners into the background. However, there are pockets of interest in etiquette and manners that suggest there is a comeback under way. Naomi Poulson, who runs an etiquette school in Silicon Valley, says, "Those who are technologically astute are becoming more aware in social situations, as techies move out of the garage or leave their cubicles to make deals with domestic and foreign investors."

Lyndy James and Sue Fox created a company called The Workshoppe, which provides etiquette courses. They looked at the high-tech industry and found what they call a "complete lack of manners." Talking, eating, and working together, manners are what they now teach Einsteins. They take 15 Einsteins to Sent Sovi, the classiest restaurant in Saratoga, California, and show them how to dine properly. Being a piglet is no longer tolerated in business even if the person "oinking" is brilliant.

*Continued*

The new economy's warp speed growth has left etiquette and manners in the dust. Being considerate, having social skills, and practicing good manners don't cost a penny, according to Liz Mirza of AML Group. Etiquette has been associated with snobbery, tea for lunch, and white gloves. A good picture is one that emphasizes etiquette as *politeness* and *consideration* of others.

As organizations become more diverse, do's and don'ts regarding etiquette and manners play a greater role. Workplace incivility is on the rise, and managers have a responsibility to help their Einsteins behave more politely and reverse the trend. If employees were not taught etiquette and manners at home, managers are going to have to become the in-house teachers in many organizations.

Einsteins have a reputation of being rumpled, abrasive, aloof, ill-mannered, and generally lacking in social graces. Einstein himself created a look, including bushy eyebrows, flying winged hair, piercing eyes, and ho-hum clothes. Of course, some Einsteins and some non-Einsteins fit this description. In fact, some Einsteins value being labeled a "dorky" dresser, possessing poor eating habits or none at all, and being so ill-mannered that everyone stays clear of them.

Business relationships, performance, and trust rely more than ever on personal contact. Courtesy, politeness, and civility are still highly valued in business and personal relationships. Many Einsteins know a lot about their jobs, technology, and how business operates, but little about how to comport themselves in day-to-day activities. The programmer who is a genius may have an abrasive manner that impedes her progress in being considered a valued Einstein team member. A systems analyst may be considered the number one conceptual thinker, but the organization is embarrassed to take him to make presentations because of his sloppy, repulsive appearance.

The ability to close a deal, entertain a client, talk politely to a user of the firm's software, and make a dazzling presentation involve etiquette and manners. There are some simple rules and suggestions that Einsteins need to know and managers must have a good grasp of so they can teach Einsteins that deals are closed, customers are retained, and current clients refer the organization to other potential clients when people are treated with respect.

## The Old Days

In the oldest guide to general behavior, *The Instructors of Ptahholep*, written by an Egyptian in about 2000 B.C., attitudes, values, and manners were discussed. The book emphasized that general behavior was expected to be handed down from parent to child through successive generations. This generational passing down has been derailed in the past three or four decades. Children used to learn some of the rules of etiquette by imitating their parents. Manners were observed in parents. Sitting around the dinner table, watching parents eat, talk, and laugh, the lessons were on display. How to use a knife, where to place a glass, and how to eat with your mouth closed while chewing were practiced and corrected.

The family sitting down to eat meals has become a thing of the past in most homes. Dual career families, single parent households, and long workdays have diminished the ability to observe others. In a large number of homes the family sitting together happens rarely, more often on holidays such as Thanksgiving. One result of the changes in society and the family has been the lack of development of social skills. Etiquette and manners now must be learned largely outside of the home.

Learning proper etiquette and displaying manners provide a common language of behavior. This common and accepted language is used when people meet, communicate, dine, travel, and conduct business. The concept of manners is based upon the notion of consideration for others. While every society has its local traditions, it's not necessary to learn a trove of tribal rules every time you step outside of the tribe's territory. Etiquette and manners transcends societies, local customs, and geographical boundaries.

When a person greets you, saying, "Hello, how are you doing, would you like to come in?" we know they're showing consideration and interest. In organizations filled with Einsteins, the language of consideration is valued, because every employee serves the larger entity—the organization. It is simple to say, but it's still true: "Good manners make sense always."

## Civility Is an Asset

The word *etiquette* comes from the French and means "ticket." The rules and regulations of the French court were written on sheets of paper called tickets, which were posted in the courtyard to be read by all citizens. Everyone could read the postings and were expected to observe and obey.

*Civility* is rooted in the Latin word for city. Civility was an indication that a person had acquired polish, as opposed to being ill-mannered, crude, or rough in dealing with others. The Latin word for polish is the root of *politeness*.

In history we know that until about the sixteenth century everyone, including kings and queens, ate their meals with their hands. Knives, spoons, and forks are modern inventions. The custom of dressing for dinner has been handed down from the Romans. They slipped into comfortable and loose robes to eat.

The first treatise on table etiquette and manners was written by a Milanese monk, Bonvicino da Riva, in 1290. Erasmus of Rotterdam wrote in 1530 on the *Civility of Children* at the table. In the first decades of the twentieth century over 65 books of etiquette were published in the United States.

As this chapter will illustrate, etiquette and manners is not a set of "must do" rules, but is a set of suggested guidelines designed to help managers coach Einsteins. The coaching is intended to help Einsteins display consideration for others. Courteous respect for the feelings of others is the keynote of etiquette and manners.

## A Quick Test

Take a few minutes to see where you are starting in understanding some of the guidelines of etiquette and manners.

---

### Etiquette Test

1. Should I stand up and shake hands when someone enters my office or work-space?

   Yes. An expression of courtesy and respect that is appreciated is displayed by taking the time and energy to stand and shake hands.

2. I received a gift from a business colleague and want to send an e-mail thank you note.

   Don't. It's better to write a personal note and send it via snail mail. E-mails lack the personal touch and give off a hint of being a little lazy.

3. Your name or a technology term is frequently mispronounced by a colleague. How should you correct these mispronunciations?

   *Continued*

---

Speak privately with the colleague and tactfully inform the person of the correct pronunciations. Don't correct mispronunciations in public.

4. I'm going to dinner with a client. Where is the best place to put my cell phone?

Leave your cell phone off and in your briefcase. If you must take a call (top urgency only), inform the people you are eating with when you sit down. When the phone rings, excuse yourself and take the call in a private area. Keep the urgent calls to no more than one. Zero is best, if possible.

5. What is too casual for a dress code?

This varies company by company. A few guidelines are: clothing should always be appropriate, clean, no beachwear or workout clothes, wear socks or hose, and keep the sleeveless blouses and shirts at home. Also, keep the sheer fabrics for private situations.

6. Is it proper to order a glass of wine?

Some firms have a no-alcohol policy. Although there are some exceptions, alcohol should not be served when business is being conducted.

7. I work with a lot of international colleagues. What are some good tips?

Know and pronounce their names correctly. Always dress conservatively. Avoid profanity. Be punctual. Learn about the person's culture (customs, religion, values, and history). This learning can be a part of the nonbusiness communication.

In looking over these seven questions and the answers, it is easy to see that common sense goes a long way. There are no laws or hard and fast rules, but there is a large dose of common sense and consideration of the other person. Einsteins are certainly intelligent, but managers need to emphasize the notion of common sense in terms of etiquette and manners in all interactions.

## The First Impression

The 80 percent common sense and 20 percent consideration of others rule applies to every business situation from meals, travel, negotiations, communications, and even the first impression. The relationship with another person starts with the first impression. The first eye contact, handshake, and words spoken set the tone for future meetings.

## Handshake

A firm handshake (not a gorilla grip) is the first physical contact. A firm handshake conveys confidence, interest, and respect. It says, "Hi, I'm interested in you," whereas a limp handshake says, "Wow, I'm unsure of myself." Eye contact and a smile while shaking hands are a nice touch.

The handshake should be brief, but long enough to introduce yourself and say a few words. The handshake, besides being firm, should be relatively stable. Shaking or pumping someone's hand should be avoided. There is no gender distinction when shaking hands, except in specific situations where the person's religious background may prohibit this custom.

## Introductions

Another part of the first impression is the introduction. If you forget someone's name, apologize politely and admit the oversight. Be considerate, smile, and make eye contact. Making good introductions requires practice, good listening skills, and observation. The purpose of a proper introduction is to get to know the other person.

In business there is a logical order to introductions, with seniority and age taking precedence. Gender is not a factor. First mention the name of the higher-ranking person, followed by the name of the other individual.

> "This is our vice president, Hailey Phillips, I would like to introduce May Cappen, a senior programmer from Technoworld in Dallas, Texas."

A few guidelines for the manager to remember. The person in *italics* is introduced first.

- Introduce the younger to the *older* person.
- Introduce our company colleague to a *colleague* in another firm.
- Introduce a junior executive to a *senior* executive.
- Avoid using nicknames.
- Use titles such as Doctor for M.D. or Ph.D, Judge (for a judge), Major (military), when you know the person uses one.
- Make a brief statement about the person (e.g., a position change, an award received, a vacation trip, a new business situation).

Sometimes the impression is formed by the way a person introduces himself.

> "Hi, my name is Hunter Zacha. I work for Management 2.0, a firm that is involved in online learning and training for corporate clients."

The self-introduction may vary depending on the setting (e.g., convention, dinner, a meeting in a client's office). A brief, fifteen-to-twenty second description of who you are and what you do comes in handy. Practicing the self-introduction is worth the work. It provides a quick glimpse of your self-confidence, energy, and openness. It also allows the self-introducer to do a little self-promotion. The emphasis should be on "little," keeping it, as mentioned, fifteen to twenty seconds.

### Names

Everyone loves to hear his or her name, especially when it is pronounced perfectly. Being addressed by a wrong or mangled name is uncomfortable. Make every effort to get the name correct. You are considered interested and caring when the person's name is pronounced correctly.

The problem with names goes beyond proper pronunciation. Forgetting names is a problem. If you forget a name, admit it: "I'm sorry, I have forgotten your name." Whenever you are unsure of a name, ask.

Many names today come from ethnic and diverse backgrounds. They really are hard names to remember and pronounce. Be patient, take time, and practice these names. If you have a hard name—I-van-ce-vich or Den-ing (Duening), for example—you know the discomfort someone has in pronouncing it correctly. Have patience and politely correct mispronunciation.

- Listen carefully. Ask the person to repeat a name if you are not sure.
- Try to remember the name and its pronunciation.
- Also remember how someone prefers to be addressed. For example, Mary Kathryn Goodson may prefer to be called Katie. Remember this for future situations.

## Grooming

An impression starts with a person's appearance. Maintaining a clean, healthy, and properly dressed appearance creates a comfortable tenor

"LOOK AT YOU! I'VE NEVER SEEN ANYONE SO POLISHED UP
FOR A PRESENTATION!"

for meetings. Individuals are not aware of problems like body odor, strong shaving lotion, and unkempt hair. There are a few companies with policies addressing odor, lotions, or hairstyles. The high-tech industries are much more open and free concerning grooming and even dress codes. However, good common sense should play a significant role in making good judgments.

Hairstyles and facial hair may be specified in a company's policies. Knowing or learning the policies before taking a job is the first order of business. If you can't give up the beard or the long hair, don't take a position in a firm with a policy against them. Companies have become much more liberal about facial hair and hairstyles. In the past two decades, clean, neat, and trimmed are the three issues that work in most organizations.

You may think that grooming concerns are silly. Yes, they may be, but they do exist. Again, being considerate about others is the guideline. Good grooming is not difficult, and it says that you care about your colleagues. This is what etiquette and manners is about. Einstein managers need to correct poor grooming situations by privately discussing concerns with the offender. Being honest, tactful, and clear, while at the same time offering suggestions, is often appreciated by the Einstein. Einsteins are sometimes so immersed in their work they are not aware of body odor, aftershave, or perfume problems.

Findings in research studies tell us that a person conveys who they are largely through visual appearance. About 55 percent of any message communicated is conveyed through visual appearance. Grooming is a large part of the visual message sent out to others.

---

### Influence Tip

Remember, doing business, striking a deal, achieving good results, is about "people." Treat people (Einsteins) like you would treat your grandparents, children, and valued friends. It's a good idea to remember what you can about each Einstein—birthdays, nicknames, family stories. People equate kindness, manners, and etiquette with how you treat them. Treating them includes knowing something about them besides work-related issues and topics.

---

## Women in the Workplace

Every day more women are joining the workforce. Five years from now having a specific section on women in the workplace may be unnecessary. However, at the moment men and women need to be reminded about a few issues about the increasing number of women in the workplace.

Many women today are increasingly striving to attain managerial and leadership roles. Einsteins may find themselves reporting to female managers. Einsteins and non-Einsteins will quickly learn that some females make excellent managers and leaders while other females will be complete failures in roles of authority and responsibility. Men or women hold no special status for being better or worse at managing Einsteins.

Einsteins' treatment of females as colleagues or managers should include manners and consideration. The issue of romance at work needs to be carefully analyzed by Einstein managers. The Einsteins' emphasis on teamwork and long work hours offers opportunities for personal relationships.

The workplace offers a favorable setting for personal romance to blossom since the special other person can be seen every day. Romance at work, however, has destroyed many careers. Damaging gossip, loss of confidence, and difficulty putting romantic colleagues together poses problems for Einstein managers.

Many companies discourage office romance, but it is very tricky indeed for a manager. The Einstein manager can monitor and intervene when excessive time is spent by an Einstein and a romantically linked colleague. The manager needs to try to make sure that the Einstein's time at work is spent on job tasks, goals, problem solving, and not on personal relationships.

Corporate travel, long hours in hotels, late night work, and weekend work are contributions to not just short flings, but to longer romances. Managers need to be aware of romantic pairings among Einsteins and cut out the opportunities for liaisons when possible.

Some firms have actually forbidden romances. Companies have nepotism policies that prohibit employment of spouses and relatives. There is a growing push to write and enforce "no romantic relationships at work" policies. The fear of sexual harassment lawsuits when and if a romance turns sour is real.

Managers also have to guard against and discourage Einsteins becoming romantically linked to customers or clients. Again, gossip, resentment from colleagues, and a poor image for the company are negative possibilities. Being linked romantically to a customer or client is not sound practice for anyone. Calling the Einstein in who is believed to be romantically linked is touchy and has to be handled with finesse and tact by managers. Be sure or fairly certain before having any fireside chat with an Einstein who is supposedly romantically associated with a customer or client.

Thus far the discussion is about Einsteins (the majority being male) and romantic partners. Silicon Valley is the home of the highest educated, highest paid Einsteins in the country. At last count there were over 68,000 more single men than women in Santa Clara County (Silicon Valley). This compares nationally to 43 million single women versus 36 million single men. Yikes! Silicon Valley is a desert for heterosexuals. Some refer to Silicon Valley, in terms of relationship potential for women, as the Alaska of the twenty-first century. Other locations around the country are not as populated with single Einsteins.

## Communication Manners

In Chapter 6 we presented the issue of communication. We dealt with communication with a capital C, or the big picture. This section covers a few specialized areas of communication to which Einsteins sometimes fail to give a second of thought.

### Telephone Manners

The use of the telephone properly is usually a nonissue. Yet, the telephone is crucial to being successful. Managers need to provide good examples to Einsteins of "how to do it right." They must show Einsteins they care about using the telephone correctly. A few simple guidelines:

- Practice and use a happy telephone voice.
- Always identify yourself. Do not presume that the person on the other end of the line knows who you are.
- Be polite. Be courteous. Be brief. Be happy.
- When taking a message, ask for the caller's name, telephone number, and the best time to have the call returned.
- Always ask permission when using a speakerphone. Identify everyone in the room. Show consideration to the other person.

---

### Black Hole

Manners about returning phone calls have become lax. Not returning calls is widespread and provides an opportunity for the well-mannered Einstein manager. Instead of not returning calls because of being busy, it might be considered exceptional if you do return calls. The choice is yours—don't return calls like most people, or do return calls, which allows you to stand out.

---

Managers who "do telephoning correctly" set an example and an expectation for Einsteins. When an Einstein is observed being impolite, curt, abrasive, and discourteous on the telephone, Einstein managers must intervene as soon as possible. Ask the Einstein to correct the behavior and explain what was observed. The explanation should include examples of how poor telephone manners cost the firm business. The quality of the company is reflected to a caller in the contact made with the firm through the telephone.

---

### Einstein Wisdom

Teaching should be such that what is offered is perceived as a valuable gift and not as a hard duty.

---

## Magic Words

A manager's vocabulary that includes some magic words can establish a good example for Einsteins. Managers, when communicating with Einsteins, sprinkle in and use the magic words. Comedian George Carlin has a routine about the "words you must not say" on television. His entire routine lampooned TV censors and how he got around the "word police." The manager's magic words are "words you should use every day." These are the opposite of Carlin's forbidden list. Saying these magic words with sincerity and meaning will pave the way for politeness and better relationships. The magic words are:

- The person's name you are talking to: get it right
- Please
- Thank you
- Excuse me
- Good day
- How are you doing?
- Can I help in any way?
- I'm sorry

These magic words work over and over. They make a difference and show that the Einstein manager cares.

### The Avoided Topics

Managers sometimes engage in and establish a topic dialogue with Einsteins, but there are a few topics to be avoided. These areas usually are considered provocative by someone on the Einstein team or the entire unit. Gossip, obscene and swear words, ethnic jokes, sexual jokes, and talking about a romantic relationship or sexual activity should be avoided and discouraged by Einstein managers. There are numerous topics to discuss, such as books, movies, business activities, sports, and career opportunities. Managers should stay away from and help their Einsteins stay away from the "to be avoided" topics. On the other hand, Einstein managers should follow the lead of their Einsteins in other areas. This assumes that some of the Einsteins want to engage the manager in topical conversations.

## Meals and Dining

A lot of business occurs over or across a dining table. Interview, negotiations, networking, conversation, and general discussion can occur at meals. A person's etiquette and manners are on display. What and how a person orders, how utensils are used, and how he or she eats are on display. Managers need to convince Einsteins that noticing how someone dines is a method of determining manners and polish.

What difference does it make how a person eats? A person with poor eating skills can put an end to a deal, can embarrass the firm, and can be interpreted as being impolite. Handling a fork like a cave dweller provides a signal that the person lacks polish.

## Formal Eating

A formal table setting is a good starting point. Managers may need a road map themselves so they can help Einsteins do a better job at the dining table. Exhibit 9.1 shows a complete formal table setting. Did you notice the position of the "fish" knife and the direction of the cutting edge of the knife? Where does the butter for your bread go? It should be placed on the bread plate. The setting is offered as a refresher or reminder for managers.

Formal eating isn't that popular today, compared to a decade ago. Still, managers of Einsteins as teachers and coaches must be up-to-date so they can lead the way. Whether at a formal or just a regular meal, business talk should be held back until later in the meal, after

**Exhibit 9.1**
Complete Formal Table Setting

A. Bread and Butter Plate
B. Butter Knife
C. Dessert spoon
D. Dessert fork
E. Salad fork
F. Fish fork
G. Dinner fork
H. Dinner plate
I. Charger
J. Dinner Knife
K. Fish knife
L. Teaspoon
M. Soup spoon
N. Oyster fork
O. Champagne flute
P. Red Wine Glass
Q. White Wine Glass
R. Sherry Glass

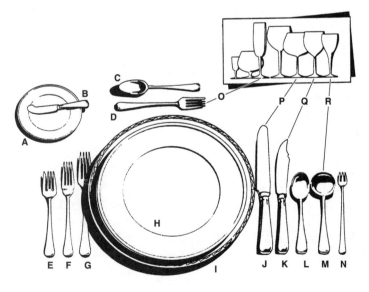

the entrée plates are removed. Serious business talk should wait until full attention can be focused. Managers must convey to Einsteins when eating meals with clients the importance of favorably representing the firm. Displaying good eating manners and knowing when to get down to serious business talk are invaluable in closing deals and furthering relationships.

Some of the common dining gaffes that Einsteins should be instructed to avoid are:

- Talking in Einstein tongue
- Getting too personal in conversations
- Using profanity
- Putting business papers on the table to illustrate points
- Wearing inappropriate clothing (use common sense)
- Eating with an open mouth
- Burping out loud

These are just a few of the gaffes that can turn a client or customer off. Yes, an open "mouth" while chewing food is impolite and is not attractive. Can any manager be successful in coaching Einsteins to take the time to display even minimum eating etiquette and manners? Maybe, if the manager is respected, displays good eating manners and etiquette, and is a good communicator.

## Business Dress

Before a person says one word, his or her clothes have already spoken. The first impression or moment of truth is communicated through the handshake, introductions, grooming, and clothing. The clothes of a person are observed within Einstein teams, in interactions outside the teams' boundaries, in videoconferences, at meetings, when making a presentation, at social events, and every time an encounter with someone else occurs. In today's frenetic-paced work environment, others take visual and social bites of Einsteins. The bites about the Einstein's intelligence, problem solving ability, logic, passion, and value are positively awesome. Einsteins "wow" others in the intelligence social bite interpretation area. The clothing, style, and wardrobe choices of Einsteins typically send a different message to others.

Managers have a responsibility to help Einsteins understand that their appearance and clothing can send a positive professional message or an "I don't care" message. Clothing, even in a work environment that accepts and encourages "casual," can be common sensically good or bad.

## Casual Dress

The Einsteins' mantra for clothing has been to "keep it simple, stupid," in terms of dress codes and expectations. The theory behind casual is to increase morale and productivity by allowing Einsteins to dress comfortably. The "casual" norm is based on the assumption that Einsteins work better without neckties, suits, white shirts, and stuffy-looking clothes. The clothing industry has seized on the "casual" dress preference of many Einsteins and non-Einsteins. Entire lines of casual business clothes have been created for men and women.

Unfortunately, what some firms view as acceptable casual and what some Einsteins interpret as casual varies dramatically. In the Einstein wardrobe mix are items such as sandals, denim, shorts, sleeveless blouses and shirts, eye-popping color combinations, and clothing with profane and, to some, obscene sayings, rhymes, or comments. The result, according to some managers, is that people act the way they are dressed. Those wearing beach clothes put their feet on the desk, slump around, and look lazy. The amount of sexual harassment complaints has increased in some firms where low tops, sheer, and tight fitting clothing are the practice. These lawsuits are costly, with settlements averaging over $225,000 each.

What does anyone think of a company when people are shuffling around in sandals, hats, shorts, and T-shirts with profanity laced across the front and back? Many customers, clients, and others outside the tribe take the quick visual bite and may decide: a bunch of losers, sloppy dress equals sloppy performance, nonconformists, interesting, wish I could do this at my place of work, or some other visually based thought.

Managers need to communicate and practice a number of appropriate guidelines without unnecessarily alienating Einsteins. What is said at the applicant's interview and what is practiced in terms of dress at work needs to be in sync. Unfortunately, too many managers fail to even mention dress expectations during the interview. The interview is the place to start the Einstein's expectations about what clothing is acceptable for the firm. The professional, buttoned-down look is favored in banking, investment, and insurance industries. This is called the "corporate" or "suit" look. Einsteins typically dislike the look and believe it is unnecessary and pretentious. Managers should spend some time in the interview explaining when or if the "corporate" look is ever necessary while working for the company.

The list in Exhibit 9.2 is simple and points toward casual dress, which is likely to continue as the accepted norm of Einsteins cloth-

**Exhibit 9.2**
Einstein Dress Guidelines
(Modify to Fit the Setting, Business, and Situation)

| *Do* | *Don't* |
|------|---------|
| • Wear clean and appropriate clothing | • Wear beach clothing |
| • Wear hose or socks | • Wear sports clothing |
| • Wear collared shirts | • Wear hats inside a building |
| • Wear belts when pants have loops | • Wear barefoot sandals |
| • Consider the color combinations when putting together the wardrobe | • Wear low neckline blouses |
| • Own a suit or one set of more formal clothes, just in case it is needed, rarely, but once in a while | • Wear tight fitting clothing |
| | • Wear clothes with holes |

ing and dress standards. Again, Einstein managers must first know the dress standards and guidelines appropriate in the firm. These should be communicated by the manager during the job interview. Managers who ignore, avoid, or forget to discuss dress expectations are likely to have a difficult time modifying an Einstein's dress behavior once he or she is on the job.

# The Etiquette Leader

Managing Einsteins concerning etiquette and manners is going to be an exceptional challenge. The issues of control and insight are in the forefront. Managers have some degree of control because of their position. Leaders have greater amounts of control because of their ability to influence based on respect, charisma, and skills. Using leadership is the preferred approach. Managers have to earn their leadership "stripes" from Einsteins. If Einsteins respect a person, he or she can become a leader and serve as an etiquette and manners coach/teacher/confidante.

## Seize the Day

Instead of sitting back and cringing about Einstein etiquette and manners, Einstein managers must address problems, situations, and events immediately. Observing barefoot Einsteins and listening to obscene comments for any extended period of time is unacceptable. True leaders "seize the day" and address the etiquette or manners debacle immediately. Preferably in private, away from other Einsteins.

Leaders must explain to Einsteins why the behavior is not acceptable and must be immediately corrected. As a leader, you must always ask Einsteins, "What can I do to help you improve or correct your display of consideration to others?" A real leader of Einsteins drives, points, convinces them that proper etiquette and manners means better business, more jobs for others, better relationships between people, and a more pleasant place to work. The leader as teacher provides Einsteins with a clear view of how to talk to others, what is appropriate dress, and even how to eat like an adult in a civilized society.

## Socialization with Einsteins

At the same time leaders are providing guidance encouragement, and actual examples of appropriate etiquette and manners, they must guard against too much "buddy-to-buddy" socializing. The less socializing leaders do with their Einsteins—beyond the minimum required, such as a holiday party, or a new, large contract celebration—the better. You don't see the dominant chimpanzee acting like "one of the guys." This may sound cold, aloof, and snobbish, but it is a fact of organizational life. If leaders become pals, buddies, or honorary Einsteins, they likely will have trouble seizing the day.

If a leader shows Einsteins concern and works carefully to help them improve their etiquette and manners, there will be an increase in respect. This is what a leader wants more than fear, love, or being a "bud." Outside of work, leaders have less control and influence. Leaders don't need Einsteins drinking with them at a bar, arguing with a drunk, or watching X-rated movies. The close "buddy" activities usually result in lost respect and the impression that a leader is less than previously thought.

## Stroking Einsteins

Leaders need to find something positive about their Einsteins' etiquette and manners at least every month or so. Praise the Einsteins about how they answered the telephone, handled an irate non-Einstein manager from another department, or dressed when meeting with an important client. The praise doesn't have to be formal, but when possible, deliver it in person. The personal touch—saying the Einstein's name, and complimenting the behavior that was observed—

never gets old. Too many compliments lose their value, so a monthly schedule is more effective. Managers should think about a number of "praise" sessions each month. The "praise" provides a message that you did observe the behavior and it was important enough to say something. Moreover, the brief "praise" session also says you care enough to recognize the Einstein. Like everyone else, Einsteins like to hear their names associated with a personal compliment. It is music to an Einstein's ears and "chicken soup" for the ego.

## Being Private

The opposite of praising Einsteins is having to call them in to correct poor etiquette or manners. Remember, as already stated, correct the problem immediately. The correction should be private and never mention other Einsteins in the discussion. Too often a manager will mention another Einstein's problem with names, in hopes of making the Einstein in the meeting feel better about the problem. This is not only poor managerial behavior, but it is not acceptable leadership behavior. Keep the discussion focused only on the Einstein sitting or standing in front of you. Never bring into the discussion other Einsteins to make a point or reduce the sting of the discussion.

## Einsteins Have a Responsibility

As good as some Einsteins may be in helping an organization succeed, they have no right to a position or an entitlement to employment. Yes, everyone can be replaced. Einsteins have a responsibility to make the firm, the team, and the manager look good. The concept of a self-fulfilling prophecy is important in order that Einsteins understand their responsibility. A self-fulfilling prophecy is illustrated in Exhibit 9.3.

The Einsteins' behavior is observed by others and influences others' (non-Einsteins') perceptions. If the Einsteins' behavior reinforces a non-Einsteins' initial perception, a self-fulfilling prophecy exists. There are good and bad self-fulfilling prophesies. A non-Einstein perceives that an Einstein is brilliant with programming. The result is that whenever a programming problem "hits the firm," the Einstein is contacted. On the other hand, if an Einstein is perceived as brilliant, but ill-mannered, foul-mouthed, and a detriment to closing business deals, leaders may, after a number of episodes, decide to get rid of the troublemaking genius.

**Exhibit 9.3**
The Self-Fulfilling Prophecy Process

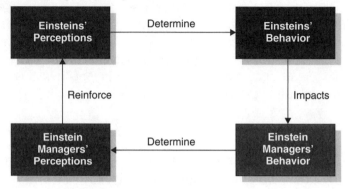

Numerous self-fulfilling prophecies, good and bad, regarding behaviors—including manners—are occurring continuously in organizations. One of the worst is that Einsteins are so intelligent they are not responsible to anyone. Einsteins have a responsibility to the organization, to their colleagues (including non-Einsteins), and to their managers. Einstein managers must communicate, display through example, make direct requests, and do so repeatedly, to emphasize that Einsteins are expected to display proper etiquette and manners.

## Stay Visible

The psychological concept of propinquity states that as managers get more distant from Einsteins in terms of any dimension (e.g., communication, slang, dress, manners), the assumptions made about the team are more negative and the attributions made about the team's behavior become less attractive. The opposite also applies. That is, the Einstein team makes more negative assumptions about the "suits," and the attributions made about managers are less positive.

Einsteins already have a natural boundary between themselves and managers—their technical intelligence. Therefore, if managers do not stay at least "visible" to Einsteins in terms of daily or regular contact, they will become increasingly distant and alien. Managers who are constantly among the Einsteins—being seen, talking, listening, and showing concern—will become part of their pattern, routine, and activities.

## CHAPTER 10

# Care and Growth of Einsteins

## Preview Einstein Story
### All Hat and No Cattle

James Kenefick founded Net-Tel and called on his employees to "treat others as you want to be treated" and "maintain a sense of humility and humor." He doled out stock options to share the wealth, but on October 23, 2000, the company sought liquidation under Chapter 7. Everyone was out of a job. What happened next was a shocker.

A group of Einsteins and non-Einsteins stormed the company, tore out videotape gear, PCs, fax machines, and printers. They wrecked the place.

Kenefick had talked a lot about freedom, autonomy, open communication, enriching work, and working conditions at Net-Tel. He provided Ping-Pong tables, dental care mobile vans, pizza blasts, and free food. Home and work life was blurred. What the wrecking crew at Net-Tel concluded was that Kenefick was a farce, a touchy feely guy who, despite the perks and rhetoric, wanted people to work like dogs. They said he was not even courteous or respectful enough to warn them about the dire financial conditions of the firm. Kenefick was accused of giving people a lot of hype, enough diversions, and feeding them occasionally so they'd never go home.

Kenefick talked about caring and supporting his Einsteins and non-Einsteins and then hammered them by keeping the financial bleeding a secret. The lesson of Net-Tel for other firms is that managers must be

*Continued*

honest. The wrecking crew was wrong and probably broke some laws at Net-Tel, but their message was loud.

Most Einsteins do not fit what is called a "zero-drag" profile and need to be considered when personal growth and care programs are designed and implemented. The "zero-drag" employee is the man or woman with no spouse, no kids, no pets, and no personal ties. Zero-drag Einsteins are expected by some managers to work through the night, take no vacations, and serve as a role model of work commitment to others.

In every element and section of this book it is emphasized that Einsteins are an extremely valuable and necessary asset to organizations. The supply and demand situation in the labor market favors Einsteins. They have choices of whether to go to work, whom to work for, and whether to stay employed. Einsteins are not able to willy-nilly switch employers every month, but they are mobile. This frequency of movement would attract recruiters' attention and may label the Einstein as a butterfly—always on the move. This is a warning signal. On the other hand, Einstein mobility is a reality. This means that smart managers and employers do what they can to make work challenging and enjoyable for Einsteins.

Quality of worklife is important to Einsteins in terms of their growth. They want to be rewarded, feel comfortable, solve challenging problems, and be surrounded by bright, interesting colleagues. They also want to feel they are making a difference. In addition, Einsteins want time for their families, pets, health and fitness, and spiritual well-being. Each Einstein defines quality of life and quality of worklife with their own script. Einstein managers need to help create supportive and growth oriented work environments to accommodate diverse Einstein needs.

## Quality of Life

Quality of life programs come in many shapes and varieties. Some include tickets to concerts, baby photo contests, exercise facilities, automated teller machines (ATMs), and free soft drinks and snacks.

There is also the practice of granting time off, since everyone, including most Einsteins, don't want to work 24/7. There are too many other things for Einsteins to do besides working continuous eighty-hour weeks. Einsteins prefer balance between work and nonwork activities. After months or years of around the clock, intense work, Einsteins need to recover some of the family, friends, and recreational sacrifices they have made.

## Management Involvement

Talking to Einsteins about work and life balance is a starting point for the involvement of managers. Respecting the needs Einsteins have is a sign that managers care and are concerned about individual well-being. As part of normal interactions, Einstein managers must ask about preferences and opinions. Managers can aggregate the input of Einsteins to tailor preferred programs instead of bestowing quality of life and quality of work balance goodies like an emperor.

The physical environment itself is important in creating a better work and life balance program. Workers enjoy displaying pictures of family, favorite places, or something they do. Color, plants, carpets, art, sculptures, and creative trinkets can make the environment feel comfortable and more like home. Bringing remembrances of home to work narrows the work and life gap.

## Involve Families

Almost every Einstein has relatives and friends outside of work. Events that include families and friends can be important in terms of morale. Sponsoring picnics, trips to amusement parks and concerts, and parties that include families and friends can be satisfying.

When family members are ill, granting Einsteins time off can be invaluable in generating appreciation and respect. Note that if time off to care for someone is granted to one Einstein, it will set a precedent and require that when other Einsteins are faced with the same circumstances, they too must be provided time off.

Welcoming the children of Einsteins at work, occasionally, is another family event that is appreciated. The "shadow" day, when children spend time with Mom or Dad at work, is educational and supportive of family values and bonding time.

# Working Conditions

There are numerous opportunities for managers to take action and intervene so that care of working conditions is a priority. The powerful impact of proper working conditions has been uncovered in studies in various industries.

## Safety at Work

Einsteins appreciate working in a safe and healthy environment. Talking about safety, watching out for hazards, and keeping the work area clean are responsibilities of managers. In order to be sure about maintaining healthy environments, Einstein managers should request periodic inspections to identify and correct environmental hazards. Pesticides, asbestos, and other hazardous materials must be identified and safely eliminated.

Incentive programs to reward Einsteins for maintaining safe workplaces can be used. Even though most Einstein work environments are generally not dangerous, there is the potential for fire, equipment accidents, and hazardous chemicals. Keeping the work area clean, organized, and safe should be a priority of every one on the Einstein team, as well as managers.

## The Right Equipment

Einsteins want to do the best job possible. They want to excel and provide superior products and service. One of their frustrations is to not have the right technology (hardware and software). Einstein managers should provide support by ensuring the right equipment is available. Purchase or lease what is needed. Service the items regularly so everything is operating efficiently. Einstein managers must be aware of the equipment needed, the furniture required, and the appropriate space and working conditions.

Three former Microsoft alumni plan to establish a Shangri-La work setting in southern India. The company, Catalytic Software, envisions a self-sustaining community of concrete domes that will house about 4,000 software engineers and about 300 support personnel. Catalytic will supply contract software engineers for technical projects.

Everyone except emergency and delivery service workers at Catalytic will have work sites with fiber-optic Internet connections in every multistory office dome. Swimming pools, tennis courts, and ice rinks will be provided on the work premises. Catalytic employees will live in 800- to 2,280-square-foot shelters gratis, and receive competitive salaries and stock options. The domed work and living structures are used because the shapes are more earthquake resistant.

## Flextime

A part of a person's working conditions is the schedule requirements for being at work. Some employees work best in the morning, while others perform better when acting like night owls. If and when possible, Einstein managers should consider the need for flexible work schedules for Einsteins. Instead of adhering to an 8:00 a.m. to 5:00 p.m. schedule, for instance, consideration of multiple schedules is appropriate. Some Einsteins may be required at all times, but a spread-out schedule to accommodate different preferences may be highly valued.

## Avoiding Burnout

Possessing the proper equipment and having flextime schedules for work have another possible benefit with regard to what is called "burnout." Individuals constantly working and spending long hours on projects results in burnout. The consequences are psychological, emotional, or physical exhaustion. Burnout is especially likely to occur when an Einstein works long hours on multiple projects and is responsible for helping other Einsteins or non-Einsteins. Burned-out Einsteins often feel that they are not helping others enough or doing enough work.

One remedy for burnout is for an Einstein manager to make sure that Einsteins take their vacations. Putting off vacations indefinitely is not good. Yes, a strong commitment from Einsteins to work is admirable, but it has risks. Without periodic breaks, many Einsteins tend to push themselves to the point of being burned out or exhausted. If Einsteins refuse to take a break, managers should make it a mandatory condition every quarter.

# Learning

Einsteins have a high need for learning and acquiring new skills. Many Einsteins assess the learning opportunities in an organization before joining up. They are interested in both academic learning and con-

"WHY DON'T YOU TAKE A DAY OR TWO OFF? YOU LOOK A LITTLE BURNED OUT."

tinuing education opportunities. Einsteins want training and development courses.

## Manager's Role in Learning

Einstein managers have to be proactive when working with Einsteins to create and maintain a learning-rich environment. Being dedicated to Einsteins' growth and development should become a routine. Anytime an Einstein discusses performance with a manager, the discussion should address steps that he or she can take to grow. Every Einstein needs a personal growth plan to which the manager refers, and helps the individual update and implement.

Managers need to help Einsteins chart out personal maps for what they don't know, or enhance and sharpen what they already know. The responsibility for learning among Einsteins rests with each individual. The Einstein manager, however, through his or her actions, can provide the time, resources, and atmosphere that encourages Einsteins to seize their learning responsibilities.

**Communities of practice.** In Einstein teams the concept of learning involves a "community of practice." The image of a solitary person hunched over a desk in a pool of light, learning new things, isn't realistic. Learning happens in a community. Teams of Einsteins often emerge on their own: three, five, or a number of people come together to collaboratively try out ideas, exchange wisdom, teach each other, experiment with new formulas. An Einstein manager can't simply create or declare a community of practice. The manager, however, by being threatening and smothering communities of practice can destroy them by overmanaging or hovering around. In Einstein terms, a community of practice is a group of Einsteins, informal, joined to one another through common interests, curiosity, or political need; a common pursuit of solutions; and creating a body of knowledge through their interaction.

By recognizing, supporting, and encouraging communities of practice, Einstein managers can help them learn and function. National Semiconductor has encouraged informal communities of practice by giving them semiofficial status. Though they do not appear on the organization chart, communities of practice have taken on increasing responsibility for a range of Einstein work.

**External training and development.** In addition to encouraging Einstein communities of practice, managers can champion the investment in external training and development. An increasing number of employers have created their own corporate universities to provide education and training to employees. Motorola, Inc., formed its corporate university in 1981. The Motorola University offers training in cutting-edge industries, business skills, and foreign languages. The university has 1,300 full- and part-time teachers in twenty countries.

Dell University, Sun U, and Verifone University have no physical campus at all. Each uses a virtual approach. Over 70 percent of all Dell courses are delivered in virtual mode. Sprint University has 50 percent of its 1,000 courses available through the World Wide Web, videos, workbooks, and the firm's intranet. Sprint's research showed that students learned slightly more online than in the classroom. The biggest gain Sprint found was that students attained their knowledge in just over half the time online. With the tight demand of people to be physically on the job, reducing the participant's time away from work is a significant benefit.

There is no magic number of how much learning, training, and education for each Einstein should be made available. Needs, results, growth, and effectiveness for individual Einsteins are difficult to measure. Some firms use a measure called "hours of classroom time invested each year." This measure is not ideal since e-learning is suitable for some training, and to be focused solely on formal classrooms is becoming outdated.

Instead of addressing what is an appropriate "seat" time amount for Einsteins' training, it is better for managers to address what learning is needed and how the effectiveness of learning should be assessed.

---

### Influence Tip

Einstein managers and team members are going to make mistakes, as everyone does. But instead of punishing or sanctioning Einsteins, you have to show the team a better way to achieve results. Einstein managers also need to provide opportunities to the team members to learn. The best teams learn continuously about other groups, each other, and the manager. The job of Einstein managers is to create learning environments so members feel they are growing and developing their talent, skills, and knowledge.

---

## Mentoring Programs

Einsteins fortunate enough to be working for managers who support, design, and implement mentor programs can personally grow significantly. In Homer's *Odyssey*, Mentor was the servant of Ulysses to whom the king entrusted the care of his son, Telemachus. Later, when searching for his father, Telemachus was supported by Athena, goddess of war, who assumed the form Mentor. Mentor's responsibilities covered a range of life development and growth, not just professional matters. Through the Middle Ages, in guilds, guild masters who were responsible for professional, social, religious, and personal habits were considered mentors.

A working definition for Einstein managers to use in designing and implementing mentor programs is that an Einstein mentor would be:

> An experienced individual, outside of the reporting relationship, who through meetings, discussions, and role modeling takes a personal interest in guiding, supporting, and encouraging the growth and development of a less experienced Einstein in progressing beyond his or her immediate role in the organization (project) (team).

### Benefits of Mentoring

There are organizational, individual, and team benefits that can emerge from mentoring. Research of mentor-protégé pairings has found motivational improvements, higher morale, stronger commitment and trust, and improved learning. In many instances the benefits of mentor pairings appear in both the mentor and the protégé.

Increased self-confidence is also a benefit received by protégés. Effective Einstein mentors can provide invaluable feedback, recognition, and support, resulting in increased confidence in work performance and risk taking on the part of mentored Einsteins.

Experienced Einstein mentors may benefit from having a network of Einstein protégés working throughout the organization. Recognition for being a developer and supporter of Einstein talent can result in increased status within and outside the immediate Einstein team.

## Key Mentor Behaviors

There are mentor competencies that Einstein managers should identify in Einsteins when instituting a formal or encouraging an informal mentoring program. What are the critical behaviors of effective mentoring? Unfortunately, an answer based on research is not available. Spotty research, discussions and debates, and observations of mentoring relationships suggest, however, that effective mentor pairings result when the mentor, as viewed by the protégé, exhibits these behaviors:

1. Good listening skills

2. Accessibility

3. Focused interest

4. Provides information

5. Supports publicly and privately

6. Is not smothering or overwhelming

7. Holds protégé accountable

8. Helps clarify views

9. Patience

There are other behaviors that suggest a higher degree of mentor-protégé benefit, but these nine are repeated again and again.

## Manager's Role

Einstein managers can support, design, and implement mentoring programs for their Einstein teams. A number of ways to get behind mentoring are available. One approach is through observation and discussion. Managers can establish a registry of those interested in serving as mentors and those who want to be mentored. The registry can be made available to possible protégés. This mentor database can be reviewed on an intranet. Another way is to put together mentor candidate notebooks for possible protégés. Under this approach the Einstein manager provides protégés with information and can schedule appointments to discuss pairing with mentors and protégés.

An important determinant of success is promoting aligned matches. *Aligned* means that the mentor-protégé pairing results in positive benefits for both parties. Some managers take a guidance role and allow pairings to happen. The manager prepares the database, sets up meetings, and monitors, but forces no matches. This is an *informal* approach to mentoring.

Simply encouraging and supporting mentoring is the best, though not always the ideal, approach to design and implement. It is not always ideal because Einsteins tend to be on the introverted side. Introverts find it more difficult to mingle, share ideas and information, and engage in the intense relationship bonding that mentoring requires.

---

### Black Hole

In the military, a leader needs unquestionable authority and instant obedience. Einsteins will reject commands, directions, and having to do something because "I say so." Caring for Einsteins requires Einstein managers to put away commands, orders, threats, and intimidation. They will not result in personal growth and respect.

---

## Managerial Motives

Mentoring, if designed and implemented carefully, has the potential to become an important part of a high-performance culture for a number of reasons. First, it can contribute to creating a sense of oneness by promoting the acceptance of the Einstein team's core values. Second, the socialization aspects of mentoring promotes a sense of cohesiveness within Einstein teams. Third, mentoring increases the interpersonal exchanges and skills of Einsteins. Finally, managers can identify mentors who have the competencies and skills needed to be promoted at a later time.

Managers will receive the benefits of having more Einsteins who are knowledgeable, skilled, and self-confident. Greater benefits to the organization are likely if managers (1) do not dictate mentor pairings,

(2) train mentors and protégés in how best to use and benefit from mentoring, (3) encourage Einsteins to mentor other Einsteins who are in need of support and guidance, (4) recognize and reward excellent mentors, and (5) recommend excellent mentors for promotions to more significant positions. The Einstein may turn down the promotion, but the recognition is appreciated and remembered.

## Managing Conflict

Conflict can stunt the growth and development of Einsteins. In work organizations, conflict is unavoidable, because human beings are involved, and people can create, perceive, or be drawn into conflicting circumstances. Conflict is a process in which one party (say, the Einstein) perceives that his or her interests are being opposed by another party (Einstein or non-Einstein). Einstein managers need to understand the dynamics of conflict and know how to intervene effectively to resolve problems before they become destructive.

### A Conflict Continuum

Einstein teams, units, or projects that experience too little conflict tend to be plagued by apathy, lack of creativity, and missed deadlines. Excessive conflict, on the other hand, can erode performance because of political jujitsu, lack of teamwork, and turnover. Aggression and violence are undesirable manifestations of lingering and excessive conflict. Exhibit 10.1 presents a continuum of conflict.

It would be great if Einstein managers somehow could pinpoint exactly when the right amount of conflict is present. This would involve finding the perfect or the most constructive amount for attaining a positive outcome.

Dysfunctional conflict (Zones 1 and 3) will hinder performance and can be very destructive and negative. Where, exactly, Einsteins as individuals and in teams are on the continuum is impossible to pinpoint.

Conflict management is more than simply reaching agreement. Managers who want to minimize dysfunctional conflict are attempting to bring about:

1. *Agreement*. But at what price? Equitable and fair agreements are best. Remember that perceptions of persons in conflict can play tricks about the meaning of equitable and fair.

**Exhibit 10.1**

Conflict Amount and Impact on Outcome

(Creativity, Teamwork, Meeting Deadlines, Morale)

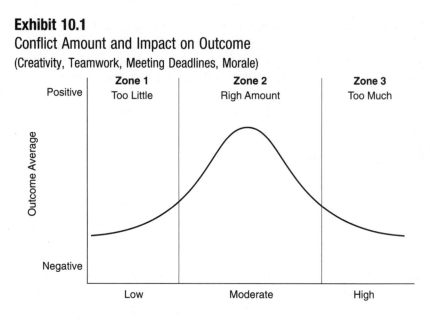

2. *Relationship building.* Fair and equitable agreements can build goodwill and trust for the future.

3. *Learning.* Functional conflict can promote positive outcomes. Successful conflict resolution is learned by being involved.

## Antecedents of Conflict

Certain situations and conditions can produce conflict for Einsteins. By being aware of the antecedents of dysfunctional conflict, managers can do a better job of minimizing their presence, or at least being aware of conflict "triggers." It would be impossible to list every antecedent. Some of the most noted, publicized, and reviewed antecedents of conflict for Einsteins include:

- Incompatible personality
- Competition for limited resources
- Interdepartment, across-project, and interteam competition
- Inadequate or poor communications
- Unreasonable deadlines or extreme time pressure
- Unreasonable or unclear policies and rules
- Decision making by consensus

Proactive, Einstein managers carefully review these conflict "triggers" and take appropriate action to correct them whenever feasible. We will discuss a few of these recurring antecedents.

## Workplace Incivility

Chronic personality conflicts often begin with seemingly insignificant irritations. For example, an Einstein team member can grow to deeply dislike another Einstein member because he continuously sings (more like a hum) off key while pounding with his left hand. These quirks build and build until a confrontation occurs. It is noted by researchers that increased informality, pressure for immediate results, and Einstein disdain for authority, schedules, and regulations have fostered an "anything goes" atmosphere in some workplaces. The result is an increase in workplace incivility and less consideration for others. This cycle can and has ended in violence in some cases.

Vicious cycles of incivility need to be quickly stopped. The caring and respectful manager serving as a courteous and considerate role model can be effective in showing Einsteins how to act and treat each other. Unfortunately, in society at large there has been a dramatic increase in incivility, disdain for appropriate etiquette, and poor manners.

Personality conflicts are a minefield for any manager. The *Diagnostic and Statistical Manual of Mental Disorders* presents 410 psychological disorders that show up at work. Managers have for decades generally ignored personality conflicts or have solved them by transferring one of the members. Today, in a more litigious atmosphere, ignoring them may result in lawsuits. Ignoring personality conflicts while serving in a managerial role is not acceptable, as more managers find themselves embroiled in lawsuits.

## Interteam Conflict

Conflict among Einstein teams is a threat to performance. Einstein teams often have to collaborate to complete projects. Managers who understand the dynamics of interteam conflict are better prepared to resolve problems. The "we" feeling within Einstein teams can be positive or negative. A certain degree of Einstein team cohesiveness can turn Einsteins into a smooth-operating unit. Too much cohesiveness ("we") can foster teamthink because members want to agree with each other. Because of the desire to get along, critical thinking is pushed into the team's background.

Increased team cohesiveness has been found to:

- Encourage teams to think of themselves as unique and view members on other teams as "not unique and similar to each other"
- Result in team members thinking they are more moral than any other team
- Exaggerate the difference between the team and other teams

The "we" thinking Einstein team occasionally engages in interteam conflict. The "we" versus them can become dysfunctional and detract from accomplishing desired goals. Einstein managers will not be able to eliminate strong cohesiveness in Einstein groups, but they need to address it when the "we" orientation hinders performance, creates ill will, or makes the firm less attractive to some members and job candidates. Managers are responsible for all the assets of an organization, not only the Einsteins they manage.

Managers, through their interactions with other Einstein team managers and team members, can display etiquette, manners, and positive attitudes. The positive style of an Einstein team manager is contagious and clearly illustrates how to work positively with others. Simple approach. Certainly it is, but the effectiveness of "showing how" should not be understated. Relentless efforts by Einstein managers to address interteam conflict is hard work and requires creative thinking, planning, plus cooperation with other Einstein team managers.

## *Encouraging Conflict*

Sometimes Einstein teams become bogged down in trivia, minutiae, and blind alleys, with nothing ever accomplished. Einstein managers can directly fan the flames of functional conflict. They can engage in what is called "programming conflict." Two methods available for stimulating conflict are the *devil's advocate* and the *dialectic method.*

An Einstein manager can assign one Einstein to serve as a devil's advocate, who is the assigned or designated critic, reviewer, or naysayer. For example, an Einstein team would come up with a new course of action. The devil's advocate is assigned and is expected to criticize the proposal. A good devil's advocate would generate debate within the team. In some cases the course of action may be modified or thrown out as a possibility.

Devil's advocates have to accept the role. They must be able to withstand the withering pressures, arguments, and attacks. In addition, the devil's advocate selected by the Einstein team manager must have strong analytical and communication skills. Astute managers pick strong Einsteins to serve in this role of stimulating conflict.

In the dialectic method, the Einstein manager frames and structures the debate. The conflict generated by this method depends on the skills and attitudes of the manager stimulating the debate. The manager is attempting to have the team explore various positions. Opposing positions require critical thinking and comparisons, which result in conflict. Through the dialectic method a final decision that has been discussed, debated, argued, and compared is eventually reached.

## Five Conflict-Handling Styles

Einstein managers have a number of styles that can be used to handle dysfunctional team conflict. Some managers are flexible enough to use one style in a situation and change to another style when faced with a different set of circumstances. The flexibility a manager possesses is personal and probably can't be easily taught in a training program. Managers, like most people, tend to use what they have become comfortable with in the past. There is no single best style. Each has its place when dealing with Einsteins, and each may be effective in a specific situation.

Exhibit 10.2 presents the five styles: problem solving, smoothing, forcing, avoiding, and compromising.

**Exhibit 10.2**
Five Einstein Manager Styles for Solving Conflict Situations

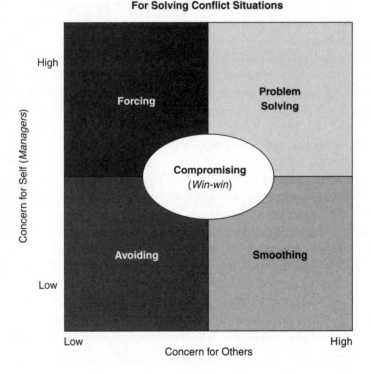

**Five Einstein Manager Styles
For Solving Conflict Situations**

A brief description of each style will illustrate the best time and place to incorporate the approach to handle Einstein-related conflict.

*Problem Solving*, in the ideal world, is the preferred choice of Einsteins and managers. In this style, the conflicted parties confront the issues and cooperatively work to solve them by selecting and implementing a solution. Einsteins are comfortable with this style, but because of personality and value clashes among Einsteins, this approach may exacerbate the problem or issue. This style takes time and patience on the part of Einstein managers: waiting for the parties to problem debate, problem analyze, and problem solve.

*Smoothing*. In this style, one person neglects his or her concerns to attempt to satisfy the other person. It involves playing down the differences and elevating the agreements. In complex circumstances, smoothing does not work well. The issues may be so interrelated and complex that reaching agreement is not possible. Smoothing also fails to confront the real problem. On the other hand, by giving up something of value to another person, it is likely that a more cooperative relationship will be built.

*Forcing* is a style of "I must win, you must lose." This style emphasizes a high concern for self. The other person is ignored. When a manager forces, he or she is using the position (manager on an organization chart) to force Einsteins to comply. If an unpopular decision is made, moving to a less preferred location, purchase of computer equipment that Einsteins do not like, or holding back on a decision to hire a software engineer who will be swept up by a competitor for later consideration, forcing may be the best style. On the other hand, in a participative Einstein climate, forcing can be resisted. The primary advantage of forcing is speed; its primary weakness is that it can breed lingering resentment.

*Avoiding* conflict by ignoring the problem may be suitable when time is needed. For example, the complexity of issues in making a decision to purchase a new computer system may warrant ignoring the feuding going on among individual Einsteins and Einstein teams. Buying time to weigh costs, benefits, issues, and different viewpoints may be what is needed. The primary weakness of the avoiding style is that it is only a temporary approach, for a decision will ultimately have to be made.

*Compromising*. A give-and-take style may be appropriate. If the conflicted individuals have the same power, authority, stature, and yet have opposite goals, the compromise style can be effective. The benefit of compromising is that the parties each take something away. One person or Einstein team doesn't get everything they want at the expense of the other person or team. However, compromise solutions can stifle creative problem solving because giving everyone something gets in the way of the "best" solution.

---

## Black Hole

### Don't Ignore Conflict

Every Einstein manager is tempted to ignore conflict within the Einstein team or between teams. Don't ignore dysfunctional conflict. You have a responsibility to act. Einsteins look to the manager for leadership. They have a right to expect help. When managers avoid conflict, they look weak, ineffective, and noncreative.

---

A variety of conflict in goals, cognition, affect, and procedures calls for management intervention to minimize or, in rare cases, eliminate dysfunctional conflict. The manager of Einsteins must be skilled at diagnosing, communicating, intervening (interpersonal), and negotiating. The ability to understand conflict, diagnose it, and take action is essential in managing Einsteins. Research can help managers weigh the advantages and disadvantages of styles. Managers should know that:

1. The smoothing style is more utilized than any other in high-performing teams and organizations. It doesn't always work well, however.

2. The smoothing style leaves more positive feelings than the other four styles.

3. The results of compromise are mixed.

4. The forcing style is the most resisted and resented approach.

5. The smoothing style has the highest chance of success when parity in power exists.

6. Forcing is the preferred style of managers who rely on command, control, and power to influence others.

In a perfect world, people would avoid conflict and handle any conflict that occurs positively. Organizational politics, human beings, supply and demand, limited resources, and poor managerial understanding of conflict get in the way. The perfect work world has never existed except for occasional brief moments.

# The Value Add of Managers

Einsteins have a need to personally grow while employed. There is no law that mandates that a firm or even its managers *must* care about and help Einsteins grow as individuals or team members. However, the high-performing organizations, those that are employers of choice for Einsteins, have managers who are champions of showing care for Einsteins at work and also away from work.

---

## Einstein Wisdom

The satisfaction of physical needs is indeed the indispensable precondition of a satisfactory existence, but in itself is not enough. In order to be content, individuals must also have the possibility of developing their intellectual and artistic powers to whatever extent aligns with their personal characteristics and abilities.

---

The added value Einstein managers can bring starts with a number of principles, including:

- Involvement through observation, diagnosis, discussion, and listening to what Einsteins prefer.
- Ignoring deep-seated conflict should never be accepted by an Einstein manager. He or she is responsible to intervene as soon as possible to minimize or eliminate conflict.
- Controlling the turnover of valued Einsteins must be a top priority that results in specific managerial intervention programs that are continuously monitored. Through intervention, the quality of life, working conditions, and growth of Einsteins can be improved to help reduce dysfunctional turnover (after all, the firm doesn't want to lose the employee.)
- There are no simple answers to improving the care and development of Einsteins. Whatever intervention is used requires creativity, time, and money.
- When managers can transmit their care for Einsteins, the results can be spectacular. Caring has to become a part of the organization's culture so that Einsteins are constantly reminded about how exceptional working for the firm is with regard to people.

Enlightened Einstein managers can differentiate themselves, add value to their organizations, and be a major part in caring for and helping Einsteins personally grow.

# Building for the Future

"I SEE SOMETHING! YES! BETTER KEEP YOUR EINSTEINS!"

## CHAPTER 11

# Humor and Fun at Work

## Preview Einstein Story

### Hum and Click Camp

Einstein talent identification, recruitment, and retention are a top priority in most companies. Talented Einsteins staying with a company is a prime source of sustained competitive advantage. Having fun at work is part of the mix and blend of activities that results in lower turnover, higher morale, and excellent performance. At Dell Computer, Vice President Theresa Garza calls the environment she works in and on a "hum." The notion of "hum" is the spirit, the lightness, the unbounded energy that we feel while at work. Garza believes that at Dell, in her team, there is a lot of "hum."

To get and sustain "hum," Garza works at having fun at work, laughing at herself and smiling. She has flung herself into Velcro walls and had Einsteins and non-Einsteins dunk her in a water tank. Garza has also belted out tunes in a stage skit, dressed up in humiliating outfits for laughs, and shot off a gun in a magician's show truck. She is an advocate of "hum," which is powered by fun and laughter.

Double Click uses fun the first day new hires arrive for a week-long orientation program called "Clickercamp." After coffee and pastries, the firm's CEO starts off with the customary words of wisdom. Before the week is over, the CEO and other managers have engaged the new hires in games of laser tag, have told jokes, eaten and drank together, and listened to music while relaxing. The orientation is all business, but laced with breaks and pauses for fun, laughter, and bonding. What Double Click believes is that building teams requires hard work, fun, and laughter.

Einsteins who laugh and have fun at work exhibit an important set of traits: laughing, smiling, and enjoying themselves. "Fun and laughing at work" shouldn't be an oxymoron. Study after study indicates direct and positive association between "fun" and productivity, creativity, morale, retention, and customer satisfaction. Yes, some fun can be transmitted through Einsteins and non-Einsteins to customers. Let's translate all of this quickly. If Einsteins have some laughs and fun at work, they see the environment as a place to be. This is exactly what Einstein managers want: a team that enjoys coming to work and working hard.

Even clinical psychologists are getting into the fun, laughter, and humor act as an adjunct to therapy. In fact, more clinicians have joined organizations. Medical experts clearly have demonstrated that laughter boosts the immune system, increasing natural disease-fighting killer cells and lowering blood pressure.

If Einstein managers can help Einsteins wear a smile, chuckle, or give off a few full-belly laughs, the work environment is going to be more enjoyable. The more enjoyment, the higher the morale and the better the performance.

## Learning from Kids

Watch a child while he or she is taking in *Snow White*, *101 Dalmatians*, or their first movie. The joy and smiles that come over their faces is exciting. Children have an ease with laughter, smiling, and enjoyment. This passion and ease somewhere along the way to adulthood becomes hidden or, at worst, lost forever. The excitement that children experience watching a cartoon character or funny movie needs to be remembered when considering "how to make working as Einsteins" more enjoyable. Creating an environment of fun at work is more than watching Roadrunner outrun the coyotes or blowing up colorful party balloons. Today's Einsteins first want to be respected, challenged, and kept informed. They expect to be rewarded fairly. But periodic breaks, pauses for fun, and some laughter is worth the manager's time, creativity, and consideration.

## A Few Fun Examples

High-performing organizations in which Einsteins are more likely to become long-timers have a knack of lightening up the surroundings and environment. A few examples can provide Einstein managers with some starter ideas.

**Have fun or get fired.**   Paradigm Communication of St. Petersburg, Florida, a software developer, has as its unofficial mission: "Have fun or get fired." Realizing that long hours, pressures, and stress are contributions to burnout, the owner pushes for a few laughs. The company's dress code and attendance policy is presented as follows: "Show up for work and wear something."

**Sleeping on the job.**   In one firm, if someone falls asleep in a management meeting, everyone else leaves the room. A group that was not present when the sleeper nodded off comes in quickly. Someone in the group says, "Bill"—assume this is the sleeper—"your plan is very risky. However, we are going to try it." Then everyone gets up and leaves the room. It is hard to do, but when it can be done, there are a lot of laughs that last a long time. The "Bills" usually laugh most at how they were caught and treated.

**Excuse bulletins.**   One firm keeps a bulletin board and an e-mail file of clever absence excuses. A few:

The dog ate my car keys. We're going to hitchhike to the vet.
I just found out that I was switched at birth. Legally, I shouldn't come
    to work because now my personnel file contains false information.
I've used all of my sick days this year . . . I'll have to use some from
    next year's quota.

**Manager of mirth.**   EDS in Buffalo, New York, annually gives a "Manager of Mirth Award." The criteria for winning are:

1. Created the Culture: leader appreciates, motivates, and inspires.

2. Knows Their People: leader gives creative, timely, and appropriate recognition.

3. Work Is Fun: leader finds ways to make serious work fun!

4. Together We're Better: leader values and fosters creativity and teamwork.

5. Sets the Example: leader has a high sense of self-esteem, is able to take themselves lightly, and thereby manages their stress more effectively.

**Warning sign.**   A little humor was posted in an e-mail circulated in a high-tech company in Austin, Texas. It read:

**Guard Against the Following**
*Prison versus Work Situation*

*In prison* you spend a majority of time in an 8 by 10 cell.
*At work* you spend your time in a 6 by 8 cubicle.

*In prison* you get three meals daily.
*At work* you get a break for your meal and you pay for it.

*In prison* you get time off for good behavior.
*At work* you get rewarded for good behavior with more work.

*In prison* you can watch TV and play games.
*At work* you get fired for watching TV and playing games.

*In prison* your family and friends can visit.
*At work* you can't even speak to your family and friends.

*In prison* all expenses are paid by taxpayers.
*At work* you pay all expenses to go to work and they deduct taxes from your pay to help pay prisoners.

*In prison* you can join many programs which you can leave at any time.
*At work* there are some programs you can never get out of.

*In prison* you have autocratic workers.
*At work* we have managers.

Where would you rather be?

**Toys for meetings.**   A number of firms use toys for people to handle while sitting in meetings. Some popular toys are Silly Putty, Koosh Balls, and Tinkertoys. As a way to relieve tension, handling glow-in-the-dark Silly Putty is fun for some people. Koosh Balls, a version with rubber-band-like loops, can be stretched, twisted, and whirled to keep the hands busy. Tinkertoys give some people a feeling of handling something they remember from childhood.

Here are six examples that suggest that fun is enjoyable and a part of the culture in some organizations. In a work environment that allows or expects fun, employees seem to have:

- Loads of energy
- A lot of smiling
- Greater self-esteem
- Enthusiasm that spreads to others
- Team spirit
- Positive attitudes

These signs and consequences of fun would fit in nicely with Einsteins. Fun is motivational because of the internal pleasure it creates. The physical nature and mechanisms of fun are usually not well-understood or considered by managers when evaluating whether or how humor and laughter can be injected into the environment.

# Humor and Fun to Combat Stress

Hans Selye, a pioneer medical researcher, defines stress as the rate of wear and tear on the body as it adapts to change or threat. Chronic exposure to long working hours, pressure to perform, time limits and deadlines, challenging problems to be solved, and managerial actions that are disliked, can lead to stress and then burnout for Einsteins. Finding humor, fun, and laughing freely with others can be an antidote for stress and burnout.

In the Middle Ages, humor referred to an energy that was thought to relate to an emotional state. It was assumed that this energy determined health and disposition. A sanguine humor was cheerful, while a choleric humor was angry and associated with bile. Today, humor is considered a quality of being laughable or comical, or a state of mind, mood, spirit. Humor then is flowing, involving basic characteristics as expressed in the body, emotions, and spirit.

The word *heal*, comes from the root word "haelen," which means to make the person whole. Bringing together the body, mind, and spirit is healing. Socrates commented:

> As it is not proper to cure the eyes without the head, nor the head without the body; so neither is it proper to cure the body without the soul.

## *Humor and Health*

Norman Cousins brought attention to the medical community of the effects of human laughter. He used both in his treatment to combat a disease he had, ankylosing spondylitis—an inflammation of nerve endings. Doctors gave him only one chance in 500 of recovering. Cousins believed that negative emotions had a negative impact on his health. He theorized that the experience of laughter could open him to feelings of hope, confidence, and love.

Cousins watched comedy films every day, especially Laurel and Hardy, *Candid Camera*, the Marx Brothers, and Abbott and Costello—

a 1940s and 1950s comedy teams. He laughed vigorously and freely. He believed that his laughter regimen enabled him to combat the pain of his disease. Cousins lived many more years than would have been predicted after being diagnosed with the nerve damaging disease. He spent the last twelve years of his life at UCLA Medical School in the Department of Behavioral Medicine, exploring the scientific proof of his theory.

### Humor and Laughter: The Body

Excessive negative stress has been shown to create unhealthy physiological changes. There is now scientific proof that laughter creates the opposite effect. Two researchers, Berk and Tan, have determined through controlled studies that the experience of laughter lowers serum cortisol levels and increases the ability of the immune system to fight off "bugs." This research is part of a field of study that has shown distinct relationships between emotions and the immune response as mediated by a person's neurological system.

Researchers at Harvard, San Diego, Ohio State, in Canada and England, have clearly displayed a mind-body connection. The emotions and moods we experience directly effect our immune system. A sense of humor allows a person to perceive and appreciate the incongruities and lack of fairness in life. The moments of joy and delight are positive emotions that trigger off neurochemical changes that appear to buffer some of the negative effects of excessive stress.

# Learning to Laugh

How does anyone learn to laugh? How can a person grasp a humorous perspective that can be so powerful in terms of the spirit, the mind, and the body? Laughing at yourself is not always easy. Often a person is so caught up in problem solving that finding or seeing humor is difficult. It can help if each Einstein team has some Einsteins who have a special flair for creating laughter. Perhaps even Einstein managers might have the special gift of humor.

Staying in touch with the "Doctor of Fun" that resides within yourself is easier said than done. The inner clown, the childlike freedom to laugh, has for many people been squelched by life experiences and life events. Researchers have found that children laugh about 400 times a day, while adults laugh maybe fifteen times a day. This is a dramatic gap that managers need to be aware of when considering how to make work and the environment of Einsteins fun.

## The Starting Point

Before Einstein managers put on Mickey Mouse ears and a clown nose, there must be some fundamental conditions in place at work:

- *Fairness*. Einsteins need to know they are working in a firm where fairness is the rule. Each Einstein must know that favoritism or bias is not tolerated. Managers, by being fair, consistent, and open, can achieve this type of condition.
- *Challenge*. Einsteins thrive on challenge. The work must be enriched and challenging before laughter can work its therapeutic magic on Einsteins.
- *Trust*. When Einsteins are accorded care and trust by others, they reciprocate. Managers need to take the issues of care and trust seriously. Being open and honest with Einsteins affirms their worth as intelligent and creative contributors.

Fairness, challenge, and trust are the starting point for working on the creation of fun at work. Einstein managers have a better chance of having fun work as a positive force in a culture that promotes, supports, and rewards these three fundamentals.

## Creating a Fun Environment

There are many ways in which Einstein managers can create a "fun" environment. First, the Einstein manager must value laughter, smiles, and humor. Starting with himself or herself, the manager needs to:

- Work at lightening up and smiling
- Plan some fun events
- Respond to fun with laughter

Humor and laughter result in positive energy, high self-esteem, and team spirit. Fun encourages and increases motivation. A few stories will illustrate firsthand how Einstein managers can contribute, plan, and sustain a fun environment.

- Music is fun tonic for many Einsteins. Researchers have found that when workers listen to music of their choice, their productivity improves, whether they are engaged in repetitive tasks or complex, analytical, or problem solving work. Also, listening to music allows employees to relax and behave enthusiastically when dealing with colleagues or customers.

• Amy's Ice Cream in Austin, Texas, started a late night tradition that clicked in right before closing. Instead of having angry service workers glowering at late arriving customers, Amy's began Wednesday night lock-ins. Customers still in the store at closing time were detained and not allowed to leave until they learned the time warp dance from the movie *The Rocky Horror Picture Show*. The result: happy store personnel, a lot of laughs carried over for days, and customers flocking to the store to be detained.

For organizations like Amy's Ice Cream, fun is a part of the overall strategy to get employees involved. Fun is a strategy tool that can be effectively used by Einstein managers to motivate Einsteins. Exhibit 11.1 points out reasons why Einstein managers should participate in creating a fun environment.

Earlier in the book we introduced Herb Kelleher, CEO of Southwest Airlines. He is the king of creating a fun environment. He is creative and sold on the value of fun. If Kelleher looked at Exhibit 11.1 (he hasn't), we believe he would wholeheartedly agree. Kelleher laughs at himself, helps others laugh, and gets his customers laughing. He has an impressive laugh-based résumé of achievements. Here are a few of Kelleher's laugh generators:

• He dressed in gold chains and a white jumpsuit, impersonated Elvis, and started a company meeting.
• One St. Patrick's Day, he dressed as a leprechaun and served coffee to passengers.
• He sang "Tea for Two" to his staff (off key) while wearing a bonnet and bloomers.

**Exhibit 11.1**
Did You Know That . . .

1. Fun relieves stress, strain, and burnout.
2. Fun improves communication.
3. Laughter has a healing ability.
4. Fun brings people together.
5. Fun eases conflict on teams and between individuals.
6. Fun creation is not very expensive to introduce.
7. Laughing energizes people.
8. Fun reduces boredom.
9. Fun results in being more considerate of others.

Kelleher creates an environment that is fun. His ability to laugh at himself is a lesson for Einstein managers to note: laughter and fun do indeed have value.

---

### Einstein Wisdom

When Albert Einstein was making the rounds of the speaker's circuit, he usually found himself eagerly longing to get back to his laboratory work. One night as they were driving to yet another rubber-chicken dinner, Einstein mentioned to his chauffeur (a man who somewhat resembled Einstein in looks and manner) that he was tired of speechmaking.

"I have an idea, boss," his chauffeur said. "I've heard you give this speech so many times. I'll bet I could give it for you."

Einstein laughed loudly and said, "Why not? Let's do it!"

When they arrived at the dinner, Einstein donned the chauffeur's cap and jacket and sat in the back of the room. The chauffeur gave a beautiful rendition of Einstein's speech and even answered a few questions expertly.

Then a supremely pompous professor asked an extremely esoteric question about antimatter formation, digressing here and there to let everyone in the audience know that he was nobody's fool.

Without missing a beat, the chauffeur fixed the professor with a steely stare and said, "Sir, the answer to that question is so simple that I will let my chauffeur, who is sitting in the back, answer it for me."

---

## Information and Fun

Einsteins are constantly communicating, sharing, sending information, and interpreting messages. Information is power in any organization. Communicating information effectively takes practice, attention, and the use of sound principles. It is important to share information in a timely fashion and to deliver it in a sensitive way. Using some fun guidelines can help Einsteins communicate more efficiently.

### The Newsletter

Some firms have an internal communication vehicle such as a newsletter. It may be circulated weekly, monthly, or quarterly in print and/or electronically. Including interesting, fun, and light information seems to draw more attention and readers. A few ways to increase the readership are:

- Crossword puzzles, mind teasers
- Jokes, cartoons, cyber characters
- Light events in colleagues' lives
- Review of local restaurants
- Funny stories that happened to customers, on a project, with a manager, to an Einstein or a team of Einsteins

The newsletter should certainly include other, more serious information. The best newsletters mix the more serious with the fun, and contain interesting writing, stories, and drawings.

A newsletter is a form of communication that can be read by everyone. It is a common reference point and a part of the organization's culture. Instead of allowing only serious communication to be transmitted, Einstein managers can lighten the atmosphere by supporting, being involved with, or using a well-done newsletter.

## Smiling

Yes, smiling is a powerful part of communication. Customers, colleagues, bosses, potential clients, alliance partners, and competitors generally respond more favorably to a person if he or she wears a legitimate smile. The smile works wonders in person or when using the telephone. People feel more comfortable communicating with a smiler than a frowner. Physicians often point out that it takes seventy-two muscles to frown and only fourteen to smile. An anonymous statement concisely captures the notion that smiling is a form of communication:

> Smiling is infectious, you catch it like the flu
> When someone smiled at me today,
> I started smiling too
> I passed around the corner, and
> Someone saw my grin.
> When he smiled I realized, I'd
> passed it on to him.
> I thought about that smile,
> Then I realized its worth.
> A single smile, just like mine,
> could travel around the earth.

So, if you feel a smile begin,

Don't leave it undetected.

Let's start an epidemic quick

and get the world infected.

## Electronic Communications

E-mail and voice mail are widely used forms of communications among Einsteins. Top Ten lists, Dilbert, and other forms of humor can be fun. The laughter, humor, and fun of electronic communication can reduce daily stress and tension. But the e-mails should be free of obscenities and offensive language. Using common sense about what is appropriate is what Einstein managers must encourage.

One manager leaves his voice mail messages in historical character, which can be funny. Imagine the Abraham Lincoln character leaving a voice message: "Four score and seven years ago, your budget for the new computer system was due." This idea can include Dick Tracy leaving a message: "I am investigating a case attempting to determine why my telephone and e-mail messages are not being returned. Lieutenant Data from the starship *Enterprise* might call with the information needed or requested."

The key to humor transmitted electronically is to ask if it is responsible. Does the receiver want to be a part of the humor connection, will it offend anyone on the receiving end, is it short and to the point, and is it really funny? The last issue is the toughest to answer because most people think they are really funny.

---

### Influence Tip

The smart leader of Einsteins understands that being in the right place at the right time is every bit as important as anything he or she brings to the position. If you can't laugh, smile, and be happy about your position and that everyone believes he or she can do it better, you don't deserve to be a leader. Smile, thinking about how fortunate you are to be working with Einsteins.

---

## Meetings and Fun

Talk about an oxymoron phrase, how about "meetings are fun"? How many hours do Einstein managers and Einsteins spend in meetings? Most would say "too many." Fun, laughter, and smiles can be a catalyst in meetings when used appropriately. It can relieve the booooor-ing tedium of sitting, talking, listening, and fidgeting. Einstein managers can enliven those long meetings with a few creative techniques. There is no one *best* technique, and the manager needs to have a good sense of timing about when to lighten it up, and some funny ideas to experiment with to breakup the boredom in meetings.

## Toys

Squirt guns, foam darts, zoom balls, basketball hoops, Nerf balls, and balsa airplanes can be introduced at meetings. Throwing around a Nerf ball appears to loosen up Einsteins who have been sitting around. It releases tension, creates smiles, and produces laughter. Kenner (401-431-8697, Pawtucket, Rhode Island), manufacturer of Nerf Arrow-storm, Nerf Sharpshooter, Nerf footballs and basketballs, and other toys has been pleasantly surprised at the thousands of annual company orders it receives.

One firm uses rubber bricks in meetings. If someone shows up late, the coworkers hurl rubber bricks as they come in to sit down. If someone says something inappropriate or boastful about themselves, they are hit with rubber bricks. Most people show up on time so they can be brick throwers.

## The Hat Trick

A number of companies have used Edward De Bono's book, *Six Thinking Hats*, in conducting meetings. The basic idea is that during a meeting participants don different color hats to represent how or what they are thinking at the moment. For example, an Einstein wearing a blue hat would be thinking or explaining the big picture or what is going to occur in the future (*Blue* Skying). The Einstein who puts on the black hat is now the team's devil's advocate. The red hat wearer is issuing a warning to the Einstein team, while the green hat signals upbeat, optimistic. The hats are passed around as individuals express different views. Some managers use a rule that everyone in the meeting must wear a different color hat at least once in each meeting.

## Skits

Acting out a skit during a meeting can have a powerful influence on the participants. Many people do not want to be laughed at or act silly. They consider it demeaning. By participating in a skit with others and having everyone laugh, a feeling of cohesiveness emerges. The energy in the meeting room is increased. Some skit advocates also suggest that the respect toward participants is noticeable and increased.

The skits can be built around a topic for the meeting, a continuing problem facing the Einsteins, or an issue that needs attention. Laughing, releasing energy, and having a little fun with the skit appears to make meetings more interesting.

# Recognition

Recognizing someone by name and accomplishment is a powerful motivational technique. Einstein managers need to put this at the top of their to-do list: recognize your Einsteins. When recognition of Einsteins is mixed with fun, it can become a memorable event. Adults need recognition as much as children do. Everyone has a need for acceptance, standing out occasionally, and being complimented. It reaffirms a person and builds self-confidence.

Einstein managers should know that if you want Einsteins to repeat outstanding performance, they should be recognized for it intermittently. Why intermittently? Because recognizing outstanding performance every time it occurs loses power; it becomes routine. If outstanding performance, creative ideas, or a project done well are important, then Einstein managers should recognize them periodically and have some fun. The fun of a recognition event can result in an energy boost for everyone.

A few of the more popular recognition gifts are presented in "Jack and Tom's Top-Ten Recognition Gifts" in Exhibit 11.2. Einsteins like little gifts that say "You are good" and "Thank you." The relatively inexpensive gifts are only a few of the many available that Einstein managers can use to recognize something special.

## *The Personal Note*

Jack Welch, CEO of General Electric (until the end of 2001, we think), is noted for his handwritten notes. He takes time to write a few sentences to recognize someone for an excellent presentation, a good written report, or some other behavior. The "Welch" notes are considered invaluable by recipients. Einstein managers are not Jack Welch, but a personal thank-you as a form of recognition is a pow-

**Exhibit 11.2**
Jack Ivancevich and Tom Duening Top Ten
Recognition Gifts

1. A dinner/lunch certificate to a popular restaurant
2. Clothing store gift certificate
3. Tickets to a concert
4. Books (or bookstore gift certificate)
5. Popcorn, nuts, fruit basket, or coffee/tea
6. Small desk clock with person's name
7. Pen and pencil desk set
8. Coffee/tea mug with person's name
9. Movie certificates
10. Tote bag, briefcase

erful morale builder. It communicates to the recipient that the Einstein manager cares. If the note includes some humor, it can also be cherished because it makes the Einstein smile or laugh.

Preparing humorous recognition notes takes time, but the consequences are worth the effort. Taking the time sends a message that everyone the Einstein knows will eventually hear. It says the Einstein manager is respectful, creative, and considerate. There is not a manager around who doesn't want to be associated with these attributes.

How many Einstein managers actually already write personal recognition notes? We have no way of accurately assessing this. However, if we assume that Einstein managers are like most other managers, the percentage is probably somewhere between 5 and 10 percent. Not very many managers appreciate the impact of a handwritten recognition note.

## *The Team*

Making awards and recognition a team event where colleagues you work closely with are involved is more memorable. Adding in some fun with the team can make it more memorable. Wells Fargo provides gift certificates to bank employees, who award them to colleagues of their choice for nice work, excellent attendance, good manners on the telephone, or being a good problem solver. This concept can be used in Einstein teams. Providing the teams once a month with a gift certificate ($50 to $100) to award the best team performer or most helpful team member would be an excellent form of recognition. Holding a special ceremony with music or snacks to award the certificate can even add some fun. The gift to an Einstein can be a way to say "Nice work" or "You're special," or "Thanks for the help," or "You are a creative genius." These are nice to get and can inspire Einsteins.

Pacific Bell created the "Gotcha" award, which is presented by anyone in the company to a colleague "caught" doing exceptional work. The certificate is just a token ($5 to $10), but everyone knows that it means "good work." The technique is to announce in front of others, when presenting a certificate, a loud "Gotcha." This signals a special person, who usually smiles for a long time because of the special and appreciated recognition.

# An Einstein Manager's Fun Kit

Hopefully by now Einstein managers know that humor and fun at work can be a performance booster and a useful approach to bonding team members. This section outlines briefly a number of things that Einstein managers can use to create fun.

### Fun Elements

Just as the artist has paint, brushes, a chair, and a canvas, Einstein managers need to develop a list of fun elements. These are things that can bring about smiles, laughs, fun, and lightness. Some of the elements are obvious, and some can be used for fun after thinking about their versatility. Exhibit 11.3 provides a starting kit for Einstein managers.

### Fun Ideas

There are numerous ideas that can be converted into laughs and humor. Here are few to consider:

- Taking laugh/job breaks—take five minutes to be devoted to non-work jokes, laughs, and smiles.
- Fun survey—ask people on the Einstein team what is fun to them. When did you have the most fun in the last few months? How can the company make work more fun? Who do you think is funny?
- Appoint a fun committee—organize a small group of Einsteins to generate ways to have fun at work. Let them plan a couple of fun events.

**Exhibit 11.3**
Potential Fun Elements

| | | |
|---|---|---|
| Balloons | Decorations | Marbles |
| Balls | Dolls | Movies/Video |
| Books | DoNuts | Paper Airplanes |
| Candy | Dunks | Ping-Pong |
| Cartoons | Excursions | Prints |
| Cards | Fake glasses | Rollerblade |
| Certificates | Films | Scrabble |
| Clown Noses | Flowers | Sing |
| Contest | Food | Sketch |
| Cookies | Games | Skits |
| Costume | Gifts | Snacks |
| Cups | Hats | Surprises |
| Dance | Helium | Toys |
| Darts | Lego | T-shirts |

- Participate in National Fun at Work Day—usually the day is April 1.
- Dress code contest—play with the dress code for one day. Have an "ugly pants" or "ugly hat" day. Award a prize to the winner.
- Guess the baby—have Einsteins bring baby pictures, place them in a common area, and let them guess who is this "baby"? Award a prize to the person guessing the best or the most babies.
- Develop an Einstein worklaw theme on the bulletin board—let Einstein team members post their own ideas in the form of "laws." A few examples (from *www.itstime.com/feb97a.htm*):

  *Murphy's Law of Thermodynamics*: things get worse under pressure.
  *Brook's Law*: adding manpower to a late software project makes it later.
  *Clarke's Third Law*: any sufficiently adorned technology is indistinguishable from magic.
  *90 Percent Rule of Project Schedules*: the first 90 percent of the task takes 10 percent of the time, and the last 10 percent takes the other 90 percent.

- Ping-Pong—table tennis is easily added to the work area. It's inexpensive, and most Einsteins can learn to play it adequately in a short period.

"SO ARE THE PARTY FAVORS MAKING WORK FUN?"

## Celebrations

Earlier, in Chapter 4, the importance of celebrations for Einstein team morale was presented. It is important enough to discuss celebrations again when examining how Einstein managers can inject fun into the work environment. Celebrations provide Einsteins with opportunities to look at positive events, situations, and behaviors. Einstein managers need to create events to celebrate; that is, they need to search for reasons to celebrate and involve all team members in the laughter, smiling, and fun. Celebrations can pop up for accomplishing a milestone, winning a new contract, anniversaries, birthdays, holidays, and even the end of the work week. (TGIF—thank goodness it's Friday.)

# The Einstein Managers' Fun Guide

Humor and fun are enjoyed by people around the world. The physical, emotional, and performance improvement benefits associated with fun are well-known, documented, and offer compelling evidence of positive outcomes achieved at work. Fun is simple—anyone can be involved. It doesn't require special training, or mandates from top executives ordering that everyone will have fun. A number of suggestions were offered to Einstein managers to perk up their imaginations and show that they are "fun" advocates. The following ten-step program is offered to Einstein managers for their consideration every day. Einstein managers need to fill out each of the ten steps to fit their approach, style, and situation. The sooner Einstein managers start with their own, tailored ten-step program, the sooner the benefits of humor, laughter, smiling, and fun will pay off.

## Einstein Manager Fun Now List

1. *You* are the master of fun. Use your imagination and come up with your own fun formula: $E = MC^2$

   E = Enjoyment at work

   M = Manager's commitment to create fun

   C = Creativity of manager in putting together fun opportunities

2. *You* serve as a fun role model. Lighten up, act silly once in a while, laugh at yourself.

3. Create a fun environment for Einsteins. Use colors, music, smiling faces, toys, Ping-Pong tables, wherever the item fits.

4. Find something funny in everything. Look at the difficult project, the lost contract, the computer crash, and find humor. You must be the fun detective, on the lookout for humor.

5. Be *spontaneous*. There is no right or wrong time to laugh. Whenever you feel like it, let fun flow. Use surprise to draw smiles and laughter.

6. Don't put off fun. Make fun a part of most daily activities. Putting if off for that special day six months from now is a fake. Live it up every single day.

7. Include all the Einstein team. Never exclude a single Einstein. The more, the funnier. Get every team member in on the laughs and joy.

8. *Smile, smile again, and smile some more.* Smiles are contagious. When Einstein managers smile, Einsteins also smile. Whenever you feel great or see an Einstein, start off the greeting with a smile. Einsteins enjoy seeing smiling faces.

9. Celebrate the day. Find excuses to celebrate and laugh. Once an Einstein manager gets on the celebration train, it will become a habit.

10. Work at becoming known as the Einstein Manager of Fun. It's a compliment and honor to be viewed and respected as being filled with fun, serving as a positive role model. There will be numerous reasons to frown, to put off fun, to grump around. Choose instead (you do have a choice) to have a fun-filled day in spite of the problems, setbacks, and events beyond your control.

---

## Black Hole

Unfortunately, too many Einstein managers do not have or show a sense of humor. Assuming that humor is not suited when conducting serious work is a mistake. The wise manager understands that laughter soothes tension and stress.

John F. Kennedy conducted the most serious business possible while serving as President. Whatever faults he possessed, one of his powerful strengths was his self-deprecating sense of humor. His press conferences, where he jousted with the White House press corps, still make memorable and fun viewing.

---

## CHAPTER 12

# Remote and International Einsteins

## Preview Story

### *Very Remote Einsteins*

It's 9:00 a.m., the start of another busy day, as Paolo Conconi logs on to read his e-mails. But instead of a business suit, he sports a bathing suit. And although his work is in Europe and China, his office is a table by the pool of his villa in Bali, Indonesia. As he goes through his mail, he sips his favorite Italian coffee. An attendant lights his cigarette.

Mr. Conconi has a lifestyle known as "extreme telecommuting"—work wholly unfettered by physical location. Pushing the promises of technology to the limit, this rare breed of telecommuters live countries— even continents—apart from their companies' home offices, indulging in a way of life others only dream about.

For American Greg LaMoshi, extreme telecommuting is the fulfillment of years of idle cubicle fantasies. Mr. LaMoshi works as the night editor for eRaider.com, a Manhattan-based financial website dedicated to corporate takeovers. He is not in Manhattan. Mr. LaMoshi makes his home along the shores of Bali, where there is roughly a twelve-hour time difference with New York. So, as night falls on New York, Mr. LaMoshi begins his overnight shift as the sun is rising in Bali, editing columns and message boards, and combing the Internet for new items. He often works from a garden terrace overlooking a water lily pond. Having long daydreamed of retirement on sunny beaches in an exotic locale, he says, "This was the opportunity to do all that, without the retire part."

Source: Kevin Voigt, "For 'Extreme Telecommuters,' Remote Work Means Really Remote," *Wall Street Journal*, January 31, 2001, B1, B7

As the new economy matures, fueled by information and driven by Einsteins, the "workplace" is no longer just a physical location. Increasingly, companies are evolving "virtual workplaces" where individuals can collaborate on projects free from time and space constraints. A new breed of remote Einsteins has emerged from the creation of the virtual workplace. The remote Einstein is rarely, if ever, seen in the office. Rather, remote Einsteins work anywhere, anytime. Frequently, the remote Einstein isn't even in the same country as his or her manager. This extreme remoteness presents greater challenges than the modern penchant for telecommuting. Telecommuting is typically a local phenomenon—developed primarily to eliminate long commutes. Telecommuting evolved primarily as an alternative to get the workers to work. The virtual workplace has evolved as an alternative to get work to the worker.

In this chapter we will be exploring the challenges of managing Einsteins in the virtual workplace. Many of these Einsteins will be from different cultures and different countries. Some may not even speak the same language as their Einstein managers. Some may never meet outside the virtual workplace. But of course they may be invaluable to the organization, no matter where they perform their work roles.

## Remote Einsteins

Before embarking on a thorough discussion of managing remote Einsteins, let's take a few moments to review the technologies that have created them. Remote work is still in its infancy. It is a by-product of the convergence of the World Wide Web and wireless telecommunications. No visionary big thinker ever sat back and decided to architect a virtual workplace. The virtual workplace is an evolutionary product. Thus, like all things evolutionary, it is riddled with inefficient systems and designs. Einstein managers should recognize these inefficiencies inherent in the virtual workplace.

The virtual workplace is based on the Internet. The file sharing and interactivity of the Web has made it possible for people to work together on projects no matter where they are, as long as they can connect to the Web. A fairly recent development is the use of corporate intranets or corporate portals for employees to collaborate on complex projects. As more employees become familiar and comfortable working online, the virtual workplace will continue to grow and evolve.

Some software firms have collaborated to build virtual workplace software. The intent is to deliver a set of project management, collaboration, and communication tools that allow employees and managers to share information, meet, and work without having to be together physically in the same location at the same time. Imagine the possibilities! How many times can you recall projects that have been delayed because you were unable to get key people together in the same room at the same time? The virtual workplace can minimize, and in some cases eliminate, this bottleneck.

The freedom engendered by the virtual workplace is becoming even greater as wireless technologies advance. Currently, remote Einsteins now must be able to at least plug in their computers to, preferably, high-speed Internet connections. The emergence of wireless technologies has enabled a new set of freedoms, untethered to any wires or need to "plug in." High bandwidth wireless connectivity has made it possible for the remote Einstein to work and contribute from literally anywhere.

Managing remote Einsteins requires many of the same strategies as working with Einsteins in a fixed physical setting. A deft managerial style with constant feedback on progress toward project goals is fundamental. Opportunities for input on project direction, and ability to demonstrate competence in their craft, is still essential for remote Einsteins.

Remote Einsteins are no less sensitive to the social and cultural environment than counterparts working on projects in the office. Einsteins have adapted themselves to remote work and feel no special need to be physically present to communicate. Einstein communications are generally direct and free of subtle nuances. Thus, they feel no sense of "loss" in being remote and removed from direct physical contact with others. The same pecking orders are established, rituals followed, and relationships established in the virtual workplace as in the physical one.

## Remote Control

Controlling the work of Einsteins from a remote location is not as difficult as might be imagined. There are plenty of software tools available to keep track of key productivity and profitability measures. The most difficult part of remote control will be ensuring that the proper data is uploaded into the system for tracking.

Einsteins are not predisposed to spending time entering information about their daily achievements. To the extent that the implemented system relies on individual Einsteins updating a log—whether online or offline—about their daily activities, you will have greater or lesser difficulty. Let's discuss the difficult task of getting Einsteins to enter this kind of information into a system.

Einstein managers should begin by making the data upload process as simple and straightforward as possible. Einsteins are smart, and they can understand a complex process. But if the process is more complicated than it should be, they will recognize it immediately and resent having to comply. A stupid process is made more stupid if it's also more complicated than necessary.

Managers should attempt to implement an online system to control remote Einsteins. There will be less resistance on the part of Einsteins to logging in their daily accomplishments if the system has a pleasant interface and appropriate prompts regarding the type of information required. An online system tells an Einstein that the data he or she is entering is wanted and, more, that it will be stored and *used*. If Einsteins are going to take time to provide regular project updates, they *must* be confident the information can and will be useful.

To close that loop, managers should ensure that there are no data collected that are irrelevant to organizational function and goals. If new data must be collected, explain to Einsteins why this information is needed and what it will be used for. *Do not* simply and suddenly require new reporting procedures without an explanation of why they are being implemented. Most important, *follow through* on what you stated you would do with the information.

Finally, there are Einsteins who, for whatever reason, simply don't comply with reporting procedures. They may be forgetful, or they may be belligerent, purposefully disruptive, or spiteful. Whatever the reason, they aren't providing managers with the information they need to control projects and allocate resources. What does the Einstein manager do now?

The first step is to get in touch with the remote Einstein and let them know that reports are due. That in itself will serve notice that, in fact, the system is being used. Often, this will be sufficient to overcome the problem. For this technique to work, the manager must state quickly that reporting problems exist. The Einstein manager must let the remote Einstein know that he or she is engaged and wants to keep track of progress.

If managers continue to experience difficulty receiving scheduled project updates from a remote Einstein, the next step is to pay a visit. A face-to-face meeting at the Einstein's location removes the sense of "remoteness" and can help reengage the individual with the organization's work requirements, reports, and processes. In fact, some Einsteins may prefer such periodic visits.

If visiting the remote Einstein still doesn't clear up reporting issues, the next step is to bring the remote Einstein to headquarters for a face-to-face meeting.

### Remote Motivation

How do Einstein managers keep the remote worker motivated? This is less of a challenge for Einsteins than it is for other types of workers. As we have pointed out, Einsteins have a high level of self-motivation. They are likely to put in the same effort whether they are thousands of miles away or within an arm's reach.

There are several key steps Einstein managers can take to ensure that their remote workers are motivated and satisfied. The most important thing is to make sure the remote Einsteins are outfitted with everything they need to "stay connected." Einsteins like the artifacts of the network age. They want to explore the functionality of the latest devices. Outfitting your remote Einsteins keeps them happy—they love the novelty—and it keeps them connected. Remember the equation: $E\text{-}MC^2$ Remote Einsteins are subject to the same forces as those working alongside managers. They want to communicate with their managers and, more important, with members of their virtual tribe. The new PDAs, Web-enabled phones, and other communication tools can easily replace the office environment as a source of motivation and satisfaction. The range of remote devices for staying in touch provides both maintenance and motivational factors. The basic tools, cell phones, and laptop computers are expected (maintenance factors). The Blackberry devices, PDAs, and other cool stuff are not always expected (motivational factors).

Of course, the most important element in keeping remote Einsteins motivated is to make sure they have an endless stream of challenging projects to work on. Just as managers engage Einsteins in the office about who should work on which projects, the same things should be done with those working remotely. The technology employed to manage remote Einsteins should include some communication and collaborative capabilities.

## Virtual Teams

Remote Einsteins don't only work alone, they also work in virtual teams. These are "cyber teams" that interact on the Web and rarely, if ever, come into physical contact with one another. Virtual teams have all the dynamic problems of real teams, with a few other, more challenging problems as well. Since we've discussed teams at length in Chapter 7, let's just focus on the unique challenges of virtual teams. The most pressing challenges of virtual teams that Einstein managers will face are:

- Establishing the pecking order
- Enabling tribal rituals

**Establishing the pecking order.** The term *pecking order* sounds petty and adolescent. We would like to preserve the meaning of the term—establishing a natural dominance hierarchy—while eliminating the sense of juvenile peer pressure. Einsteins routinely measure themselves in their craft by comparing their competence to other Einsteins.

Not only do Einsteins measure themselves this way, they place all others in their tribe on a continuum of best to worst. This dynamic hierarchy is unspoken, but is known by team members and among Einstein teams. Einsteins within a tribe normally have deep and subtle knowledge of each other's strengths and weaknesses in their craft. One's place in the pecking order is typically hard-won through performance on projects over a period of time where the other Einsteins in the tribe can observe and mentally record results.

Virtual teams typically don't have established pecking orders. They form and dissolve quickly, without allowing time for Einsteins to develop mental records of each other's skill levels. There is no way to completely overcome this deficiency of virtual teams. However, managers can and should take two steps to minimize the problem.

One step that can help establish the pecking order in virtual teams is to include a directory for team members to peruse. This should include biographical information on each team member. Members should be encouraged to keep their bios up-to-date, including a history of projects they have worked on for the firm (or other firms) and the role they played. They should also list their formal education, degrees and certificates, and employment history. Second, and importantly, they should list personal information—including leisure pursuits and interests. The directory helps encourage Einsteins to swap stories informally with one another on similar interests and experiences. While this will have little effect on the pecking order—which is determined primarily by results—it does help personalize the virtual team environment.

**Establishing tribal rituals.** Tribal rituals emerge naturally among Einsteins who work side by side in a physical location. These rituals serve to cement the bonds within the group, and helps preserve it during difficult stretches. Ritualistic behavior might include private names for supervisors in the corporate hierarchy, inside jokes about historical events in the tribe's past, or secret techniques for getting in a little play between grueling periods of work. Such rituals are typically private—intended for member participation only. No outsiders allowed.

In cyberspace, privacy is difficult to get and preserve. Online work forums, where people can go to work on projects together, aren't sufficiently private. Anyone using such a forum to cast off a ritualistic "inside joke" or refer to a superior using tribal slang might be called out by a snooping manager. On the Internet, no one knows if you're a dog—or a manager. Einsteins will not feel comfortable practicing private tribal rituals in a public forum—even a forum "protected" within the walls of the corporate intranet.

Without ritualistic behavior the tribe does not form strong bonds—it is little more than a work team. This is not a bad thing, but it does limit the level of effort you can extract. A tribe bonded by ritual and galvanized by a common mission will work on and on until tasks and projects are completed. The pressure to stay true to the tribe and not let it down compels individuals to contribute at levels they might not have thought possible. Teams, on the other hand, will not inspire as high a level of personal commitment. In general, people are motivated to contribute to team goals. This motivation is far less intense than that which drives individuals in tribes.

Managers must allow remote Einsteins to establish tribal bonds through private, ritualistic behavior. How? Several techniques can be used:

1. Enable instant messaging

2. Provide a "members only" online forum

3. Provide offline multiparty communication

Instant messaging has been made famous by America Online. Millions of kids around the world type furiously into the night as they chat online in real time with an unlimited number of "buddies" simultaneously. This technology enables people to talk one-to-one and one-to-many. It's private and between buddies. An instant messaging system could be included in a virtual workplace to allow individuals to "chat" with one another beyond the eyes of any possible lurking managers. With such a private channel, some ritualistic behaviors will arise.

A "members only" online forum is a good place for multiple parties to chat all at the same time. While instant messaging is one-to-one or one-to-many, an online forum can be either of these plus many-to-many. It's like an online cocktail lounge. The problem with a "members only" forum is that it cannot be absolutely secure, and it can leave a record. Although members need a password to enter, no one can be sure that someone outside the tribe—a prying manager, for instance—might not have access. Online forum conversations can also be stored and printed. Einsteins may be reluctant to practice ritualistic behaviors in a forum that might be recorded and later recovered for legal or other purposes.

To encourage Einsteins to practice ritualistic behavior in an online forum requires absolute privacy. The tribe itself should be placed in charge of the forum and password distribution. The sanctity of the forum should never be invaded without tribal permission. Any violation of this will jeopardize forever the future use of this tribal communication channel.

Perhaps the most reliable and trustworthy technique for enabling ritualistic behavior to emerge among remote Einsteins is through multiparty telecommunications. You have probably participated in conference calls yourself. You know how this works: everyone calls a number at a prearranged time and a "bridge" is established between all the callers. Now everyone can talk and rituals can emerge. To be effective, the multiparty calls must be regular and they must be easy to use. Technical glitches, hard-to-hear connections, or inadvertent disconnects will interrupt the free flow of conversation required to establish behavioral and linguistic rituals.

The power of this approach can be enhanced if remote Einsteins are outfitted with desktop video cameras that will allow them to see one another. Voice-over-IP is not reliable enough yet to allow free-flowing conversation, but the video quality over the Internet with the telephone-based voice communication can be a powerful combination. To even greater effect, instant messaging can also occur simultaneous to the voice-over-phone and video-over-IP. This complete and private communication network among remote Einsteins will allow them to build the tribal bonds that can promote incredible levels of effort on projects.

## International Einsteins

With the exceedingly tight Einstein labor market, many firms have turned to international regions for sources of talent. Indeed, there are certain pockets of the world—India, for example—where there is an abundance of fresh new Einsteins. Finding, recruiting, retaining, and leading those workers presents a wide range of new challenges. These include:

1. Cultural Barriers

2. Language Barriers

3. Ethical Barriers

---

### Einstein Wisdom

*More Jobs and Work Moving Overseas*

As the century progresses, the migration of white-collar jobs around the globe will force managers to become far more accustomed to virtual corporations. Millions of clerical workers in developed industrial countries will have to retrain themselves as jobs shift to other locations. The good news is that corporations will have access to much wider talent pools. But companies will have to groom cosmopolitan managers—equally at home in Madras and Manhattan.

Companies are seeking workers to take jobs ranging from basic clerical, accounting, customer support, and legal services, to software design, scientific research, and pharmaceutical development. "This is a huge transformation—much bigger than what happened in the blue-collar world," says management guru Tom Peters. He estimates that as many as 90 percent of today's American white-collar and clerical jobs could be outsourced over the next ten to fifteen years.

From: Mark Clifford, Manjeet Kripalani, and Heidi Dawley, "Different Countries, Adjoining Cubicles," *Business Week Online*, August 28, 2000

---

### Cultural Barriers

Despite great similarities across cultures, there are vast differences as well. An Einstein in India, for example, might perceive a corporate cell phone as a maintenance factor, whereas an Einstein in China may regard a cell phone as a motivational factor. The difference is part cultural and part environmental. India is now well-regarded for its high-tech workforce. China is just beginning to be recognized.

Sensitivity to the practices and rituals of the foreign culture is very important. International Einsteins usually make their cultural rituals a part of their work life. Attempting to separate work and projects from the practice of cultural rituals will be met with resistance and hostility. The smart manager will be aware of the type of rituals international Einsteins practice, their timing, and their meaning. Accommodations especially designed for maintaining ritualistic practices will be recognized, appreciated, and rewarded with loyal effort and productivity.

Nothing can substitute for firsthand experience in dealing with international Einsteins working in international settings. Deep understanding of a culture and its effects on worker attitudes and behaviors can only occur over time through direct experience. Managers of remote international Einsteins should endeavor to spend ample time at the remote site living and working with the team. The purpose of this is not to "become one of them," but rather, to better understand the challenges local managers must face in meeting objectives, deadlines, and goals handed down from headquarters.

## Language Barriers

Managers of international Einsteins will often encounter language barriers. This can be very disconcerting at first. Managers who have not previously led employees who spoke another language will feel disempowered by this barrier. Direct communication beyond rudimentary gestures or facial expressions is impossible. When language barriers are present, all communication requires the intervention of translators. Translators are third parties to the communication process. Effectively managing language barriers with international Einsteins involves getting used to and comfortable with translators.

Due to translation process problems, there is a need for unique checks and balances when breaching language barriers. It would be wise, for example, to use one translator to deliver your messages to your international Einsteins, and a different one for their feedback to you. This will give Einstein managers a clearer picture of the message their Einsteins received than by having the same translator do both jobs. Another important technique is to have more frequent project updates from international Einsteins. Frequent project updates, at least in the early stages of a project, will help ensure that your project is on the right track.

A final comment about language barriers is to watch the emerging translation software. This technology is making rapid progress and will in the near future eliminate the need for translating, allowing direct (albeit, computer mediated) communication with international Einsteins who don't speak your language.

## Ethical Barriers

Ethical barriers also pose difficulties when working with international Einsteins. Einstein managers unfamiliar with the customs and norms of foreign cultures may be ethically challenged by practices encountered. For example, many cultures consider bribery and influence peddling to be a natural part of doing business. An Einstein manager who encounters this for the first time may do the right thing and refuse the bribe, but he or she may afterward not trust the individual who offered it. *This* would be a mistake.

---

### Influence Tip

*Employee Loyalty Around the Globe*

A global study conducted by Walker Information Global Network and the Hudson Institute asked more than 9,700 full- and part-time employees around the globe what makes them loyal to a company. The study included employees from thirty-two countries and regions as varied as the United States, Bolivia, Finland, and Hong Kong. The conclusion: the cultural differences that we observe in cuisine, clothing, and sport as we travel around the globe should not be confused with differences in workforce issues.

The study confirms the useful cliché that people are people wherever they live, and that most people care deeply about the same few things. In the workplace, people everywhere ask, "Am I fairly compensated for my work?" "Am I well suited for my work?" "Does my employer trust me to do that work?"

The study found that employees who perceive their company as ethical are more likely to be proud to be associated with the company. Fully one-third of the worldwide employees studied do not believe their organization is highly ethical, and only 60 percent believe that their senior managers are people of high personal integrity.

From: Katherine J. Sweetman, "Employee Loyalty Around the Globe," *MIT Sloan Management Review*, Winter 2001, 16

---

Overcoming ethical barriers *doesn't* mean that managers should adopt the ethics and ways of the cultures in which your international Einsteins reside. It *does* mean learning to live with the differences in a nonjudgmental way. International Einsteins will not accept foreign managers preaching to them about their ethical norms. *They* will respect you if *you* respect their uniqueness.

At the same time, Einstein managers should never compromise their own ethics to do business in a foreign country. If an Einstein manager works with an existing foreign company, they should do the necessary due diligence ahead of time on their business practices. If they are doing something that is ethically wrong (child labor, for example), then don't work with them. It is a mistake to think that you will change their practices after the contract is signed. Time is too short, and the difficulty too great, to change ethical practices from afar. It simply can't be done.

Often it is useful for Einstein managers to set up a foreign office of their own and recruit local workers to staff it. If managers do this, they can follow your company's ethical norms in setting the policies and procedures of the remote office. Nonetheless, the individuals recruited will not share the manager's ethics completely. Einstein managers must design the foreign office in a manner that doesn't unduly constrain individuals from practicing their own ethical principles. For example, in Moslem countries many faithful individuals require breaks throughout the day for prayer. It would be unwise and unduly restrictive to establish office policies that forbade this activity. Einstein managers can lessen the instances of conflicts of this type from occurring by developing an understanding of the varieties of ethical norms among the pool of people they will be recruiting.

## Where Are the International Einsteins?

Firms are struggling to find new pockets of untapped Einstein talent all over the world. There is a rich vein of Einstein talent in India. Software firms, engineering firms, and even manufacturers have rushed to India to mine this wealth of talent. Some enlist Indian recruiters to scour the universities, which are turning out Einsteins in large numbers. Others set up shop in India and do the searching and recruiting themselves. More often than not, firms are able to find the talent they need at a price that is less than domestic talent. Of course, the added costs of conducting a foreign recruiting effort can offset lower labor costs. However, firms that hire a lot of Indian Einsteins will save money.

But India is not the only source of international Einsteins. Large populations of Einsteins abound in Southeast Asia, including Taiwan, Hong Kong, Thailand, Vietnam, and China. Fresh talent also is untapped in many of the former Soviet Republics. Little known places such as Estonia, Latvia, and Belarus are home to Einsteins who were trained in the premier Soviet academies and now are underemployed in their struggling countries. The educational programs of the leading Soviet (now Russian) academies are among the best in the world in the sciences and engineering. Top graduates of these programs have achieved and innovated on the same scale as top-flight American scientists and engineers, and they have done so with fewer resources. Many companies have opened plants in the Baltic countries to take advantage of this underutilized talent. Many have stepped away due to the uncertain political and economic environment. If you can stand the state of flux these countries are in, you will find hardworking, intelligent Einsteins ready and eager to join your firm.

The Middle East has also earned a reputation for talented Einsteins. Israel, in particular, has turned out a number of innovative high-tech ventures in the past few years. Looking beyond the Mediterranean, Ireland has its share of Einstein factories. Surprisingly, Ice-

"SO THAT'S WHY PEOPLE ASK ME ABOUT ASIA? NO WONDER! I'M NOT FROM INDIA, I'M FROM INDIANA!"

land and Finland also have high-tech cultures that breed a stable supply of Einsteins.

Latin America has some rich sources of Einsteins. Leading academic institutions in Brazil and Mexico, in particular, have been hot spots. Outside of these countries, the supply of Einsteins does not exceed local demand. Recruiting in markets where local jobs are easy to find is expensive and difficult.

Managed effectively, remote and international Einsteins can be an important source of labor and competitive advantage. Organizations large and small should learn to tap this vast reserve of talent that is eager to contribute.

## A Final Comment

Remote and international Einsteins will become more of a reality facing many managers. Technology advances will be adopted by Einsteins and adapted to fit their most comfortable surroundings. Einsteins preferring to work away from fixed work sites will present challenges to managers in terms of establishing project goals, monitoring progress, reviewing and rewarding performance, and creating loyalty bonds. These and many other challenges will need to be addressed if the talents of remote and international Einsteins are to be optimized.

CHAPTER 13

# Managing, Leading, and Facilitating Einsteins

## Preview Einstein Story
*The Real World*

In reality, the world of managing, leading, and facilitating Einsteins for a non-Einstein is like Alice's experience and story in Wonderland. Alice played croquet under the command and direction of the Red Queen. We read in *Alice's Adventures in Wonderland* that when the Red Queen shouted, "Get to your places," there was confusion, chaos, and bewilderment. After a few minutes Alice found that the croquet ground was full of holes and furrows; the mallets were live flamingos; the balls were live hedgehogs; and soldiers formed the hoops by bending at the waist and touching the ground.

Alice's first difficulty was in handling her mallet (the flamingo). Twisting, turning, and tracking required agility, adaption, and creativity from Alice. The hedgehog, instead of sitting still, moved around. When Alice took aim, a furrow was in the way. The soldiers got tired and moved, and the hoops they were supposed to form were not there. Mallets shaking, balls moving, ground holes; and walking around, standing erect hoops. Alice soon realized that croquet was a very difficult game; little productivity, limited control, and constant changes. This is just like what faces the Einstein manager.

Flamingos, hedgehogs, furrows, and soldiers are not a part of the Einstein managers' work world, but uncertainty, challenges, diversity, surprise, and the need to be flexible, agile, creative, patient, and motivated to learn are realities. Single, one-best solutions are just not pos-

*Continued*

216

sible in the real world of Einsteins. The future awaits managers who can embrace and utilize the intelligence, skills, talents, styles, and personalities of Einsteins. The realm of nurturing and developing Einsteins is within the grasp of what we refer to as managers (M), leaders (L), and facilitators (F).

The infrastructure of labor markets has shifted dramatically in the past two decades. Service-oriented firms that need to find, attract, retain, and motivate exceptionally talented Einsteins now dominate the labor market. Of course, industrial manufacturing firms, now in the minority as well, have a need for Einsteins to work on technology and to keep productivity racing ahead.

There are likely to be blips in labor market supply and demand as the economy forges ahead, dips, or falls back. In this book, we've discussed the management, leading, and facilitating of Einsteins in the twenty-first century. The challenge and actions required of Einstein managers fill each chapter. At this point you know that perfect, right answers to managing, leading, and facilitating Einsteins are not available. Among the points we've made:

- Referring to super-intelligent, curious, passionate, often introverted, talented individuals as "geeks" is outdated. Although Einsteins can call colleagues "geeks," it is not appropriate or cool for non-Einsteins to refer to computer, technology, systems, and software geniuses as geeks.
- Einsteins are super intelligent and very diverse.
- Einsteins identify with their craft.
- Einstein talent is needed, difficult to find, and hard to hold on to.
- Einsteins love freedom, autonomy, problem solving, excellent colleagues, supportive, and facilitative non-Einstein managers, being treated fairly, laughter and fun, and talking in their own tribal slang and language.
- Einsteins dislike formality, rigid policies, uninformed and noncommunicative managers, oppressive authority, worrying about issues involving etiquette and manners, and individuals (like presidents or bosses) who threaten to fire them.
- Einsteins occasionally need to be disciplined, and some also have to be fired. Doing these difficult tasks correctly, tactfully, and with sincerity is the only way to manage and lead them.

- Not all managers rise to the level of being leaders of Einsteins. The Einstein leader pantheon is reserved for those special people who have created a relationship of trust, respect, and commitment through action.
- Not all Einsteins are Americans. There are international Einsteins working throughout the world and in the United States. Their backgrounds and experience may be different than their American counterparts, but their intelligence and personality profiles are similar as well as their connection to their craft.

In this final chapter, we offer advice, suggestions, and proven recommendations to Einstein managers. We hope that what is offered ties the book's chapters together, offers useful guidelines that can be returned to again and again as reminders, and that you commit to at least some of the guidelines. The Einstein manager already realizes that Einsteins are like no other group they work with and attempt to lead. Einsteins are truly the first free agents in the new economy. They will go, move, and gravitate toward opportunities, challenges, and problems that they're fascinated with and interested in solving.

The free agent, free-thinking, open-minded, talented Einstein is a central figure in the new economy. Einsteins are self-confident, entrepreneurial, computer and technology literate, skilled, curious, innovative, and not impressed with hierarchically imposed authority. These characteristics mean that Einsteins possess a certain amount of negotiating power and attractiveness, which requires clever management and a blend of solid leadership and facilitation. The recommendations we provided on the roles of Einstein managers are a starting point in managing, leading, and facilitating the work, careers, and worklife balance of Einsteins. The emphasis is on the words *starting point*. Some of these suggestions are obvious, while others may be counterintuitive.

## The Roles of Einstein Managers

Even a quick look at the business landscape finds changes happening at breakneck speed. Although Einsteins are free thinkers and free agents, experienced managers are needed more than ever. The manager needs to help, facilitate, and support each Einstein so that his or her intelligence and talent can be channeled into performance. The manager plays a vital facilitation role.

A facilitator (Einstein manager) helps others complete their work, improve the way they work as a team, and personally grow and develop.

"DON'T WORRY ABOUT TAKING RISKS. I'M READY TO STICK OUT MY NECK FOR YOU!"

Facilitators help Einsteins make the connection between the quality of their work, the way they treat each other, and their own personal growth.

In the context of Einsteins' work assignments, tasks, and projects, managers must manage, lead, and facilitate. This MLF trifecta is the ideal to remember. *Managing* means to be concerned with doing the work right. *Leading* means focusing on doing the right thing. *Facilitating* means helping, supporting, and encouraging.

In offering the remaining guidelines the thinking should reflect back on the MLF concepts: managing, leading, and facilitating. The ideal person working as a representative of the organization's administrative team is hopefully a MLF in the eyes of Einsteins.

## Observing and Asking

MLF results are not possible if you do not know your Einsteins. Observing them at work, in recreation, and in other settings is a step in learning how to cope and support Einsteins. Asking and listening are skills that the MLF must perfect. Many individuals are afraid to ask Einsteins about themselves. This fear results in not probing or asking about their likes and dislikes, career plans, impressions. Some managers use the time excuse to get out of asking: "I don't have time." Not asking, and guessing instead, is short-sighted, and failing to work effectively with Einsteins because of a lack of knowledge about them is the likely result. By observing Einsteins and asking questions, a manager will also have an emotional impact, conveying to Einsteins: "This manager must care about me." Asking employees in general why they like working for a particular company usually results in comments about:

- Meaningful work and making a difference
- Being a part of a great team
- Career opportunities and personal growth
- Autonomy and a sense of control
- Fun on the job
- Fair pay and benefits
- Pride in the firm
- Flexibility on work schedules and dress codes

Whether these reasons fit Einsteins is an individual and organizational issue. Asking Einsteins what they like and dislike, want or prefer, from their work is the starting point of the education of a person performing the MLF role. Answers to the questions will provide the MLF with information to develop the appropriate work environment, career path, and future discussions.

## The Respect Imperative

An MLF cannot respect and honor Einsteins unless he or she values the differences in people. Einsteins come in "thirty-one flavors." Most effective MLFs accept the notion that diversity of Einstein talent and perspective strengthens the team and adds to results. The problem sometimes is that tolerating and valuing differences is difficult. We tend to place a premium on "similar to me thinking." That is, if Einsteins are "similar to me" in religion, size, age, political attitudes, likes and dislikes, etc., we rate them higher, prefer their company, and are comfortable with them. It's important for MLFs to recognize their "similar to me" bias and prejudices.

## Think in Terms of Work

In the old economy, most organizations hired full-time employees to complete a job. The individual tasks to be completed were specified in tightly written job descriptions. Today, Einstein managers should think more in terms of completing work or projects. The work may require flextime, part-time, or as remote Einsteins. The fixed, full-time, job-centered model has yielded to numerous work arrangement models. Flexibility by Einstein managers in staffing is the preferred approach.

Einstein managers need to assess the work: exactly which tasks, responsibilities, and projects need to be done, and when. Then the question is: How can I assemble and motivate the Einstein team needed to complete the work? The Einstein manager might have to creatively put together full-timers, part-timers, remote workers, and outsourced personnel. Harold Leavitt, a Stanford professor, calls the new era of a mixed or blended group of Einsteins a "hot group." The group completes the work, and then parts of it are disbanded and a new "hot group" is created. This type of work-based staffing is more complex and requires a more difficult MLF set of competencies than existed under the rigid, job-centered approach.

## Enrich the Work

When work becomes ho-hum for Einsteins, they begin to look around for other positions and opportunities. By definition, Einsteins are creative, energetic, curious, and intelligent. They need stimulating work, opportunities for growth, and challenges. If and when Einsteins find that the work no longer provides these necessities, they will conclude that they have outgrown the challenge.

There are many Einsteins who suffer work discontent yet remain in their present position. Instead of leaving, they find ways to disengage psychologically. This shows up in increased absenteeism, daydreaming, and merely average performance. Disengagement, like departure, means a loss of Einstein talent. Einstein managers need to be alert to pick up signs of discontent, which involves asking, observing, and listening.

One approach MLFs have at their disposal is work enrichment. Restructuring, reengineering, or redesigning work to eliminate or diminish discontent requires creativity from Einstein managers. The creativity starts by determining what work features Einsteins feel can and should be enriched. Rotating assignments, combining tasks, providing more feedback, and expanding the autonomy and freedom to make decisions are possible enrichment steps.

## The Right Fit

Einstein managers have to find the right Einsteins to do the necessary work. Finding a good fit is tricky. A first step is identifying what skills, interests, and talent is needed to complete the work effectively. Second, the hired Einstein has to fit the team's culture. Finally, the hired Einstein must fit the overall organizational culture.

In assessing an Einstein's fit, remember that he or she is also conducting a "do I fit here" analysis. Einstein managers have to assess the fit and sell the work, team, and organization at the same time. Knowing the work, Einstein team, and organization will make the selling role easier, more accurate, and more convincing.

One firm, after several years of unsuccessful recruiting of Einsteins, concluded that its managers were not selling the firm. The Einstein managers were reluctant to brag about the organization. Once they provided realistic work previews and told the real company story with passion, the Einstein recruitment success rate took off.

In preparing for the right fit, Einstein managers, like anyone, must guard against the "similar to me" bias. Right fit doesn't mean that the Einstein looks, acts, and talks like the recruiter. Managers need to pause, look at the work, team, and organization, and recruit who is right for the mix.

## *The Rules Barrier*

Many managers are afraid to tamper with rules. When Einsteins come up with new ideas, concepts, or rule benders, they would like to hear an occasional, "Let's try it" or "That could work." They want to be thought of as innovative, and they want some Einstein manager support. The odds of keeping skilled and talented Einsteins are higher if on some occasions a rule (not a law) is tweaked or modified.

Questioning rules started thousands of years ago. In the twentieth century a few who questioned the rules were:

- The Wright Brothers. Why can't we fly?
- Fred Smith (Federal Express). Why can't we deliver packages anywhere in the world overnight?
- Mark McGwire (St. Louis Cardinals). Why can't I break Roger Maris's sixty-one home run record?

Einstein managers will be constantly tested by Einsteins regarding rules. If the manager is always rigid, Einsteins will be less inclined to ask questions, will not consider the workplace open to new ideas, and will be less enthusiastic about the work. Rules and questions are continuously evaluated. Some of the breakthroughs on rules include:

- Casual dress codes
- Maternity leaves

- Child-care centers
- Flextime
- Telecommuting
- Employee ownership
- Stock options
- Contests at work

Rules, policies, and guidelines are needed to bring some order and stability to the team or firm. However, in some cases rules become barriers or shortcut answers for "no we can't do that—it's the rule." Rules need to be reexamined, occasionally modified, and sometimes discarded. If Einsteins are bogged down in rules, it detracts from their performance. Loosen up a little and enjoy the energy this will create among the Einstein team.

## Recognize Einsteins

Rosabeth Moss Kanter, author and management consultant, stated it correctly: "Compensation is a right, recognition is a gift." Recognition works for everyone.

- *Publicly*. Recognize an Einstein in the presence of other Einsteins.
- *Impromptu*. Catch Einsteins doing exceptional performance and recognize them immediately.
- *Pinpoint*. Recognize exceptional performance by pointing out exactly what is exceptional. Say it in detail and link the recognition to a specific achievement.

Don't assume that more money is the preferred recognition. Again, individual differences among Einsteins exist. Einstein managers have to develop recognition programs that fit Einstein needs and preferences. Also, remember that needs and preferences change over time, so do not assume that what was desired last year is the same this year.

---

### Influence Tip

Although, some Einstein managers believe that money is the primary way to keep Einsteins, it isn't. The match between Einsteins' values and the organization's values is a more powerful factor by far. It is your responsibility to determine these values by inquiring, listening, and discussing. Once this is done, Einstein managers must then help Einsteins acquire what they value.

---

## Space

Dilbert, the cartoon character, constantly depicts managers as control freaks who give their subordinates no choice of space (the cubicle crunch) or overwork flow. Space can be a physical element or a psychological factor.

The physical element refers to the work environment and includes the work area, the dress code, or the location (e.g., at work or at home). The psychological factor includes the autonomy to experiment with new approaches, managing a schedule on time, or working free of close supervision or oversight. Einstein managers can make various adjustments to allow Einsteins more psychological space.

Homes, offices, and cubicles can be designed, decorated, and arranged to reflect personal preferences. In many organizations, preferences are controlled by having no room for personal touches. This rigid space and design control leaves little freedom or choice for Einsteins. There is no evidence that perfect uniformity improves performance. On the other hand, research shows that Einsteins given some freedom of physical space and design choice have higher morale and more work satisfaction.

Space to dress as preferred must be buffered somewhat. Meeting customers barefooted or with no shirt on is not going to be permitted in most firms. Concerning dress, common sense and consideration of others should be the guideline. Microsoft has no dress code in many departments, and the productivity and commitment to the firm have become legendary. Allowing workers to dress as they wish is a small concession. Communicating the dress code, if any, should be made to the applicant at the time of recruitment. Being casual, using common sense, are reasonable guidelines that most Einsteins can live with, especially if they know the expectations before joining a firm.

## Being Honest

Einsteins prefer honest feedback, comments, and communication from their MLFs. They want to hear the truth about their performance, and about the firm's plans, financial performance, and career opportunities. Truthful, tactful feedback and communication to Einsteins will enhance the stature and respect of Einstein managers. Being honest and direct in pointing out successes, failures, disappointments, enthusiasm, and achievements is appreciated. Of course, it is more difficult to point out areas in which improvement is needed. But negative feedback, when performance or behavior is not up to par, must also be delivered by Einstein managers.

Einsteins want to continually know how they are doing. Research from the Center for Creative Leadership determined that lack of honest feedback is a major reason for poor managerial performance. Even the superstar Einstein performers need honest and truthful feedback. In fact, lack of honest feedback stunts the growth and development of Einsteins. MLFs have a responsibility to help their Einsteins progress. Without honest feedback, Einsteins can develop major blind spots about their performance.

Einsteins also need to know how the organization is doing. They want to be trusted with the facts of market, product, and financial performance. Informing them results in more trust in managers, and more trust in return from the managers to Einsteins. It is a powerful trust cycle.

There are situations when sharing information about a merger, a firing, or a security breach is not advised. In these few sensitive cases, holding back is acceptable. However, it is not acceptable to hold back poor financial information in order to retain Einsteins until improvement occurs, which may not happen. This is a devious reason for holding back information. It is difficult when the truth is bad news. However, research indicates that satisfied, trusted Einsteins in the know are productive. When bad news is available, share it, and as a manager you will find your respect and trust ratings increase.

Ideally, Einstein managers should, through example, build a culture and work environment in which Einsteins can handle the truth about themselves. And MLFs should also encourage feedback about their own performance. The truth and honesty of feedback flowing in all directions creates a healthy, trusting, developing, and loyalty-centered organization. Einsteins working in this kind of organization are committed to staying around, to enjoy this special kind of energy.

## The Time Factor

As an Einstein manager, try this exercise. On the left-hand side of a piece of paper, list in descending order the names of your best performing Einsteins, starting with the best at the top. On the right hand side, list the names of your Einstein team in descending order in terms of the time you spend with them, the first name being the Einstein with whom you spend the most time. Now connect the left side name with the same name on the right side. Do the lines cross? Usually, they do. Einstein managers often spend the most time with their least productive team members. Intuitively, this seems like the right way to practice MLF. The common assumption is that superstar Einsteins don't need management, leadership, or facilitation. However, research indicates that this is not the most effective allocation of time. The most effective MLFs have pages with horizontal lines. They spend the most time with their superstars.

Great Einstein managers are in favor of fairness to all members of the team. This means treating members as they deserve to be treated. Every Einstein, including the superstars, wants attention and recognition. Spending the most time with the best communicates to others that performance is the "attention getter," the sine qua non of MLF. Telling your best Einsteins that they are super, telling the truth about their importance, and praising them often is invaluable. Don't assume that your best Einsteins already know about their talent and value to the team and organization, and the trust you place in them. They may sense these things, but telling them and showing them through giving them your time is what's needed.

Another value of spending the most time with superstar Einsteins is that you will learn more from the best Einsteins than from the average team members. MLFs learn why something works, how to improve or enrich the work, what barriers block progress of the team, and how to meet and set deadlines, goals, and requests. Being around and observing excellence in performance creates within an Einstein manager a new "gold standard" of what he or she should expect from Einsteins. This new gold standard can then be used in recruiting new Einstein team talent, evaluating current team members, and creating applied motivational approaches that work effectively.

## Career Path Options

Einstein managers have to creatively work with Einsteins on their career path questions, concerns, and needs. The reality of the talent wars for Einsteins means that MLFs must be aware of their team members' career path expectations. The career paths for Einsteins are unlimited, but they can benefit from guidance and wisdom offered by knowledgeable MLFs. Einsteins want interesting, meaningful, and challenging work. They are willing to work hard and long hours when necessary. They prefer to work on their own schedules. Einsteins also want to work with smart people, in a fun environment. And they want to make money, a lot of money. Don't we all? Yes, but Einsteins have the skills, talent, intelligence, and limited labor market supply conditions working in their favor. When Einsteins ask for new work, everyone listens.

Research findings indicate that besides money (which a lot of people like to say is not important—we disagree), there are five crucial nonfinancial factors that Einsteins and non-Einsteins care the most about:

1. When to work (schedule)

2. Where to work (location)

3. What they do (tasks and responsibilities)

4. Who they work with (colleagues)

5. What they are learning while working

If Einsteins could customize these five factors, they would come up with their own enriched work positions. Managers erroneously assume that their best talent is being lost to other firms only because of money and perk-filled packages. Do not underestimate the money factor, but these five factors are extremely important. Einstein managers are advised to pay close attention to these five factors, and at the same time keep an eye on market pay rates for Einstein talent. You must keep up with the competition.

The worklife balance issue is another career path consideration. Women entering the labor force in the 1980s have changed the thinking about one-size-fits-all career paths. Women have challenged many of the old norms of when to work, how long to work, and what fringe benefits are important. Women were the first to pressure employers to consider and adopt family leaves, telecommuting, sabbaticals, daycare at work, preventive sexual harassment training programs, and flexible work schedules. As the demand for worklife balance accelerates, the pressure on MLFs to consider multiple career path options continues to grow. The one-size-fits-all path doesn't fit all women or all Einsteins.

Beyond multiple career paths upward, Einstein managers should also give some thought to what is referred to as "career downshifting." This allows Einsteins to step off the organization for pauses and still remain a part of the team. That is, some Einsteins want to get off the fast career track because of personal reasons (e.g., family issues, burnout, return to school). This is not a litmus test of loyalty and commitment, but is a choice that some Einsteins want to make. They still want to work, but on a different path. Einstein managers should be aware of "career downshifting" preferences. You do not have to lose your Einstein talent entirely if this type of career path option is available and can be customized on a case-by-case basis. Not all Einstein work can accommodate customized career paths. Projects, clients, special demands, and business goals may not permit unique customization across the board. Einstein managers, however, need to ask, observe, and listen to Einsteins.

The goal of Einstein managers in providing multiple career path support is to attempt to accommodate Einsteins. The effort and work Einstein managers put into such accommodation itself will have an impact. The Einstein tribe will respect the work and the attempt, and will appreciate the concern it shows for personal growth. Considering career path customization is difficult, yet it can be very rewarding to hardworking and creative Einstein managers.

---

### Black Hole

Not talking to your Einsteins about the B word is a mistake. It is considered by too many managers to be off limits to discuss the "balance" between an Einstein's work and personal life. Don't ignore the B word, since you may be able to help him or her achieve a better balance.

---

# Epilogue

The great practicing managers of the world do not have much in common. They employ different techniques, styles, and energy. They are of different sexes, races, and ages. What we have attempted to illustrate in this book is that managers are different and so are Einsteins. One size, one description, one picture doesn't fit everyone. The best Einstein managers are learners, listeners, and people builders. They are honest, truthful, and clearly display integrity every day. The best Einstein managers are also leaders and facilitators. They get the meaning, intent, and tone of the differences in the M (Managing), L (Leading), and F (Facilitating).

Even the best Einstein managers, however, have some flaws. They might play favorites and politics. They might not always be good at providing feedback. They might not really understand the language, work, and idiosyncrasies of Einsteins.

In the lessons presented and noted in this book, a theme is that humans, Einsteins, and non-Einsteins are social primates. If Einstein managers are up on their social primate lessons, they know that primates share a number of characteristics. A visit to the primate house at the zoo illustrates that primates:

- Form into groups (teams)
- Do not like to live on their own (tribes)
- Bear helpless infants who must be nurtured and cared for (new hires)
- Have an authority structure (management)
- Form small groups within larger ones (cultures and subcultures)
- Avoid conflict when they can (dislike dysfunction)
- Do not violate group norms of behavior (follow the team lead)

A visit to the zoo will show that the need for and recognition of authority is hard-wired into primates. Leaders act like leaders, expect to be obeyed, and are given deference by other members. This fact of primate and human life is real. The MLF manager is admittedly underskilled or deficient in the technical aspects of Einstein work. However, Einsteins who dislike authority, commands, and directives are part of the hard-wiring system established millions of years ago.

Doctors must attend seminars, workshops, and read research studies to update their knowledge and skills. CPAs must continue their learning and education to maintain certification. Lawyers constantly update themselves on the law, precedent cases, and court rulings. Likewise, to become a full-fledged MLF you must continually learn, update, and upgrade. The work never ends. Books, journals, seminars, courses, workshops, observing others in action, and working with coaches and mentors are the efforts required to become the very best MLF.

---

### Einstein Wisdom

If A equals success, then the formula is:

$$A = X + Y + Z$$

X is work, Y is play, and Z is keep your mouth shut.

---

Richard Farson in his book *Management of the Absurd* provides an appropriate story to end our book. He discusses Ludwig von Beethoven as follows:

> In music there is a very common sequence of chords known as the two-five-one sequence, referring to the second, fifth, and first notes in a scale. When the chords are played in this sequence on the piano, the listener experiences a feeling of comfortable closure when the third and final chord is played. If, however, only the first two are played, the experience is a tension that comes from the sequence's not being completed.
>
> Legend has it that Frau von Beethoven, Ludwig's mother, used to wake him up when he was a little boy by playing two-five and not then playing the final one chord. Even though asleep, he would experience the missing chord and become so disturbed that he would get up to complete the sequence.

This book is ending at this point, and as an actual or aspiring Einstein MLF you feel that the final *one* chord is missing. It is missing. The next lessons, learning, and applications of serving as an MLF are yours to play. The journey of managing Einsteins will continue as you search for the one chord of how to improve and become the best you can. Good Luck!

# Appendix

## Resources for Einstein Managers

*www.ddj.com/ddj*
**Slogan**: Grounded in real world experiences.
**About**: Since 1976 provides information on practical technology. Authors and readers are professional software developers who want to explore new technologies and share tricks of the trade. Site includes articles, book reviews, source code, mailing lists, and a store.

*www.dice.com*
**Slogan**: High-Tech Jobs Online
**About**: The leading online Information Technology (IT) job board, with high-tech permanent, contract, and consulting jobs, and home to a world of career development resources and technical expertise to the world's IT professionals.

*www.geekculture.com*
**Slogan**: The Joy of Tech
**About**: This site has everything for geeks. Links on the home page include: Computer Window, Geek Erotica, Geek TV, Geek Love, Geek Jane, Movie Review, Mind Numbing Magazine, Date-Mate Cards, and Awards!

*www.girlgeeks.com*
**Slogan**: The source for women in computing.
**About**: Newletters, chat rooms, information on technology, career news, and events for female geeks. Women come to this site to help advance their careers, find appropriate training opportunities, and connect with other women who have similar questions, experience, and interests.

*www.nerd.co.uk*
**Slogan**: Idealistic Information Society
**About**: A Web-based community of professionals. It claims to function like a small town. Everyone, including subscribers, have their own function and responsibilities. It's a place of work for professionals to function, communicate, navigate the Web, keep in touch with news and events, solve problems, learn new skills, get a job, ask for guidance, get certified, and choose and order new computer equipment.

*www.nerdworld.com*
**Slogan**: Your source for Nerdly Culture, Life, and Work Styles since 1995.
**About**: This is the premier destination site for nerds who seek cool, offbeat lifestyle and work-related content, entertainment, and services. Nerds have long been both ridiculed and celebrated in movies, television, and the press. But recently nerds have reaped revenge, as Internet billionaires have been thrust into the limelight of high culture. Nerdworld reaps revenge in its own right by relaunching Nerdworld.com and thriving among tired, old B2B e-commerce and infrastructure plays.

*www.pbs.org/nerds*
**Slogan**: Did you like *Triumph of the Nerds?* Then you'll love Robert X. Cringely's weekly column.
**About**: The companion website for the PBS special *Triumph of the Nerds: The Rise of Accidental Empires.* Includes online resources such as history of the computer and "Who are these nerds?" Also, Q&A with computer industry gossip columnist Bob Cringely.

*www.sabram.com/site/slang.html*
**Slogan**: The slang zone
**About**: The ultimate Silicon Valley slang website. Created in 1996 on a lark with a few words, it has mushroomed into one of the most popular and irreverent slang sites on the Web. Individuals are invited to submit slang, and words and phrases are reviewed for inclusion. Includes latest slang, favorites, and links.

*www.salon.com*
**Slogan**: Now in seventeen different varieties
**About**: An Internet media company that provides ten original content sites as well as two online communities—Table Talk and The Will.

The content sites are updated daily and include news, technology and business, life, people, and comments. Founded in 1995, won the "Best Online Magazine" award in 2001 from Yahoo Internet Life.

*www.slashdot.com*
**Slogan**: News for nerds. Stuff that matters.
**About**: Created in September 1997 by Rob "CmdrTaco" Malda. Today it is owned by Andover.net. Slashdot is run primarily by Jeff "Jomos" Bates, who posts stories, sells advertising, and handles the book review; and Robin "Roblimo" Miller, who has recently come on board to help handle some of the managerial side of the site, as well as (surprise!) posting stories. You can read more about each of the authors, find contact information, and figure out who to blame for what by reading The Authors Page. But the majority of the work is done by people who e-mail stories.
*Other creds*: The cool Wilber the Gimp image was by Tuomas Kuosmanen, and the famous Tux Linux Penguin is a creation of Larry Ewing. Anything that is copyrighted or trademarked or registered to anyone else is theirs.

*www.strafe.com*
**Slogan**: If you can't talk the talk, who'll even notice if you walk the walk?
**About**: Definitions, words, trivia, and a forty-six page book for cyberpunks. Streetspeak is the special language portrayed on the website.

*www.techies.com*
**Slogan**: To improve the work and life of the technology professional.
**About**: An exchange for technology professionals, and for businesses that want to recruit, market to, and interact with these professionals. The company was incorporated in 1994. In March 1999 it became techies.com. Since its inception, it has done business with more than 2,200 companies, and has grown its member base to more that 730,000 technology professionals.

**techies.com** provides its clients with the resources to plan for, acquire, and retain technology professionals, by giving them access to an extensive pool of technology professionals, customized recruiting services, market intelligence, and a marketplace to sell technology-related products and services.

*www.woz.org*

**Slogan**: Welcome to a free exchange of Information, the Way It Always Should Be.

**About**: An online recruiting site with a Steve "Woz" Wozniak (one of the original Apple Computer founders, with Steve Jobs) orientation. That is, news, comments, letters, Q&A, and links that deal with media, software, interface, architecture, and information. A lot of information. A lot of data and information about Macs.

# Notes

## Introduction

Borsook, Paulina. *Cyberselfish*. New York: Public Affairs, 2000.

Eenger, Win, and Richard Poe. *The Einstein Factor*. Rocklin, CA: Prima Publishing, 1996.

Gimein, Mack. "Smart Is Not Enough." January 8, 2001, 124–34.

Queenan, Joe, "Five Crappiest Tech Jobs," *Forbes ASAP*, November 27, 2000, 129.

Sacks, Peter. *Standardized Minds*. New York: Perseus, 1999.

## Chapter 2

Butler, Timothy, and James Waldroop. "Job Sculpting." *Harvard Business Review*, September–October 1999, 144–52.

Farr, J. Michael. *America's Fastest Growing Jobs*. Indianapolis: JIST Works, 2001.

Jana, Reena. "The New Brain Game." *Industry Standard*, January 1–8, 2001, 88–89.

Seaberg, Jim. "Talent Crunch." *Business 2.0*, October 10, 2000, 276–78.

## Chapter 3

Dronsfield, Angel. "Recruiting and Retaining IT Staff." *Syllabus*, January 2001, 18–21.

Maslow, Abraham. *Motivation and Personality*. New York: Harper & Row, 1954, 93–98.

## Chapter 4

Chung, Kae H., and Monica F. Ross. "Difference in Motivational Properties Between Job Enlargement and Job Enrichment." *Academy of Management Review*, January 1977, 114–15.

Drucker, Peter. "Knowledge Worker Productivity: The Biggest Challenge." *California Management Review*, Winter 1999, 79–94.

"Money for Something." *Business 2.0*, November 14, 2000, 46.

Shactman, Noah. "Mainstream Companies Pay the Price for IT Workers." *Information Week*, March 20, 2000, 112–16.

Stettner, Morey. "How to Keep a Millionaire on the Payroll." *Investor's Business Daily*, October 26, 2000, 1.

## Chapter 6

Kipnis, David, Stuart M. Schmidt, Chris Swaffin-Smith, and Ian Wilkinson. "Patterns of Managerial Influence: Shotgun Managers, Tacticians, and Bystanders." *Organizational Dynamics*, Winter 1984, 58–67.

McCall, Jr., Morgan W., and Michael M. Lombardo. "What Makes a Top Executive?" *Psychology Today*, February 1983, 26–31.

## Chapter 7

Adams, Bud. *Managing People*. Holbrook, Massachuseets: Adams Media Corp., 1998.

Bruce, Anne, and James S. Pepitone. *Motivating Employees*. New York: McGraw-Hill, 1999.

Katz, Jon. *Geeks*. New York: Random House, 2000.

Kellaway, Lucy. *Sense and Nonsense in the Office*. London: Prentice-Hall, 2000.

Manz, Charles C., and Henry P. Sims, Jr. *Business Without Bosses*. New York: John Wiley & Sons, 1993.

Mitchell, Russ. "How to Manage Geeks." *Fast Company*, June 1999, 174–76.

Toropov, Brandon. *The Art and Skill of Dealing With People*. Paramus, New Jersey: Prentice-Hall, 1997.

## Chapter 9

Casperson, Dana May. *Power Etiquette*, New York: ACACOM, 1999.

## Chapter 11

Adams, Bob. *Managing People*, Holbrook, Massachusetts: Adams Media Corp., 1998, 81–102.

Boyadjian, Berge. *Create Fun at Work*. Long Beach, California: Knowledge Capture and Treasure, 1999.

Hemsath, Dave, and Leslie Yerkes. *301 Ways to Have Fun*. San Francisco: Berrett-Koehler, 1997.

Weinstein, Matt. *Managing to Have Fun*. New York: Fireside, 1996.

## Chapter 13

Brown, Erika. *High Tech Titans*. New York: McGraw-Hill, 2001.

Buckingham, Marcus, and Curt Coffman. *First Break All the Rules*. New York: McGraw-Hill, 2001.

Farson, Richard. *Management of the Absurd*. New York: Simon & Schuster, 1996.

McCormack, Mark H. *Staying Street Smart in the Internet Age*. New York: Viking, 2000.

Rosner, Bob. *Working Wounded*. New York: Warner Books, 1998.

Tulgain, Bruce. *Winning the Talent Wars*. New York: W.W. Norton, 2001.

# Index

# About the Authors

**John M. (Jack) Ivancevich, DBA**, has a long and distinguished career as a professor, dean, provost, and recognized authority on management and management issues. Dr. Ivancevich is the author or coauthor of over 60 books—as well as an increasing library of Web-enabled courseware—on management, human resource management, and organizational behavior. He serves on a number of boards, business associations, and organizations, and is the recipient of numerous academic awards.

**Tom Duening, Ph.D.**, is a visiting assistant professor in the department of marketing and entrepreneurship at the University of Houston Bauer College of Business. Author of *Management 2.0: Managing in the New Economy*, Dr. Duening has published numerous articles on entrepreneurship and small business. He consults on business development and new-venture creation for clients of every size, from small to multinational.